BULLISH ON UNCERTAINTY

Bullish on Uncertainty provides rare insight into the secretive world of Wall Street high finance, which has shaped influential business, governmental, and cultural leaders and keeps supplying new business practices to other organizations in dynamic and complex environments. The book studies how two highly successful Wall Street investment banks managed the uncertainty of their high-velocity environment through different work practices. One bank chose the familiar route of decreasing bankers' uncertainty. The other bank used the novel and effective practice of increasing bankers' uncertainty to make them more alert to new situations and more likely to draw on the bank's entire range of resources. Through vivid accounts of newcomers during their first two years, the book traces how the two banks' initially similar participants were transformed into fundamentally different kinds of persons by the different kinds of work practices in which they participated.

Alexandra Michel is assistant professor in the Department of Management and Organization at the Marshall School of Business, University of Southern California. Before receiving a Ph.D. from the Wharton School of Business, University of Pennsylvania, and beginning her academic career, she worked as an investment banker in Goldman Sachs's mergers and acquisitions department, and she worked under Goldman's chief of staff, helping the firm implement a new approach to executive education, with topics that included leadership, banker development, and building client relationships. Her interdisciplinary publication record includes such journals as *Administrative Science Quarterly*, *Theory and Psychology*, and *Learning Inquiry*.

Stanton Wortham is the Judy and Howard Berkowitz Professor of Education at the Graduate School of Education, University of Pennsylvania. He is the author of *Learning Identity* (Cambridge University Press, 2006).

Bullish on Uncertainty

HOW ORGANIZATIONAL CULTURES TRANSFORM PARTICIPANTS

Alexandra Michel

Marshall School of Business, University of Southern California

Stanton Wortham

Graduate School of Education, University of Pennsylvania

CAMBRIDGE UNIVERSITY PRESS
Cambridge, New York, Melbourne, Madrid, Cape Town, Singapore, São Paulo, Delhi

Cambridge University Press
32 Avenue of the Americas, New York, NY 10013-2473, USA

www.cambridge.org
Information on this title: www.cambridge.org/9780521690195

First published 2009

Printed in the United States of America

A catalog record for this publication is available from the British Library.

Library of Congress Cataloging in Publication Data

Michel, Alexandra, 1967–
Bullish on uncertainty : how organizational cultures transform
participants / Alexandra Michel, Stanton Wortham.
p. cm.
Includes bibliographical references (p.) and index.
ISBN 978-0-521-86996-6 (hardback) – ISBN 978-0-521-69019-5 (pbk.)
1. Corporate culture. 2. Bank management. 3. Investment banking.
I. Wortham, Stanton Emerson Fisher, 1963– II. Title.
HD58.7.M526 2008
332.660973–dc22   2008025660

ISBN 978-0-521-86996-6 hardback
ISBN 978-0-521-69019-5 paperback

CONTENTS

FOREWORD

One may detect a slow but profound shift in both the concept and practice of the contemporary organization. To be sure, the metaphor of the organization as pyramid continues to dominate, along with the familiar practices of command and control. However, as was once said of cultural modernism, it is dominant but dead. In the present context it is to say that we inherit organizational practices from the past, while simultaneously realizing that they are becoming increasingly ineffectual. And, because there is so little understanding of viable alternatives, a death-like atmosphere prevails. In the present work, Alexandra Michel and Stanton Wortham not only illuminate the problems with the traditional, modernist organization but also judiciously demonstrate the possibility for a viable field of alternatives through a powerful combination of theoretical reasoning and careful observation.

How are we to characterize this field of alternatives? Broadly put, the authors characterize the new organizational form as *organization-centered.* This is in contrast to the modernist organization in which the individual is the basic unit within the organizational machinery. In the organization-centered orientation, participants view each other not as isolated competitors but as resources. The stress on over-arching rules of action is replaced by a more situated or contingent view of what may be effective. The definition of the person as singular is replaced by an emphasis on multiplicity and plasticity. Any person may, at some point, be able to substitute for any other. The ethos of competition and conflict is replaced by an emphasis on collaboration. Policies aimed at reducing uncertainty are replaced by an emphasis on both learning from contexts of ambiguity and moving sensitively and reflexively with the flow of events.

Michel and Wortham are scarcely alone in their focus on the potentials of relational process in the organization. There are ways in which their concerns reflect and amplify a movement of broad significance. The signals of a relational turn have been apparent for some years – in movements toward creating democracy in the workplace, flattening organizational structures, and establishing cross-functional teams, or more recently in practices spawned by the emphasis on organizational learning, information sharing, and appreciative inquiry. As many now see, the major innovations in many fields – technology noteworthy among them – emerge from collaborative processes. These workplace developments are also echoed in the sphere of organizational scholarship. The early indicators were there in the form of open systems theory, network theory, and chaos theory. More recently, however, critics of the modernist organization have explored the potentials of postmodern and critical theory to locate alternative visions of the organization. We variously find scholars likening the newer forms of organization to polyphonic singing groups, jazz musicians working improvisationally, or an extended array of conversations. Research on discursive and dialogic processes has now become a mainstay in the organizational literature, committed as they are to a view of conversation as the central ingredient of organizational efficacy.

Leadership studies are also moving away from an emphasis on the "great man," poised at the apex of the pyramid, commanding and inspiring the minions below. Slowly it is being realized that none of the qualities attributed to good leaders stands alone. Alone, one cannot be inspiring, visionary, humble, or flexible. These qualities are achievements of a co-active process in which others' affirmation is essential. To say anything about the leader as a single human being is to miss the relational confluence from which the very possibility of "the leader" emerges. Increasingly, both theorists and training programs are abandoning the endless and often contradictory lists of what it takes to be a good leader. In their place we find increasing emphasis on collaboration, empowerment, dialogue, horizontal decision-making, sharing, distribution of leadership, networking, leaderful organizations, and connectivity. The concept of individual leadership is slowly being replaced by a view of *relational leading*.

Yet, while Michel and Wortham add important theoretical depth to these emerging ventures, they also add a vital and virtually unparalleled comparison of individual and relation-centered practices in motion. They trace the differing forms of executive training in the two organizations, the differing assignment of roles, and the forms of feedback on which participants depend. They illuminate the way information is shared (or not) within the organization, the assignment or distribution of responsibilities. In certain respects, one finds here descriptive information that could inform the development of practices across a broad organizational spectrum. At the same time, Michel and Wortham are to be credited with their judicious conclusion that, while there were many ways in which the relation-centered organization was superior, the individual orientation was not without its strengths.

For me, the central question raised by this comparison concerns the comparative efficacy of these organizational forms in terms of the broader world context in which they function. This question is also related to the fact that there is such broad and active interest and activity surrounding the move to more relation-centered theory and practice. Is this shift in sensibility simply a contemporary fad, or are there more profound issues at stake? Does the contemporary world context favor the kind of organizational functioning illuminated by Michel and Wortham? In particular, these authors have selected organizations that function effectively within a rapidly changing, complex, and unpredictable environment. Under these conditions, we gain special appreciation of relation-centered practice. Now, we may ask, is there not reason to suppose that this shift in the working context of the contemporary organization represents the "way of the world" today?

In my view, the technologies of communication, information transmission, research, and transportation act in concert to transform the challenges faced by contemporary organizations.

Specifically:

- Organizations are increasingly fragmented – through geographic expansions and the diversification of functions.
- Information accumulates more rapidly, becomes increasingly complex, and is more rapidly outdated.
- The speed of change, in economic conditions, government policies, and public opinion, outpaces assimilation. Long–term planning becomes increasingly ineffectual.
- New organizations constantly shift the terrain of competition and cooperation.
- Personal commitments to organizations diminish. Ties based on trust and long-term understandings are eroding.
- The opinion climate can change at any moment, and the range of opinions to which the organization must be sensitive constantly expands.

In my view, it is precisely in these conditions that the kind of organization illuminated and envisioned by Michel and Wortham is most effective. In this sense, the present volume may not only be understated but indeed may be prophetic.

I wish to add a touch of idealism to this vision of the future organization. Traditionally, the organization has been treated as a self-contained unit. Similar to our conception of the individual, it is generally held that the organization primarily seeks its own well-being. Indeed, organizations *should be* seeking their own success. However, as the organization increasingly recognizes the significance of relational process *within*, we may hope to see an associated transformation in the conception of the organization in its relationship to the environment. Rather than seeking its own prosperity, we may hope to see a new consciousness of relationship take root. Here, the organization would understand that its own well-being is intimately tied to its surrounds, and that a collaborative posture is essential. In their attempt to serve themselves, most organizations – business, governmental, and religious alike – have contributed to a world of alienation, conflict, and suffering. Should such organizations place their major investments in the well-being of relationship, we might anticipate a profound increment in global well-being. We might replace the Hobbesian dystopia of "all against all" with a vision of "all with all." When relational well-being is the center of our concern, we may move toward a life-giving future.

Kenneth J. Gergen

ACKNOWLEDGMENTS

We would like to thank various institutions and colleagues who have made this work possible. Our informants at the two banks taught us much through their actions. They also worked with us to develop the ideas in this manuscript through stimulating conversations and generous comments on drafts. The Wharton School at the University of Pennsylvania supported the initial data collection. The Marshall School at the University of Southern California supported follow-up interviews and provided research assistance. The University of Pennsylvania Graduate School of Education helped support the writing of the manuscript. The study benefited from exchanges with and suggestions by faculty and students at the Wharton Management Department, the Wharton/Penn GSE Executive Program in Workplace Learning Leadership, Boston College, the Bren School at the University of California Santa Barbara, the University of California Riverside, the University of Southern California, and the UCLA Templeton Lecture Series on Ethics. We also benefited from exchanges with colleagues at the Research on Managing Groups and Teams Conference, the European Conference on Identities in Amsterdam, and the meetings of the Academy of Sciences, the American Anthropological Association, the International Society for Cultural and Activity Research, the Academy of Management, and the Society for Psychological Anthropology. We are grateful for the skilled research assistance of Elaine Allard, Ken Chen, Tim Chen, Vivian Lim, Jocelyne Liu, Bryce McFerran, Jaimie Ucuzoglu, and Tiffany Young. Betty Deane provided careful copyediting. Phil Laughlin, Eric Schwartz, and Simina Calin have been skillful and supportive editors. Beth Bechky, Mauro Guillén, Karen Jehn, Greg Urban, and Steffanie Wilk shaped the data collection and analysis. Seth Chaiklin, Dorothy Holland, Jay Lemke, Martin Packer, and Greg Urban provided helpful comments on the manuscript. We also thank other friends and colleagues for their comments on this data set and support: Paul Adler, Susan Ashford, Corinne Bendersky, Tom Cummings, Carol Dweck, Martha Feldman, Adam Grant, Sandy Green, Alex Haslam, Linda Johanson, Peter Kim, Jennifer Overbeck, Chris Porath, Mike Pratt, Nandini Rajagopalan, John Wagner III, Karl Weick, Batia Wiesenfeld, and Maia Young. We are grateful to Ken Gergen for contributing the Foreword. Bertram Michel helped with access to experts, insights into industry practices, endless enthusiasm for the project, and extensive comments on many drafts of the manuscript. Alexandra would like to dedicate this book to him.

Los Angeles, California, and Philadelphia, Pennsylvania
Spring, 2008

1

Bullish on Uncertainty

Our research uncovered a puzzle. Two highly successful investment banks were experiencing high uncertainty because globalization and industry deregulation demanded a new way of doing business. The two investment banks advised top executives of Fortune 100 companies about raising capital, taking companies public or private, and restructuring businesses. These tasks were becoming more complicated in the 1990s, however, because the environments around investment banking were changing rapidly. To assist bankers in making effective decisions amidst this turbulence, the banks designed work practices that managed uncertainty. But the two banks, "Individual Bank" and "Organization Bank," managed uncertainty in divergent ways. Individual Bank used familiar practices to *reduce* uncertainty for employees – explicit strategies and organizational structures, clear role definitions, careful feedback to bankers, and extensive training. Organization Bank, in contrast, used puzzling practices that *amplified* uncertainty, highlighting and even intentionally creating additional uncertainty for bankers. It deemphasized explicit strategies and roles, feedback was difficult to interpret, and training was full of contradiction and viewed as relatively unimportant.

THE TWO BANKS' APPROACHES

Individual Bank's approach followed traditional organizational theory. From this perspective, uncertainty is pervasive in business and, because it can impede decision making, its reduction should be a central priority for management (March and Simon, 1958; Simon, 1976). The management literature describes this priority clearly. Uncertainty reduction is viewed as a "fundamental need" for individual employees (Hogg and Mullin, 1999: 253;

Hogg and Terry, 2000), who experience uncertainty as frustrating, disorienting, and aversive (Katz, 1985; Schein, 1978). Reducing uncertainty for employees is thus crucial for organizational design and socialization (Ashford and Black, 1996; March and Simon, 1958). Companies have successfully adopted uncertainty reduction for decades (Colvin, 2006).

Run by managers with MBAs from prominent business schools, Individual Bank followed the advice of management theorists. It reduced uncertainty for its bankers by narrowing the amount of information they attended to and by providing them with guidelines – such as organizational concepts, values, goals, and standards. For example, as recommended by classic organizational theory (March and Simon, 1958; Simon, 1976), top management devised strategies that dictated the actions of bankers at lower levels, letting them know which clients to pursue, which opportunities to pass by, and how much revenue to generate. Bankers were reviewed and paid based on the goals that top management gave them. This reduced uncertainty because bankers did not need to evaluate business opportunities independently. All a banker needed to know was whether a company was on the banker's client list. Quarterly revenue goals further simplified the bankers' decision making because they did not need to attend to more complex considerations such as the longer-term implications of a particular deal or the resources they spent to get the business.

Individual Bank also cultivated "superstars." These were senior bankers with extensive experience in a given area and strong client relationships. They were celebrated for their expertise and courted publicity by commenting in the press and developing colorful public personalities. The bank developed banker expertise by repeatedly staffing superstars on deals in their areas of expertise. When a new deal came in, the bank assembled teams with the most relevant experience. This reduced the bankers' uncertainty because they were consistently confronted with familiar situations. The bankers advertised their deal-specific expertise to the client, and clients rarely made expert bankers feel insecure by challenging their knowledge.

Clients were pleased with this practice. As one client said, "We always invite at least three or four banks to pitch to us and we give the business to the bank that gives us the best banker team." Bankers from Individual Bank believed that its uncertainty-reduction strategy contributed to the bank's high performance. In response to an open-ended question about critical factors for a bank's performance, thirty-four out of thirty-eight senior Individual Bankers mentioned uncertainty reduction. They said that banks fail when bankers "are overwhelmed with the information they get or the tasks they have to do," "aren't given clear goals or directives," "do not get the training they need to know how to do their job," and "get inconsistent messages from the different HR [Human Resources] processes we have in place." The bankers also acknowledged the downside of their uncertainty-reduction approach, however. When one of its superstars left, the bank often could not fill the gap in that area of expertise, and this sometimes caused colleagues and clients to defect as well. Some of these mass exits forced the bank to abandon entire business lines – not an uncommon event in knowledge-intensive industries.

Individual Bank's uncertainty-reduction practices followed the advice of organizational scholars, the judgment of its bankers, and common sense. These practices were also successful, as indicated by the bank's leading position in the industry. Our puzzle is why Organization Bank, which faced the same challenges as Individual Bank and was just as successful, flaunted the time-honored uncertainty-reduction approach and *deliberately amplified uncertainty*. Organization Bank purposefully broadened the amount of information that its inundated bankers had to attend to, it withheld clear goals and directives, and it did not give bankers the training they needed to do their jobs. Even though outsiders admired the bank for its extraordinary profitability ("a money-making machine") and also considered the bank as "among the best managed in the industry," they derided these uncertainty-management practices as "organized chaos," "completely incomprehensible," and "defying everything we know to be true about how to manage a firm."

Organization Bankers did not, for example, receive client lists or goals. Instead, every few days they were given comprehensive information about the consequences of their actions – the amount of time they had spent on various types of projects, deals that were done by other teams, and the cost of the resources they used, including the time of other bankers and support staff and even the cost of their color copies. The bankers were supposed to use this information to determine which business opportunities to pursue and with which combination of resources. Strategies emerged only retrospectively, when many bankers had noticed and seized the same market opportunity. The absence of lists, goals, and strategic direction amplified uncertainty because bankers had to attend to more information, as compared to the Individual Bankers, and because they received few guidelines to assist them in making decisions. As one vice president commented, "The sheer demands on your attention and concentration are just mind-boggling. Not to mention the frustration that comes when you are trying to make sense of this mess of contradictory trends and information."

Another puzzling practice at Organization Bank involved the assignment of bankers to projects. Like Individual Bank, Organization Bank hired graduates with diverse educational backgrounds, including degrees in music, poetry, and the social sciences. Knowledge of finance was not a prerequisite. Unlike Individual Bank, however, it put these graduates to work on complicated deals immediately, asking them to produce leveraged buy-out analyses, common stock comparisons, and other products that most new bankers had never heard of. Newcomers often had to deliver these products overnight for deals in which billions of dollars, the careers of client employees, and sometimes the fate of an entire industry were at stake. Not surprisingly, the newcomers experienced uncertainty and extremely high anxiety. As one new associate said: "This is really difficult for me. I have always been the best at everything I took on. Now I am constantly in situations in which I feel completely helpless and incompetent."

The bank's puzzling practices ensured that even relatively senior bankers experienced persistent uncertainty. Unlike Individual Bankers, Organization Bankers were not assigned to projects based on relevant expert knowledge, but solely based on availability. When one Organization Banker went on vacation or was overloaded, other bankers seamlessly substituted on projects. One Organization Bank vice president said about this practice: "Even at my level I am still regularly confronted with deals about which I know relatively little." This was "unthinkable" at Individual Bank, as a senior Individual Banker noted: "It just doesn't work that way. You can't replicate what your colleague knows at the drop of a hat."

As a result of its unusual staffing practices, Organization Bank clients were presented with teams that included relatively junior and inexperienced bankers – and they often complained vigorously. As one potential client CEO said:

> What is this? The high school science project team? I have a granddaughter who is older than you are.... My ass is on the line here and this is the best that you can come up with? You know what this is? [pointing to a stack of business cards in front of him]. These are business cards from other bankers I am dealing with. [Reading off the name of the bank and the bankers' title] ... head of investment banking, ... head of sales and trading, ... head of global corporate finance. These banks send in their superstars, their most experienced bankers. I want the same kind of attention from Organization Bank.

The Organization Bankers routinely declined such requests, responding: "We are fungible. We all do the same thing. We all draw on the resources of the organization."

Despite the fact that some clients were initially displeased, Organization Bank was at least as successful as Individual Bank. On some dimensions of performance, it was more successful. Both banks had comparable league table standings. (League tables are important performance indicators in investment banking. They rank banks according to how many deals they have done in a given area and according to the size of the deals.) Even though both banks were profitable, Organization Bank was relatively more profitable and had been so for a long period of time. In fact, industry observers often remarked on Organization Bank's profitability as the "envy" of the industry.

Organization Bank has also consistently adjusted to unanticipated market changes more successfully than Individual Bank. Like most of its peers, Individual Bank was known for being "one step behind the market," as an Individual Bank director noted:

> Look at the example of our [name of group]. We used to be number one in the industry. After the market [for that group] tanked, we became so nervous that we overreacted. We let go of 90 percent of our senior bankers, leaving a bunch of analysts, associates, VPs to work for two senior people. But that was at a time when Organization Bank was already ramping up its business [in this area] because it correctly anticipated that the market slump would be over soon. By the time it had dawned on us that this market was going strong again, we were way behind the curve in hiring. We couldn't get any business during that time because, with only a few senior bankers, clients questioned our commitment to the market, and they were right. And then, of course, we swung too far in the other direction as a result and overhired. By the time we had a big team together, ready to go, the market was heading south again and a new round of headcount reductions started.

Organization Bank was known as an innovator that noticed changing conditions early and also created important market changes, such as new types of products that other banks subsequently copied. For example, commenting on a draft of this book, one Individual Banker said about Organization Bank:

> One example that supports your theory is our industry's turn toward [a particular type of service offering]. While most of us are stuck with the typical investment banking products, at least for now, Organization

Bank has reinvented itself and now is a completely different type of animal than it was only a few years ago, and it is raking in unheard-of profits.

During many unanticipated market changes, Organization Bank was among the few industry participants that either were buffered from losses or even profited as other competitors suffered substantial losses. This consistently superior performance in the face of uncertainty led competitors and outside evaluators to conclude that Organization Bank's repeated successes were extraordinary and "defied logic."

Even when very senior and experienced bankers left the bank, Organization Bank did not suffer knowledge gaps or additional attrition. Clients stayed with the bank because they believed that the expertise they were buying resided in the organization as a whole, not in a particular banker. Commenting on the lack of a superstar culture at Organization Bank, one client said: "The advantage of having drones working on your account is that they bring in the knowledge of the whole hive." For similar reasons, other employees did not defect when senior bankers left. They were confident that the loss of one knowledgeable colleague would not mean that their group was doomed to collapse, as was sometimes the case at Individual Bank.

THE PUZZLE

The Organization Bank puzzle is this: A knowledge-based organization usually sells the expert knowledge of particular employees and reduces uncertainty so those employees can implement their expertise. How can a knowledge-based organization be consistently effective in situations where its participants do not have the requisite knowledge? Why would an organization deliberately structure itself so that its employees regularly confront unfamiliar situations and persistently face uncertainty?

Even though organizational theory and common sense would find these practices puzzling, uncertainty amplification is increasingly practiced by other successful organizations. Examples include Apple Computer's R&D unit that exploits employees' uncertainty for innovation (Walker, 2003), Google's "chaos by design" (Lashinsky, 2006: 86), U.S. Army officer combat training that creates "ambiguity and uncertainty" (Wong, 2004: 17), and John Seely Brown's former job as Xerox's "chief of confusion." Moreover, anthropological studies suggest that uncertainty reduction is a cultural choice – rather than a human imperative or a fundamental need –

and that other responses are possible. Levy (2001), for example, describes how certain Nepalese communities continuously place adolescents into new situations and deliberately create high levels of uncertainty for them.

Organization Bank had an unusual but effective view of what causes high performance. As already noted, Individual Bankers believed that banks fail when bankers are overwhelmed with information or do not get clear and consistent directives. In contrast, Organization Bankers believed that banks fail when "people think of themselves as experts and don't realize that their knowledge doesn't apply to a new situation," when "bankers develop these recipes for how to do things and forget that each situation is different," when "people put too much faith into what they think to be true," and when "bankers rely too much on what they think they know and too little on the organization's resources." Out of forty-two senior Organization Bankers interviewed, thirty-seven made similar references to uncertainty amplification. Not one Organization Banker mentioned uncertainty reduction. They said that banks succeed when they "continuously remind people of how little they know" and "create the 'insecure overachiever', someone who compulsively doubts what they know all the time." One managing director said: "Our most catastrophic problems came about because people thought they were the experts. They thought they knew what was going on even though the market had changed.... What we do around here has to do with dispelling these illusions."

The two banks thus managed uncertainty differently. Individual Bank sold the knowledge of its *individual* superstars. Because individuals have limited information processing abilities, Individual Bank's work practices reduced the amount of information that bankers had to cope with, thus allowing its bankers to function competently. The bank's reliance on individual experts is typical for contemporary professional service firms coping with environmental uncertainty and complexity. This departs from the approach taken by traditional industrial companies, which typically face more stable business environments and can rely on the resources and procedures of a whole organization. They could, for example, script individuals on how to conduct activities. Standardized procedures, however, do not work in investment banks where each client problem is different and where markets change rapidly. Contemporary banks therefore rely on the flexible judgment of highly educated and trained professionals to devise appropriate solutions in each situation (Nanda, 2005). As one Individual Bank director said, "When the environment is that complex, you cannot rely on an organization. Organizations are simply not agile enough. You need to rely on really smart, brilliant individual minds."

Organization Bank approached uncertainty from a third and less common perspective. Instead of providing rigid scripts like traditional industrial companies, and instead of depending on individual experts like Individual Bank, it spread cognitive demands across a higher-capacity *organizational system*. Because they had the resources of the entire organization at their disposal, bankers did not have to rely on their own judgment to make sense of difficult situations. This organizational system avoided the rigidity of traditional organizations because it did not consist of standardized procedures. Bankers were not scripted on what to do, but instead relied on interaction with the organization's resources to devise the best solution. For example, an inexperienced banker who was staffed on a healthcare sell-side merger assignment could speak to experts in the healthcare market, rely on project templates from previous sell-side transactions, and get feedback from other bankers. Organization Bankers did not rely heavily on their personal expertise, because they were consistently confronted with situations for which they had not developed much prior knowledge. They were forced to treat each client problem as unique and to devise appropriate solutions from the bottom up, driven by the situation's requirements instead of the banker's preconceived notions. The Individual Bankers, of course, also depended on the resources of the bank, but not to the same extent. Individual Bankers would not, for example, ask peers to comment on their client solutions because this was seen as a sign of incompetence.

Organization Bank did not tell or encourage its bankers to use the bank's resources. It *forced* them. In the following chapters, we describe in detail how incoming bankers at both banks initially preferred to rely on their own resources. They wanted to work as independently as possible to prove how competent they were. Other businesses that depend on knowledge professionals often experience this independence in the form of "silo effects," which keep professionals from interacting with and cross-selling the services of other departments, or the "not-invented-here syndrome," in which professionals do not utilize solutions that have been discovered outside their immediate group. As one of our informants, an industry expert, remarked: "The most important – and the most difficult – thing that banks have to do is get their people to talk to one another." Organization Bank counteracted its bankers' tendency toward self-reliance by repeatedly placing them in situations for which their own knowledge was insufficient. It believed that bankers only made effective use of the bank's resources when they were uncertain about the applicability of their own knowledge. Only by drawing on others could bankers who were lacking personal expertise deliver high-quality products under extreme time pressure.

It makes sense for a firm to want its employees to make good use of organizational resources. But was Organization Bank going too far? How could it expect inexperienced bankers to deliver complex products the next day when they did not understand basic things about the type of deal they were working on? This book answers these questions in two parts. Part One describes the two banks' approaches in more detail, explaining why the banks managed uncertainty in contrasting ways. It explores how and why Organization Bank made its unconventional choices, comparing these to Individual Bank's more familiar practices. We argue that Organization Bank's practices seem counterintuitive partly because of familiar cultural notions about what it means for individuals to be knowledgeable. We tend to think that individuals are knowledgeable to the extent that they *possess* concepts and skills that they apply to new situations. In this view, if a person does not have relevant concepts and skills he or she will not be able to complete a task. Organization Bank took a different approach to problem solving in which individuals *suspend* their concepts and skills to seek out the best combination of resources in a given situation. This approach is based on the view that the knowledge of one person does not matter because whatever the person does not know can be supplied by a different resource.

The second part of the book describes how junior bankers were transformed by their work in these two different contexts. It describes how newcomers at both banks learned to use cognitive resources in different ways – psychological resources, such as identity, cognition, emotion, and motivation, as well as social resources, which include other people, data, objects, and technology. We show how Individual Bank's practices caused bankers to internalize knowledge and guidelines such that bankers thought, felt, and acted in terms of concepts that they brought to a situation. Organization Bank, in contrast, intentionally withheld guidelines and forced bankers to think, feel, and act with respect to the details of particular situations. Organization Bankers became highly sensitized to the unique aspects of each problem, noticing changes in the environment and rapidly marshalling organizational resources to assemble unique solutions. We describe how the Organization Bankers did more than learn a different way of solving problems. They also were fundamentally transformed as persons. In addition to describing this transformation, the second part of the book describes how the banks' divergent practices yielded different performance consequences. We suggest that Organization Bank's less common approach is valuable because of beneficial consequences for both the participants and the organization, but we also acknowledge the costs and limits of this approach.

WHY STUDY INVESTMENT BANKS?

Investment banks are excellent places to study uncertainty-management practices, problem solving, and socialization for several reasons. First, these banks work in extremely dynamic, complex, and competitive business environments. They must innovate constantly, adopting new technologies, routines, and procedures often long before similar practices find their way into more traditional organizations. As bankers work in these rapidly changing environments, their basic psychological processes – such as cognition, emotion, motivation, and identity – can take new forms. Study of investment banks can thus illuminate the interdependence of psychological processes and organizational contexts, as well as the plasticity of basic psychological processes. We can also observe psychological processes in investment banks that may soon appear in other contexts as other sectors adopt practices from trailblazing organizations such as these.

Second, investment banks are prototypical knowledge-based organizations, a type of organization on which Western societies increasingly rely. Investment banks and other knowledge-based organizations use knowledge as a primary input, in the form of employees' expertise, and as the principal output, as, for example, advice to clients. Observations about our "technological society" (Berger et al., 1974), "information society" (Lyotard, 1984), or "knowledge society" (Drucker, 1993) describe how the West is increasingly governed by knowledge and expertise. Our research suggests that the idea of expertise as the property of an individual, which is prevalent in Western societies, is only one way in which expertise can be understood and enacted. Our comparison of the two banks' work practices shows that organizations differ in how they define what it means to be knowledgeable. The book articulates an alternative, distributed model of expertise that is not yet well understood, and we explain its consequences for knowledge-based organizations, their employees, and their clients.

Third, responding to uncertain environmental conditions, investment banks have developed unusually adaptive work practices that are increasingly used by more traditional organizations (Eccles and Crane, 1988;

Covaleski et al., 1998). Firms such as IBM and Xerox have shown how traditional companies can transform themselves into knowledge-based organizations, drawing on the kinds of work practices described here. Our description of the banks' uncertainty-management practices thus illuminates processes that structure significant parts of the economy. Understanding that there are different kinds of uncertainty-management approaches available, with different implications for organizations and individuals, is important for the increasing number of organizations that adopt these practices.

Fourth, investment banks influence the distribution of scarce social resources, the life chances of other organizations, and thereby products, services, and employment opportunities in the larger society. In contemporary Western societies, the investment banking industry is a pillar of the corporate economy. Microeconomics textbooks frequently use the metaphor of Robinson Crusoe to emphasize that, without something to invest, one cannot aspire to produce much. Crusoe first has to invest his own time and labor to create some productive capital infrastructure. Intermediaries such as investment banks can shorten this process. Organizations do not have to wait for profits to accumulate, but can instead create an infrastructure with money from investors. Strange (1994) has argued that the enormous economic growth of recent decades reflects this access to external financing. The decisions bankers make can thus improve the prospects of some organizations and hold back others. But the processes bankers use to make their allocation decisions are not well understood. This book describes important aspects of these processes in detail, showing how different types of uncertainty-management practices yield different outcomes for individual bankers, their firms, and their clients.

Fifth, and finally, investment banks are important because they attract many talented young people and produce influential economic, government, and cultural leaders – including Henry Blodget, Jon Corzine, Michael Lewis, Michael Milken, Hank Paulson, Donald Regan, Robert Rubin, John Thain, and Gary Winnick. These leaders are often chosen because their work in investment banking has trained them to respond successfully to unexpected challenges. Mandel (2006) differentiates between the "old economic thinking" embodied by government officials drafted from the industrial sector, such as Paul O'Neill and John Snow, and the current thinking, embodied by current Treasury Secretary Hank Paulson among others. Mandel calls Paulson "Mr. Risk," referring to the importance of risk management in an investment bank and Paulson's ability to apply his experience to government, where "risk shows up in virtually every economic issue of the day." Our perspective on investment banking does not emphasize the excesses and extravagant personalities that have captivated the public imagination in books and movies including *Wall Street*, *The Bonfire of the Vanities*, *Liars' Poker*, and *Money Culture*. We focus instead on the extraordinary discipline and sacrifice investment banking demands of participants and on the human resources that can be produced in the process. The book describes two very different ways in which investment banks produce individuals who often go on to play important roles in society.

We studied Individual Bank and Organization Bank intensively, over a period of two years, using information from four overlapping data sources. First, we used participant and nonparticipant observation. The most intensive observation took place during the first year of the study, when Michel observed 5 to 7 days a week (between 80 and 120 hours per week), mirroring the bankers' own schedules. The total observation time was about 7,000 hours. Michel both worked alongside bankers and observed them while they worked. She followed more than two dozen deal teams at the two banks, attending both team and client meetings and interviewing some clients. Her prior experience in investment banking assuaged the banks' concerns that the research might interfere with the bankers' work because they trusted her to be sensitive to the bankers' high pressure and fast pace. Michel's personal experience also made her more empathic toward informants and positioned her as an in-group member. This facilitated more trusting relationships. Bankers frequently invited her along to non-work events and sought her out for informal conversations, which provided important insights into the psychological processes this book explores. Second, Michel conducted 136 formal, semi-structured interviews, each lasting between 30 and 45 minutes. She interviewed the incoming junior bankers at both banks – who answered questions about socialization processes, specific learning situations, and their own development – as well as the senior bankers who interacted with these newcomers while doing their own jobs. Third, Michel conducted informal interviews with about 120 informants, including Individual Bank and Organization Bank employees and clients, employees of other investment banks, and industry experts. The informal interviews with the two cohorts of junior bankers, conducted at least once per month across the two-year period, focused on their learning and development. Fourth, we collected comparable documents at both banks, including training and recruiting materials and new bankers' work products, which consisted mostly of client presentations and the repeated rounds of feedback on these.

Researchers only rarely gain access to investment banks because of the industry's high confidentiality concerns. Our study is unique in the amount of detail we offer about these closed settings. Michel had such extraordinary access because of contacts she developed while working as a Wall Street investment banker herself for four years. As a banker, her primary responsibilities included conducting financial analyses, helping assemble client presentations, and managing some of the daily client interactions. During her fourth year, she worked in the bank's training department, which was re-evaluating its approach to professional development. Michel participated in this process by conducting a survey of best practices among comparable firms. The personal relationships she established during this research helped her gain access for the present investigation.

CONTRIBUTIONS OF THE BOOK

Our account of Individual Bank and Organization Bank makes four important contributions. It describes a counterintuitive but promising way that organizations can manage uncertainty, by amplifying instead of reducing it. It describes how individual development can take different pathways in different organizational contexts. It describes how basic psychological processes like cognition, emotion, motivation, and identity can function differently when organizations adopt divergent work practices. And it describes how apparently incompatible theories of human cognition can usefully be construed as local theories that account for different practices in the world. The next few paragraphs summarize each of these points, and the following sections elaborate on each in turn.

Uncertainty is central to contemporary organizations because it strongly influences how organizations structure their activities (Lawrence and Lorsch, 1967; Thompson, 1967; Williamson, 1981; Weick, 1979). It is also a crucial construct in the psychological literature on human development because uncertainty can catalyze cognitive development (Acredolo and O'Connor, 1991). Existing organizational and psychological accounts, however, assume that organizations can only manage uncertainty by reducing it. We challenge this fundamental assumption and describe *uncertainty amplification* as an alternative strategy for productively managing uncertainty in rapidly changing environments. We show how uncertainty amplification can yield counterintuitive results – how experts with less knowledge can be more effective, how giving people too much and contradictory information can help them think more clearly, how strategies work best when they are developed after the fact, and how employees can organize work more effectively when managers do not plan their activities.

We are not interested in uncertainty-management only for its own sake. Organizations' uncertainty-management practices influence how participants develop as individuals and employees. Few have studied how specific organizational practices transform individuals over time (Bauer et al., 1998), even though this type of transformation is at the heart of what it means to study socialization (Van Maanen and Schein, 1979). For a period of two years, we traced how a relatively homogeneous pool of participants, who all attended top American universities, became very different types of people as they experienced the banks' different uncertainty-management practices. Working in an environment that spells everything out for the individual – the kind of environment that Individual Bank and many other organizations aspire to create – provides different experiences than an environment that challenges participants to muddle through one crisis after another. As a result, human development takes different pathways. In describing the unusual pathway taken at Organization Bank, we introduce a novel and counterintuitive mechanism for learning and development. Learning is normally conceived as the accumulation of scripts, concepts, or texts that people *build up* through their participation in an organization, possessions that the individual can then use in new situations. At Organization Bank, in contrast, bankers learned by *clearing away* preexisting concepts and identities, such that that they were free to recognize situation-specific resources and devise unique solutions.

The longitudinal study of psychological processes not only is a separate "developmental" concern but also has to form the "very base" (Vygotsky, 1978: 65) of cognitive research: "it is possible to understand . . . mental processes only by understanding . . . the transitions they undergo" (Wertsch, 1991: 87). Our developmental research informs the book's third contribution, demonstrating how basic psychological processes work differently in different contexts. Traditional cognitive theory assumes that the laws of human identity formation, cognition, emotion, motivation, and development are the same everywhere (cf., Molden and Dweck, 2006; Higgins and Kruglanski, 1996). Research on organizational socialization examines organizational tactics and strategies separately from individual behaviors and outcomes, assuming that the laws of individual psychology remain constant (Bauer et al., 1998). But our analysis shows that there is considerable variability in basic psychological processes, within one society and even within one industry, when individuals experience divergent work practices. Our approach to the bankers' psychological functioning is distinctive in that we focus on whole persons, exploring an unusually broad range of psychological processes ranging from cognition to emotion, motivation, and self-identification. Most prior work, in contrast, has conceptualized development in terms of decontextualized "component parts of persons" (Lave, 1991: 64). We describe how these various psychological processes come together into two distinct modes of psychological functioning manifested by Individual Bankers and Organization Bankers.

Our analysis illuminates a debate between the two preeminent theories of human cognition. Traditional cognitive theories (Fiske and Taylor, 1991; Higgins and Bargh, 1987; Markus and Zajonc, 1985) locate psychological processes primarily within an isolated individual, as intramental phenomena. Sociocultural theories (e.g., Brown et al., 1989; Cole, 1996; Suchman, 1987) describe psychological processes as woven more deeply into their contexts, as distributed across people, cognitive tools, and the situations within which cognition occurs. Our study shows how organizations can enact one or the other of these orientations toward cognition, depending on how they organize their work practices. Individual Bank enacted traditional cognitive theories, emphasizing individuals' intramental resources. Organization Bank enacted sociocultural theories, emphasizing distributed cognitive processes.

Cognitive and sociocultural theories are typically presented as rival academic approaches, competing to explain how human cognition works (Anderson et al., 1996; Greeno, 1997). Our analysis shows that they are theories about not only the world but also practices in the world. We describe how the two banks adopt these theories, both explicitly as beliefs and implicitly in the organization of their activities. Instead of merely judging a theory by its accuracy, we suggest that theories should also be evaluated based on what they make possible for the people and institutions that adopt the theories in practice. We focus on the different types of individual transformation and organizational performance that these theories-as-practices facilitate, both the psychological development that they encourage in new bankers and the historical development that they encourage as the banks react to changing environments.

UNCERTAINTY REDUCTION AND UNCERTAINTY AMPLIFICATION

Uncertainty management is central both to the practice of investment banking and to academic accounts of how individuals and organizations function. All individuals and organizations face uncertainty. How they choose to address uncertainty shapes much of their behavior, including both everyday work practices and more fundamental transformations in individual and organizational functioning.

We became interested in uncertainty management because it was an important concern of our informants. Discussions of rapid and unpredictable changes dominated many weekly staff meetings at both banks. As described in Chapter 2, the banks confronted uncertainty caused by historically unique events, such as industry deregulation, as well as the chronic uncertainty that results from unpredictable business cycles. As external circumstances changed, bankers had to change deal strategies, the ways in which they thought about clients, the division of labor on projects, and the tempo of deal execution. Bankers routinely confronted unanticipated complications that could put their deals at risk. Clients and other firms involved in deals often failed to reach agreement over minor points, due diligence could reveal negative surprises, shareholders could threaten to reject the terms of a deal, regulatory issues could render planned business combinations illegal, or participants could simply change their minds. Because these external circumstances often changed in unpredictable ways, bankers routinely experienced uncertainty.

Our informants used "uncertainty" to cover a set of related issues, including both unpredictability and degrees of complexity that made situations difficult to understand. They used the term to describe the state of the business environment as well as the state of the person struggling to understand that environment. When we need to differentiate between these meanings, we use the term *uncertainty* to refer to the business environment and the term *cognitive uncertainty* to refer to a person's psychological state. Most of the book is concerned with cognitive uncertainty, however, and when this is clear we sometimes use the simpler term. Bankers who experienced cognitive uncertainty felt that they could not effectively solve a problem because they were missing important information, they possessed conflicting information, they could not discern cause-effect relationships, they sensed ambiguity about available courses of action and their potential consequences, or they were unable to distinguish between relevant and irrelevant information (Berlyne, 1970; Daft and Macintosh, 1981; Piaget, 1985; Trope and Liberman, 1996).

Both banks believed that their performance hinged on how effectively they could manage bankers' cognitive uncertainty. But they differed in their approach to this challenge because they had different beliefs about how cognitive uncertainty influences banker cognition. As noted above,

Individual Bank considered cognitive uncertainty a problem because it could overwhelm bankers and impede their decision making. The bank therefore structured work practices to reduce uncertainty – providing strategy and structures, organizational roles, staffing, feedback, and training. In contrast, Organization Bank believed that cognitive uncertainty made bankers attend to the unique aspects of new situations and forced them to make good use of organizational resources. It also believed that, because people experience cognitive uncertainty as unpleasant, they are likely to find ways to avoid it – by, for example, confining themselves to familiar situations. Organization Bank wanted its bankers to experience persistent uncertainty, so it deliberately implemented work practices that amplified uncertainty. The two banks' divergent approaches to managing uncertainty shaped both how bankers solved problems and how new bankers developed during their socialization to the firm.

Uncertainty has been an important topic in academic research on organizations. Because the rational administration of people and tasks requires predictability, organizational scholars have viewed uncertainty as negative. Considerable research has investigated different forms of uncertainty that an organization can experience and has devised ways for managers to reduce this uncertainty (see Scott, 1992, for a review). Weick (1979) even suggests that the reduction of participants' uncertainty is the central purpose of an organization's existence. Most organizational research recommends that businesses reduce uncertainty by orienting employees toward shared concepts. These concepts often take the form of plans, visions, and strategies. They can also be embedded in organizational culture, routines, technology, and managerial systems (Leonard-Barton, 1992; Scott, 1992; Simon, 1976). Shared concepts reduce employee uncertainty because they impose consistency on messy facts, they restrict employees' attention to focused organizational goals, and they provide premises to guide action. It is important to recognize that this approach to uncertainty management orients participants toward *abstractions*. Employees make decisions by referring to organizational concepts, which are abstract entities meant to describe a class of actual and possible situations. Effective decision making, in this view, does not require that employees attend closely to situational complexity. It only requires that employees identify the type of situation they face and then follow organizational concepts and rules appropriate to that type (Scott, 1992).

Researchers have also recognized that uncertainty reduction comes at a cost (Bartunek et al., 1983; Weick, 1979; Walsh, 1995). Because they orient people toward abstract concepts, uncertainty reduction techniques can distance participants from concrete situations. They thus make it difficult to notice and act on information that diverges from participants' preexisting concepts (Gioia, 1992; Harrison and Carroll, 1991; Leonard-Barton, 1992; Tushman and Rosenkopf, 1992; Weick and Quinn, 1999). Fransman (1994), for example, explains how IBM had difficulties in the early 1990s adapting to a changing environment because of "a mistaken belief in the ability of the mainframe computer to sustain its profitability, growth and size, *despite the information which it possessed (and processed) contradicting this belief*" (p. 751, emphasis in original). The abstract, orienting concepts that IBM's leaders had developed in a previous market prevented them from noticing the readily available information indicating how the new environment contradicted those habitual assumptions.

Others have described similar problems with uncertainty reduction. Rubin (2003: 80) writes about his experience in the Goldman Sachs trading department:

> The now famous Black-Scholes formula was my first experience with the application of mathematical models to trading, and I formed both an appreciation for and a skepticism about [mathematical] models that I have to this day. Financial models are useful tools. But they can also be dangerous because reality is always more complex than models. Models necessarily make assumptions. . . . But a trader could easily lose sight of the limitations. Entranced by the model, a trader could easily forget that assumptions are involved and treat it as definitive. Years later, traders at Long-Term Capital Management, whose partners included Scholes and Merton themselves, got into trouble by using models without adequately allowing for their shortcomings and getting heavily over-leveraged. When reality diverged from their model, they lost billions of dollars, and the stability of the global financial system might have been threatened.

Rubin describes how these experts over-relied on devices that were designed to simplify their decision making, and he notes the negative consequences. As the Organization Bankers might have predicted, these experts acted according their abstract models without noticing how the market had changed.

A dramatic illustration of the dangers associated with uncertainty reduction comes from the "mortgage crisis" of 2007, when several highly regarded financial institutions incurred unusually high losses. Observers attributed these problems to experts' over-reliance on models that diverged from the reality they were designed to represent. "A recurring characteristic of the 2007 trouble in financial markets was that many lenders, funds and brokerages were following statistical models that grossly underestimated how risky the market environment had become" (Sender and Kelly, 2007: C1). In this risky environment, seemingly unrelated markets affected one another. Stocks also "started moving not only in ways that commonly used models didn't predict, but in precisely the opposite direction from what was expected. Equally troubling, the moves were far more volatile than models based on decades of testing assumed were likely" (Whitehouse, 2007: B3). Speaking of this experience, Rothman, "a University of Chicago Ph.D. who ran a quantitative fund before joining Lehman Brothers [said]: 'Events that models only predicted would happen once in 10,000 years happened every day for three days'" (Whitehouse, 2007: B3). Summarizing the mechanistic nature of the uncertainty-reduction approach that underlies these problems, a consultant at Oliver Wyman (as cited in Silver-Greenberg, 2008: 62) commented: "banks have seen risk management as an industrial process where you have the machine, you have the data, and then you crank the handle."

Traditional businesses, the type of business considered by classic organizational theory, experienced relatively stable environments. In such settings, experts can use similar strategies repeatedly, and the resulting cognitive rigidity is less of a problem. Productive innovation has always been desirable, of course, but in more stable environments innovation can be located in a subset of the organization and implemented from the top. The rapidly changing environments now faced by organizations such as investment banks demand a new approach, however. They struggle with a historically high level of uncertainty caused by rapidly changing markets, globalization, and political instability. The habitual use of proven methods often is not effective in these environments. Uncertainty amplification, even though it has costs, is one successful way of combating cognitive rigidity and creating a more adaptive organization.

It is important to note that both banks were highly successful, which means that the uncertainty reduction practiced by Individual Bank can be a viable strategy even in rapidly changing environments. We argue that Individual Bank continued to succeed for two reasons. First, most of the banks' competitors also used uncertainty reduction as a central strategy. In times of market turmoil, such as the 2007 mortgage crisis, Organization Bank significantly outperformed Individual Bank and other competitors because it noticed and responded to early signs of the crisis. Individual Bank, in contrast, incurred substantial losses because bankers only noticed the market change when it was too late. Individual Bank did not lose its position in the industry, however, because almost all competitors made similar mistakes.

Second, both banks were aware of the vulnerabilities entailed by their respective approaches and structured their practices to compensate. Individual Bank recognized that its experts relied on personal resources and habitual strategies too often. Individual Bankers hesitated to ask questions of colleagues because they feared that they would look incompetent, which is a serious flaw in an expert-centered system. The bank compensated for such problematic self-reliance by requiring that bankers solicit input from other experts, with the types of relevant experts specified according to the type of deal. By mandating these interactions the bank removed the stigma that would otherwise be attached to the information-seeking banker, who under this arrangement was not admitting ignorance but merely doing his or her job. Some of Individual Bank's competitors did not have such compensatory techniques, and Individual Bank might have bested most competitors in part because it more effectively mitigated the problems caused by its uncertainty reduction strategies.

DIVERGENT DEVELOPMENTAL PATHWAYS

We focus on uncertainty management not only because it has far-reaching consequences for organizations but also because uncertainty plays a central role in psychological development. Uncertainty serves as a catalyst for psychological transformation (Acredolo and O'Connor, 1991; Campbell and Bickhard, 1986; Piaget, 1980, 1985). When they experience uncertainty, people often open themselves to new information and recognize alternative ways of understanding. Organizations' uncertainty-management practices influence participants' cognitive uncertainty and can thus influence their psychological development. When both sets of bankers began their jobs, they were similar on many dimensions. After about six months, however, the Organization Bankers diverged from the Individual Bankers' more typical trajectory. This happened because Individual Bank's uncertainty reduction practices oriented bankers toward abstract context-independent scripts, while Organization Bank's uncertainty amplification practices oriented bankers toward the concrete details of specific situations. This difference in the bankers' orientations caused them to display distinct forms of psychological functioning over time, which we discuss in the next section.

Since the cognitive revolution, cognitive psychologists have recognized that individual psychology is shaped by social processes (Asch, 1952; Bruner, 1957; Kelly, 1955; Piaget, 1985). Mainstream cognitive research, however, is dominated by a laboratory tradition that studies mental processes in a context-free way. Nonetheless, human mental functioning does not involve stable, universal mental processes that are simply applied to different contexts. Psychological processes are instead interwoven with social and cultural processes, such that thinking, feeling, and self-identification often happen differently in different times and places (Brown et al., 1989; Cole, 1996; Shweder, 1991). To capture how psychological and social processes coevolve, it is necessary to study people in a more contextualized and longitudinal way. Cognitive psychologists have recognized this (Levine et al., 1993) and sometimes study individuals in their natural environment. This research tends to assess the attributes of the individual alone, however, without measuring aspects of the context and developmental processes (e.g., Higgins et al., 1995). Our research, in contrast, studies persons and social situations together. The ethnographic methods we use are ideal for examining people as they are engaged in their daily activities and the mechanisms by which social and psychological processes codevelop over time.

Organizations such as investment banks are productive sites for studying how such psychological processes as cognition, motivation, and self-identification change in practice. Organizations must compete for advantage based on the expertise of their participants, so they experiment with different practices and thereby facilitate distinct developmental pathways for employees. New developmental conditions are more likely to emerge in rapidly changing organizations than in larger, less competitive, more conservative national and occupational cultures. By comparing practices and developmental trajectories across organizations, we can observe a relatively broad range of developmental processes in a relatively economical and systematic way. We thus propose a different type of conversation between psychology and organizational studies. Currently, this conversation flows one way, as organizational scholars apply "basic" psychological research to organizations. We demonstrate the merits of a reciprocal exchange in which organizations become one promising site for generating insight into fundamental psychological processes.

Our contrast between two investment banks allows us to control for many potentially confounding factors. Our subjects moved from a shared culture – with new recruits to both banks coming from the same elite American universities – into the banks' divergent workplace cultures. Chapter 4 explains in detail how the shared culture of origin holds many relevant variables constant. The two banks also differed primarily in their uncertainty-management practices and were comparable on many other dimensions that could affect psychological development. The banks were both located on Wall Street, had comparable numbers and types of employees, performed similar tasks in giving financial advice to the same set of clients, and paid bankers similar salaries at comparable levels of seniority and performance.

At entry, both Individual Bankers and Organization Bankers showed high uncertainty about their new work and their identities. To find out how things worked in the new context, both sets of junior bankers eagerly sought information and paid careful attention to specific situations. As one new Organization Banker said, "priority number one is to listen closely so that you can figure out the rules and norms around here." When bankers had questions, they went to the person who was most likely to have the needed information. As a new Individual Banker said, "This is a great way to learn the ropes and to meet important people." The junior bankers' behavior is consistent with the cognitive literature on life transitions (Higgins et al., 1995; Ruble, 1994). People prefer to use abstract concepts to guide their actions, but when they enter a new context they recognize that their existing concepts might not apply and attend to the concrete details of new situations.

After six months, the new Individual and Organization Bankers had experienced the distinct uncertainty-management practices of the two banks, and as a result they began to behave differently. For Individual Bankers, their initial uncertainty was transient. It spiked at entry and subsequently declined. After six months, the bankers knew what kinds of deals they would be working on, they had learned general concepts that they could apply to each specific deal situation, and they knew how to conduct themselves. At this point, the bankers could project the type of expertise that clients and colleagues expected. This expertise had a cost, however. Bankers sometimes misclassified new situations as familiar ones and applied their existing knowledge with undue confidence. They failed to inquire into the situations' unique aspects and failed to modify their standard scripts. As we describe in Chapter 2, these failures tended to occur when bankers were preoccupied with maintaining their identities as experts. In addition, because they did not want to reveal ignorance, Individual Bankers did not often consult other experts in the organization – instead asking only allies, even if the allies did not have as much relevant knowledge.

The Individual Bankers' developmental progression toward abstract understandings and scripts and toward preoccupation with their own identities, as well as the associated costs of this approach, are described by cognitive research on life shifts. As people become familiar with a context, knowledge representation becomes more abstract (Ruble, 1994: 167) and information processing more schematic (cf., Fiske and Taylor, 1991), which means that "information is organized in terms of existing conclusions and information consistent with these conclusions is more easily retrieved" (Ruble, 1994: 168). Because people know how to complete their tasks, they can shift attention to identity-relevant concerns and to "draw self-relevant conclusions that guide future action" (Higgins et al., 1995: 216). Eventually, "new information is not sought actively, and information that could change conclusions is resisted" (Higgins et al., 1995: 217). This cognitive research on problem solving and identity development accurately describes new bankers' development at Individual Bank.

This supposedly universal developmental pathway did not occur at Organization Bank, however. The Organization Bankers experienced *persistent* uncertainty. Throughout the two years of the study, they were staffed on deals for which they lacked relevant knowledge and in which they could not develop solutions by themselves. Because the bankers did not have enough abstract guidelines and scripts to direct their actions in these unfamiliar situations, they continued to attend closely to concrete, situation-specific information and to draw more widely on organizational resources. During their first six months, new Organization Bankers, like new Individual Bankers, were preoccupied with the identity-relevant implications of situations, they tried to project identities as competent bankers, and they failed to attend to task-related information. After six months, however, identity concerns were eclipsed by task-related concerns. Organization Bankers developed two types of behaviors that serve people well in a complex, dynamic business environment: sensitivity to the concrete and a prioritization of task concerns over identity concerns. The persistent uncertainty at Organization Bank also had costs, including the bankers' high stress level and the failure to meet clients' expectations that they would be served by individual experts. We describe more fully in Chapter 3 how the Organization Bankers mitigated these costs much of the time.

Our description of Organization Bank shows that the practice of uncertainty reduction and the associated development from close attention to the habitual application of established knowledge – processes which are presented as universal and "natural" in most cognitive psychological research – are only one way that organizations can structure task environments and develop their participants. When development takes the new form observed at Organization Bank, cognition, emotion, motivation, and self-identification function in different ways.

DIFFERENT FORMS OF PSYCHOLOGICAL FUNCTIONING

As we describe the divergent developmental pathways at Individual Bank and Organization Bank, we attend to a broad range of basic psychological processes that over time came to work together in two distinct ways. Identities, cognition, emotion, and motivation functioned together to focus Individual Bankers on abstract concepts and banker identities and Organization Bankers on concrete situations and resources outside the individual. Chapters 5 and 6 describe how these differences in overall psychological functioning formed different ways of engaging the world that generated different possibilities for action. We refer to these overall stances as different types of *involvement*. When individuals exhibited these two different forms of involvement, they oriented differently both toward their own psychological processes and toward external resources. The divergent developmental pathways that we describe, then, involved not only changes in the component processes of individuals but also changes in larger systems that included persons-in-situations.

Individual Bank cultivated in its bankers an identity as members of the bank and one or more of its subgroups (e.g., "I am a merger banker at Individual Bank"). Such identities are abstractions that contain theories about the self in relation to social context (Haslam, 2004). These identities carried social expectations about how to behave. To be a "good" Individual Banker, one had to be smart and an expert in some relevant domain. These expectations became very significant to Individual Bankers and influenced their behavior. When meeting with clients and other bankers, for example, Individual Bankers noticed whether other participants accepted their claims to expertise. When others did not, bankers often focused their attention on reaffirming their abstract identities even when this distracted them from the concrete task.

These abstract identities became focal points for Individual Bankers' other psychological processes as well. We call this configuration of identity, cognition, emotion, and motivation *identity-induced involvement*. Individual Bankers developed abstract concepts – including trait-based accounts of their own and others' identities, models for understanding standard situations, and guidelines for action – and they applied these concepts to understand and act in new situations. Bankers' emotions often registered the degree of alignment between identity goals and the actual situation. Alignment yielded positive emotions such as pride, while lack of alignment yielded emotions such as anxiety and fear. These emotions often distracted bankers from task-related concerns. Bankers were highly motivated to sustain their favored identities by realigning situations with them. Self-identification, cognition, emotion, and motivation thus all worked together as one integrated system that oriented Individual Bankers inward, toward their own abstract concepts, in ways that often disconnected them from concrete, situationally relevant cues.

One would not expect this outcome, given the praise that organizational and cognitive psychologists have for organizational identities. The literature promotes such identities as valuable tools for making participants think, feel, and act on behalf of a collective (e.g., Brewer and Gardner, 1996; O'Reilly and Chatman, 1996). Because these identities orient employees toward an organization's goals, some researchers even portray the creation of organizational identities as a "fundamental task of organizations" (Pratt, 1998: 171). As this literature would predict, the Individual Bankers did work very hard to reach the bank's goals. But their abstract identities distracted them from concrete problems and thus, ironically, undermined the achievement of these goals. Chapters 2 and 5 describe in detail how this happened.

Organization Bank provides an alternative. Instead of being oriented toward abstract identities, people can "forget" their identities and think, feel, and act in response to the concrete situation. Organization Bank's uncertainty amplification practices impeded the formation of organizational identities by continuously confronting bankers with unfamiliar situations and undermining their claims to expertise. The bankers could not apply preexisting concepts to determine appropriate actions because they often did not have any concepts relevant to the novel situations they faced. To complete tasks successfully, they needed to attend closely to situations and marshal organizational resources appropriate to particular problems. Organization Bankers realized that their successes were not the result of their own traits but instead reflected their use of organizational resources. Because personal identities, concepts, and scripts did not explain successful action, Organization Bankers focused more on situational cues and less on applying abstract knowledge. Wicklund (1986: 65) describes how individuals can "forget" their identities in situations like this: "it would serve no function ... to engage in the self-ascribing or other ascribing of dispositions. Each person is actively ... focusing on the relation between act and environment. To turn one's thoughts to membership in such categories as 'aggressive', 'creative', 'sportsmanlike', or anything of the kind would constitute moving one's thoughts away from task-related preoccupations."

We refer to the Organization Bankers' orientation as *direct involvement* because abstract identities, scripts, and models were cleared away and their cognition, emotion, and motivation engaged situations more directly. Unlike Individual Bankers, their actions were not mediated by standard, abstract resources imported from outside the situation. This does not make their actions unmediated. Instead, Organization Bankers used mediating resources attuned to concrete situations, with different configurations of resources used in different settings – whatever was appropriate for the task at hand. Bankers' emotions registered the relative progress that participants made toward situational goals, not the alignment of the situation with abstract standards and goals. Organization Bankers also experienced a broader range of emotions than Individual Bankers, including emotions that were unfamiliar. Unfamiliar emotions moved them to take actions that they experienced as relatively atypical compared to previous behavior. This further reinforced the bankers' perception that being a self does not involve exhibiting relatively stable traits and ways of behaving. Cognition, emotion, motivation, and identity thus worked together, as one integrated system, to orient the Organization Bankers *outside*, toward the current situation, connecting them to relevant social resources that they used to get the task done.

In identity-induced involvement, the person starts with his or her own concepts and molds the situation accordingly. With such an orientation, people act as if knowledge were the property of an individual. Individuals consistently apply their own ideas, and this reinforces a dualistic sense of being separate from the context. Psychological processes are consequently directed *inside*, toward the person's ideas and goals. They function as the intramental faculties of a person and serve the person's interests. Direct involvement, on the other hand, orients the person toward concrete, social resources, many of which exist outside the individual. People behave as if knowledge is the property of a system, even when the individual is working alone. Because psychological processes are directed outside, toward the concrete aspects of situations, they function in more relational ways, serving the interests of the overall situated system that includes but is not limited to the person.

As an example, consider the contrast between how Individual Bankers and Organization Bankers structured client meetings. Individual Bankers used client presentation books. These usually captured the bankers' understanding of the client's financial situation and their expert recommendations. In client meetings, most bankers walked through the book, page by page. The Individual Bankers used this strategy "to look prepared," "to show the client that we know what we are doing," and because "that's why they hire experts, to tell them what to do." This strategy applied preexisting banker models to client situations and helped assert the bankers' identities as experts. The book itself was relatively passive and static, merely expressing the banker's thinking without generating new ideas. Organization Bankers, in contrast, often approached clients with rudimentary materials instead of polished books, sometimes bringing only preliminary spreadsheets. As bankers and clients gathered around these spreadsheets, unreasonable assumptions were modified, new ones were introduced, and new potential solutions became salient. The Organization Bankers used this collaborative strategy when they were unfamiliar with client situations and therefore "could not make assumptions," "needed to gather more information," and "worked together with the client to figure out what is important and what is not and what solution would work best." In these situations, the spreadsheet was dynamic and active, not packaged and inert. It evolved as participants provided new data and bankers entered these into the spreadsheet. This prompted next steps, such as modifying assumptions, and often led to new insights. Like the persons who used it, the spreadsheet participated in generating ideas, acting together with the individuals' ideas and actions.

Our account of Individual Bank and Organization Bank shows that managing knowledge effectively might require more than individual expertise and more than sophisticated tools. Knowledge professionals must also use knowledge resources effectively in context. Surprisingly, this may be best accomplished not by providing abstract guidelines on how to use resources, but instead by clearing away people's preexisting identities, scripts, and models so that they can notice and use resources flexibly.

COGNITIVE AND SOCIOCULTURAL THEORIES AS PRACTICES

Individual Bank and Organization Bank adopted different practices to manage uncertainty, and bankers' individual paths diverged as they developed in the two settings. We propose that these differences can be productively understood as the banks' instantiation of two different psychological theories: *cognitive* and *sociocultural*. Individuals in the two banks explicitly and tacitly made the assumptions articulated by these academic approaches. Participants acted as if they were cognitive or sociocultural theorists without necessarily being aware of it. This book describes how the two banks enacted distinct psychological theories and how they created different kinds of people – as individual development would be predicted by these two theories – through the banks' divergent socialization practices. We document two distinct forms that human action can take and the social practices that create such distinct psychological processes.

Theories about psychological processes "embody a particular way in which human beings have tried to understand themselves ... [and have also] played a constitutive role in shaping the ways in which we think of ourselves and act upon ourselves" (Rose, 1999: vii). All people have folk psychological theories that influence how they talk and think about themselves and others. In societies such as ours, formal academic theories also enter popular consciousness and combine with circulating folk theories. Thus, we must understand psychological theories not only as being about the world but also as things in the world. They are part of everyday practices and they influence people's actions, for good and for ill.

It turns out that the psychological theories enacted by Individual Bank and Organization Bank are the two dominant approaches to cognition in contemporary academic discussions. Psychology and related fields have recently experienced a "conceptual upheaval" (Sfard, 1998) in how to think about problem solving and individual transformation, a "sociocultural revolution" (Voss et al., 1995) that challenges the traditional cognitive perspective. Under cognitive perspectives, we include theories of social cognition (e.g., Fiske and Taylor, 1991; Higgins and Bargh, 1987; Markus and Zajonc, 1985) and cognitive developmental theories (e.g., Berlyne, 1970; Ruble, 1994; Piaget, 1980, 1985). These theories share an "unabashed commitment to mentalism" (Fiske and Taylor, 1991: 14), which means that they construe psychological processes as attributes of individual minds. From a cognitive perspective, development involves the accumulation and transformation of mental knowledge structures that people construct about a concept or domain. Sociocultural perspectives include work in *activity theory* and *situated cognition* (e.g., Brown et al., 1989; Cole, 1996; Greeno et al., 1998; Lave, 1988; Packer and Goicoechea, 2000; Scribner, 1999; Scribner and Cole, 1981; Suchman, 1987; Rogoff and Lave, 1999) as well as *practice theory* (e.g., Schatzki et al., 2001; Turner, 1994). These approaches all construe psychological processes as woven into social systems. Individuals participate in social settings and relationships, and their psychological functioning essentially involves both internal and external resources. From a sociocultural perspective, development involves changes across persons and social resources in addition to changes in mental representations and processes.

Debate continues between cognitive and sociocultural approaches (Anderson et al., 1996, 1997, 2000; Greeno, 1997). Our data reframe the debate. Instead of simply taking sides, we describe these theories as things in the world. We show how the theories are enacted in practice, how they are reproduced as individual participants are socialized into systems that presuppose one theory or the other, and how the theories have distinct consequences for the individuals and organizations that adopt them. Instead of treating the theories as mutually exclusive logical and explanatory systems, we propose that each theory facilitates a viable type of human functioning. The theories thus can be evaluated not only for how well they describe particular situations but also with respect to their consequences for the institutions and participants who enact them.

Sociocultural theorists criticize the traditional cognitive focus on abstraction, decontextualized knowledge, and the resulting dualism between mind and world (e.g., Lave, 2003; Lave and Wenger, 1991). Dualism presupposes two different types of entities, such as mental and material substances, and it is difficult to explain how these different substances can interact. Dennett (1991: 35–7) explains this problem in the following way:

> It [dualism] is the same incoherence that children notice . . . in such fare as Casper the Friendly Ghost. . . . How can Casper *both* glide through walls and grab a falling towel? How can mind stuff *both* elude all physical measurement and control the body . . . [since] anything that can move a physical thing is itself a physical thing. . . . This fundamentally antiscientific stance of dualism is, to my mind, its most disqualifying feature, and is the reason why . . . I adopt the apparently dogmatic rule that dualism is to be avoided *at all costs.* (Emphasis in original)

While sociocultural scholars have mostly shared Dennett's rejection of dualism, others have argued that the abstraction, decontextualization, and dualism presupposed by cognitive theories are best understood not as bad theory but as accurate descriptions of many Western practices. Lave (2003: 23), for example, describes this cultural preference:

> Abstraction from and generalizations across "context" are mechanisms that are supposed to produce decontextualized (valuable, general) knowledge. Along with this way of talking about decontextualization go several other claims. First, that movement toward powerful (abstract, general) knowledge is movement away from engagement with the world, so that distance "frees" knowers from the particularities of time, place, and ongoing activity.

Lave describes how many Western institutions encourage individuals to represent knowledge in an abstract form and to act as if their knowledge were independent of particular contexts. Our cultural preference for abstractions means that dualism has a "robust existence in *practice*, in the contemporary world. Euro-American culture instantiates it, and in many ways is predicated upon it. Beliefs, institutions, and a great deal of action operate in its name" (Lave, 2003: 24, emphasis in original). Individual Bank is a typical Western institution in this respect because it treats individuals as bearers of expertise who independently represent the world.

Sfard (1998) makes a similar argument. She describes how cognitive and sociocultural theories differ in the basic metaphors that they use to understand learning. Cognitive theories construe learning as the accumulation of concepts, the mind as a kind of container, and the learner as possessing durable attributes. Sociocultural theories use a participation metaphor to understand learning in more relational terms. From this perspective, the mind does not store abstract concepts but instead becomes attuned to and learns how to work with heterogeneous resources in specific situations. Like Lave, Sfard argues that the cognitive perspective has dominated educational practice in the West. It is thus difficult to conceptualize and organize learning in a way that does not aim at "generating," "constructing," "delivering," and "accumulating" knowledge and concepts. Sfard describes how sociocultural theories make these taken-for-granted assumptions about learning visible and begin to reveal alternatives.

This book takes the suggestions made by Sfard and Lave seriously. We take a *practical* approach to the debate between cognitivism and socioculturalism. Instead of treating cognitivism as an incorrect theory and dualist accounts as erroneous descriptions, we treat them as things in the world, as theories that people and institutions sometimes instantiate. Individual Bank did in fact orient bankers toward abstractions. In order to reduce uncertainty, it provided abstract concepts and guidelines that "freed" bankers from needing to think about the specifics of situations. These abstract, decontextualized concepts were an important part of dualistic practices that separated the person from the situation.

Once we treat cognitive accounts as situated practices, not incorrect theories, we can explore their consequences and the mechanisms through which these dualistic practices are sustained. We can also investigate alternative choices that organizations might make. Alternative organizational structures often exhibit the attributes described by sociocultural theories, such as a tendency toward understanding individuals in more contextualized ways, a focus on concrete and embodied activities, and a nondualistic understanding of persons and social contexts. Organization Bank, for instance, oriented bankers away from abstractions. It amplified uncertainty by withholding abstract guidelines and counteracting their formation. The overwhelmed bankers thus had to rely more on social resources instead of their own mental concepts and they enacted the distributed cognitive processes that sociocultural theory has described. In this book, we study Organization Bank's sociocultural practices in order to explore the practical consequences of enacting sociocultural theory.

One purpose of the book, then, is to give a detailed empirical portrait of decontextualization and contextualization, dualism and nondualism, as situated practices. We describe how the banks' distinct training, project assignments, role definitions, strategies, and procedures made contrasting aspects of persons and contexts salient to participants and how their different approaches to uncertainty management yielded more cognitivist and more sociocultural practices. We argue not only that the bankers held divergent implicit theories (Dweck, 1999) but also that they developed and enacted complex social arrangements, both material and ideological, that maintained the two distinct approaches.

The banks made these divergent choices not because of academic theories, but for practical reasons that we examine empirically. Organization Bank was originally structured in more dualistic, cognitivist ways. Like Individual Bank, it sold the expertise of particular individuals and its experts had preconceived notions about how markets behave that blinded them to sudden market shifts. During one rapid and unexpected market shift, the bank incurred severe losses and had to fire many employees. In reflecting on this experience, Organization Bankers decided that they must orient away from abstract concepts and toward the concrete aspects of particular situations. The bank also had limited resources and was forced to deploy bankers outside their areas of expertise. Instead of causing more chaos, this practice turned out to encourage in bankers a situational alertness that Organization Bankers aspired to. As a result, bankers self-consciously created practices that encouraged the desired mindset in individuals, such as staffing bankers fungibly, and eliminated practices that caused undue self-confidence in bankers, such as hiring superstars and providing extensive training.

We can only speculate about how Individual Bank and most other investment banks adopted more individualist, cognitivist practices. Individual Bank's management practices followed well-established management principles based on cognitive theories (March and Simon, 1958; Simon, 1976). These academic theories encouraged the bank's practices, both as bankers read publications and as recruits brought business school training with them to the bank. The bank also worked with management professors to devise training, feedback to bankers, and leadership strategies. Bankers used the practices described by professors and management consultants, priding themselves on "following the gold standards of management" and "doing management the right way." In addition, as Lave (2003) points out, a variety of interlocking Western institutions – including law, many media, popular culture, and schooling – enact cognitivist and individualist practices. These probably influenced bankers, making the individual expert and abstract knowledge seem natural. Individual Bank was also successful, so they saw no reason to change.

We do not claim that the banks exhibited "pure" versions of the academic theories, if such exist. While Individual Bank primarily instantiated cognitive theory, it also exhibited elements from sociocultural theory. Individual Bankers often learned through apprenticeship and followed the orderly trajectory from peripheral to central participants outlined by Lave and Wenger (1991). Similarly, despite their sociocultural tendency to question whether concepts transfer from past experience to new situations, Organization Bankers did believe that they acquired concepts and heuristics that helped in new situations. The two banks were not ideal versions of the two theories, but they differed substantially in their tendencies to instantiate one or the other theory.

Our argument, then, is that we can fruitfully treat cognitive and sociocultural theories as practices in the world that organize institutions such as Individual Bank and Organization Bank. We can then judge the theories not only on epistemological but also on practical grounds, in terms of their consequences for clients and participants. We inevitably adopt aspects of these theories ourselves as we make this argument. We focus on *practices*, as do sociocultural researchers, and we formulate abstract concepts that apply across situations, of the sort described by cognitivists. Borrowing an element from a theory has consequences, but one has to use the resources of available traditions to communicate effectively, and this does not necessarily require that one endorse the whole theory (Gergen, 2001b). Similar tensions remain in other theories. After critiquing cognitive theory for its focus on abstractions, for example, Lave and Wenger (1991: 38) point out the contradiction in their effort: "How can we purport to be working out a theoretical conception of learning without, in fact, engaging in the project of abstraction rejected above?" Sfard (1998) concludes that such tensions cannot be resolved.

Our analysis describes the performance consequences of the two approaches, and we note the costs and benefits of each. It turns out that Organization Bank outperformed Individual Bank in both adapability and profitability. It also created more cognitively flexible individuals, which we consider a desirable attribute. But in most market conditions Individual Bank performed very well. Furthermore, when one is navigating a society that constructs individuals as discrete bearers of expertise – as almost all of us learn in traditional individual-centered schools and as assumed in most other important Western institutions – Individual Bank's practices often may be more successful.

PLAN OF THE BOOK

Section 1 describes the banks' contrasting uncertainty-management practices. Chapter 2 shows how Individual Bank used five different work practices to reduce bankers' cognitive uncertainty: strategy and structures, roles, project staffing, feedback systems, and training. These practices oriented participants toward abstractions such as organizational guidelines and an organizational identity, which bankers were advised to internalize and apply across different situations. Chapter 3 describes how Organization Bank managed these same five practices quite differently to amplify bankers' cognitive uncertainty. The bank withheld organizational concepts and even counteracted their formation, forcing bankers to forego preconceived concepts and attend closely to concrete cues.

Section 2 shows how the newcomers who entered these distinct settings experienced different types of uncertainty and took divergent developmental pathways across their first two years on the job. Chapter 4 describes the comparable recruiting practices that the two banks used, establishing that Individual Bankers and Organization Bankers were similar at entry. This eliminates an important alternative explanation for our findings – that the bankers might have acted and developed in different ways because they were different to begin with. Chapter 5 shows how junior Individual Bankers experienced uncertainty as transient. They faced high uncertainty at entry, but it decreased rapidly as the bank provided newcomers with the knowledge they needed to perform competently. We describe how these uncertainty reduction practices reinforced in bankers an orientation toward abstract identities, scripts, and models, an orientation that they had entered with. Because the bankers felt that work demands were manageable, they monitored situations relatively more with reference to implications for their identities and they often applied abstract concepts instead of noticing specific situational cues. Chapter 6 describes how Organization Bank's uncertainty amplification practices caused junior Organization Bankers to experience persistent cognitive uncertainty. At first they tried to use abstract guidelines and protect their own identities as experts. The bank's practices blocked this, and in the first six months they experienced much higher anxiety than incoming Individual Bankers. After six months, however, they learned to orient toward organizational resources and function as part of systems – which included their own capacities together with those of other bankers plus physical and symbolic resources. Their earlier preoccupation with their identities moved into the background and they attended much more closely to the affordances of concrete situations. Chapters 5 and 6 also explain how these two distinct types of orientation made different types of performance possible for the individuals and the organization.

Chapter 7 returns to the constructs of identity-induced involvement and direct involvement, integrating patterns from the empirical analyses and outlining our theoretical contributions. The concluding chapter also discusses the implications for cognitive and sociocultural theories, and it presents implications for managers.

PART 1

WORK PRACTICES

Handling uncertainty is one of top management's primary concerns, and it has been a central topic for organizational scholars since the inception of the discipline (e.g., Thompson, 1967; Lawrence and Lorsch, 1967). How organizations manage cognitive uncertainty is of great interest because this influences the organization's ability to act effectively in a dynamic environment. This section describes how decisions about managing cognitive uncertainty also influence almost every aspect of the organization and thereby influence most daily activities.

Their approaches to cognitive uncertainty influenced how both banks that we studied embarked on strategic courses of action, such as their plans for entering new markets and the organizational structures they used to coordinate bankers' activities. In Individual Bank's uncertainty reduction approach, this coordination took place among bankers who were thought of as occupants of abstract roles – individuals who operated within the organizational structures created by top management, fulfilled management's top-down directives, were trained and staffed in their areas of expertise, and received feedback on how they were performing in relation to the organization's explicit standards. This approach reduced the bankers' cognitive uncertainty by creating an internally consistent system of premises and resources that bankers could use to make decisions.

In Organization Bank's uncertainty amplification approach, coordination happened through more situated processes. Roles were merely one of many resources for action. The bankers decided on relevant participants and approaches for each situation based on the concrete cues that they attended to as they solved problems. Organizational structures were more like processes. They emerged out of bankers' conversations when there was a need for additional resources, and they dissolved when this need disappeared. Training and feedback did not involve the dissemination of abstract strategies, but were instead opportunities to discuss the complexities of bankers' daily activities in an environment that facilitated reflection instead of resolution. This approach amplified the bankers' cognitive uncertainty because the bank actively withheld concepts and structures that could help bankers frame and guide decisions and because the bank created processes that highlighted and even created inconsistencies.

2

Practices That Reduced Cognitive Uncertainty at Individual Bank

Individual Bank designed its practices to reduce the uncertainty that confronted bankers. When asked an open-ended question about factors that were critical for a bank's performance, thirty-four out of thirty-eight senior Individual Bankers (vice presidents, directors, and managing directors) mentioned the reduction of banker uncertainty. They said that banks fail when bankers "are overwhelmed with the information they get or the tasks they have to do," "aren't given clear goals or directives," and "do not get the training they need to know how to do their job." Individual Bank helped bankers manage uncertainty by giving them relatively abstract concepts – such as expert knowledge, norms, and goals – to narrow the bankers' range of attention and guide decisions. The central practices that Individual Bankers considered important for managing uncertainty were strategy formulation, role definition, training, staffing, and feedback. Table 2.1 summarizes how the two banks organized these practices differently.

STRATEGY AND STRUCTURES

The Individual Bankers believed that strategy was crucial to a bank's success and that devising strategies was the task of top management. When asked what makes a bank successful, one Individual Bank director emphasized the power of a strategy to focus and coordinate bankers who struggle with a complex and rapidly changing environment:

> If you want to understand why bankers in some banks are able to do their jobs, while bankers in other banks are running around aimlessly, you have to look at top management first and at the kind of strategy that they are putting in place. That's what helps people make sense in a chaotic environment. That's what focuses everyone and brings people onto the same page.

A vice president explained how a good strategy reduced the uncertainty that would otherwise confront individual bankers and impede coordination: "Just think about it. Think about the hundreds of bankers we have. There are no managers here. No one tells you what to do. You don't have to get approval for your decisions. How would you make sure that these people are all pulling together? ... You need to have a strategy."

Other Individual Bankers also argued that strategic directives reduce uncertainty by coordinating the efforts of different bankers:

> Every banker could in principle strike out in many different directions, depending on where he or she sees opportunity. But we are not a set of independent contractors. We are a firm. We need to all go in the same direction. ... But bankers are so mired in deal execution. They don't have the time to look at the big picture. They don't really have the information to decide where to focus their time and effort. That's what you need leadership for.

A strategy reduces uncertainty because it summarizes a complex environment in a convenient way for bankers who are overloaded with information. Individual Bankers did not have to make sense of this environment themselves because they relied on the abstract schematization of the environment that was provided by top management. As one director said: "It sounds so simple when one talks about *the* business environment. But in order to really understand all the factors that impact our business, you would have to follow an inordinate amount of dimensions and the relevant business indicators and you would have to interpret it correctly. This is impossible to do for a banker."

Another director also explained how management's strategy facilitated his work: "[Managers] here look at the big picture. That is their job. They worry about statistics and trends so that I can do my job. They tell me what kinds of clients matter and what kinds of deals need to get done and I worry about how to get it done."

Thus, the abstract schematization embedded in top management's strategy reduced banker uncertainty and it freed bankers from worrying about extraneous aspects of particular deals. Individual Bankers could assume that a certain kind of deal should be pursued, while others should be rejected, because the firm's strategy provided general principles that dictated this.

Individual Bank's reliance on top-down strategy as key to uncertainty management thus created a separation between the abstract thinking of top management – who thought about the "big picture" – and the practical activities of Individual Bankers who had direct contact with clients. In this respect, Individual Bank was following the directives of traditional cognitive theories, which construe more abstract knowledge as more valuable. It differs from the focus of sociocultural theories, which emphasize the embedded and contextualized nature of useful knowledge. Individual Bank valued abstract thinking, making it the prerogative of the highest-status bankers and using it to guide the practical activity of others.

Individual Bankers believed that the most important part of a strategy was the vision that top management formulated. For example, one director explained that "the hallmark of a good leader is a great vision." Another vice president said that "leading is about strategy formulation . . . [having] a vision of what kind of bank you want to be – how you are going to be unique and different from the pack." Bankers construed a vision as a set of abstract ideas that organized the firm's priorities. An abstract vision guides the activities of bankers in different sections of the bank. It is not linked to a particular type of situation. Another director said that a vision consists of "priorities," such as "global presence," "market share," or "CEO recognition." He claimed, for instance, that the bank's strategic focus on "CEO recognition" was designed to reinforce the bank's identity as a "white shoe" investment bank and to thereby differentiate it from competitors who also had a lot of relatively "low-brow" brokerage business. A strategy thus helps to construct a shared understanding of the bank's identity. As a vice president said: "Part of what you are selling to your client is a story about who the bank is. The vision gives you a way to think about what you do and to position it to the client."

Individual Bankers believed that an organizational identity reduced uncertainty for bank employees themselves, not only for clients. One vice president said: "Everyone needs to have a story about who they are. Otherwise life just doesn't make sense and you don't know what to go after and what to pass by. That is also true for a business." A managing director explained how the abstract goals contained in an organizational identity could also motivate participants: "A vision of the firm helps people understand what they stand for. It makes you different and proud and willing to put effort into the goals that we stand for." This banker claimed that Individual Bankers identified with the bank by making the bank's goals and standards their own. We found that this was in fact the case. Bankers also believed that, when they identified with the bank's goals, they were more likely to act on behalf of those goals. For example, one director said: "When you identify with being a trusted advisor, that means you act differently in front of the client." The strategy thus reduced banker uncertainty by providing bankers with a narrative that they could use to make sense of situations and by providing goals that could inform behaviors. The Individual Bankers' beliefs about strategy are consistent with how cognitive psychology explains behavior – as guided by a relatively abstract set of principles, such as values, identity-related goals, and ideas. This differs from the more tacit and embodied understandings that sociocultural theories use to explain behavior.

Another distinguishing feature of strategy formulation at Individual Bank was the kind of information that top management used as input for the vision. In contrast to their counterparts at Organization Bank, Individual Bank's top managers did not consult extensively with other bankers to gather input into their decisions. One managing director explained why: "People here believe in strong leadership, someone with a unique and firm vision. I don't think people here would respect someone who goes around asking others what the right strategy and vision should be." This echoes a dominant theme at Individual Bank – that knowledge is vested in individuals. It corresponds to the principles of cognitive theory, which also focuses on the individual knower, and contrasts with sociocultural theory, which construes knowledge as embedded in a distributed system. If an Individual Banker sought input or advice from others, other bankers often concluded that the banker's own knowledge fell short. Conceiving of knowledge as a property of individuals in this way helped reduce uncertainty because it allowed bankers to divide up the cognitive and practical labor. They divided an overwhelming body of expert knowledge into smaller pieces that were more comprehensible for individuals and they expected that each individual would master his or her own piece.

The information that top management used to formulate strategy was mostly in the form of aggregate statistics generated by the heads of the various business groups and divisions. For example, one division head said:

> There is a certain set of indicators that we follow. At different times, depending mostly on the leadership, we focus on different indicators. In the past, everything that related to revenue was crucial and coming up with a strategy was all about finding new sources of revenue. Now the pendulum has swung to cost cutting and the kind of indicators that we are looking at have to do with who spends how much on what and why.

Another managing director also highlighted the statistics-driven nature of the strategy formulation process: "To come up with a strategy you have to pore over reams and reams of statistics or have your people do that for you." In contrast, Organization Bank formulated its strategy based on concrete information solicited from clients or from bankers who had regular contact with clients. Individual Bank's top managers, however, rarely had direct exposure to clients. Even though they generally assumed their leadership positions because of their effectiveness as revenue producers, markets changed so rapidly that this knowledge quickly became obsolete. Therefore, leaders were not trusted to possess authoritative insight into what clients wanted or what bankers at lower levels worried about. One director said: "I think they [top management] quickly lose touch with business conditions. If you haven't been involved in any deals for more than a year, I just don't think you still know what's going on." This division between top management and client service helped establish the dualism between abstract thinking and practical doing that characterizes traditional cognitive theories.

The Individual Bankers believed that the bank's strategy coordinated the activities of bankers in a cascading, top-down fashion. As the following director explained, each layer of management was responsible for translating the goals it received from above into more concrete directives:

> Our new top management has decided that we need to raise our profile among CEOs. That's the directive that was communicated to us. From that we decided that we need to shift away from the focus on equity that we had so far, because equity decisions are made by CFOs and treasurers. If you want to start a strategic dialogue with a CEO, you have to talk about issues that are of more strategic importance to a company. How to build a bigger empire or, more likely, how to dismantle the inefficient behemoths that have been created in the last decade or so. This kind of strategic repositioning is what CEOs worry about when they lie awake at night. That's what you want to get involved in.

Mid-level management accomplished this change in focus by aligning reporting relations with this new set of priorities. For example, they expanded the responsibilities of bankers with merger experience and formed merger-oriented subgroups to penetrate lucrative business segments, while consolidating equity-focused subgroups and demoting their leadership. These changes in responsibility and status were made highly visible by, for example, relocating the demoted groups to lower floors in the building and removing their perks. As one vice president said: "As a rule of thumb, the higher you are in the building, the more important you are to the business. If your group has been underperforming for a few months, the entire team moves a few floors down. I am not kidding." A director said: "When times get rough, groups that are less important to the business are

TABLE 2.1 *The banks' different uncertainty-management practices*

	Individual Bank	Organization Bank
Overall approach	Reduce uncertainty Narrow banker range of attention Convey abstract concepts	Amplify uncertainty Broaden banker range of attention Withhold abstract concepts and counteract their formation
Strategy and structures	Top bankers formulated abstract vision that guided lower-level bankers (deductive)	Top bankers facilitated self-organizing processes General strategies emerged from lower-level bankers' daily tasks (abductive)
Roles	Predetermined roles on each deal Titles on business cards Roles associated with specific tasks, behavioral norms, and relative status	Deemphasized roles No titles on business cards Fluid relation between roles and tasks Norms difficult to infer Status less important
Staffing	Based on expertise Banker biographies in pitch book Bankers were "public personalities" who often spoke to press	Bankers were fungible Pitch book highlighted organizational resources, contained no banker biographies Bankers were discouraged from talking to the press
Feedback	Review criteria determined deductively, from industry "best practices" Focus on quantitative assessments Senior bankers: Primarily revenue goals	Review criteria determined inductively, through interviews with bankers Focus on qualitative assessments Senior bankers: Ongoing feedback, no revenue goals
Training	Conducted by HR department Based on best industry practices Focus on general principles and abstract concepts for classifying people Bankers valued internal consistency Viewed as critical for improving banker performance	Conducted by bankers Based on concrete situations Focus on practical activities Emphasized contradictions Viewed as less potent than other work practices for improving performance

affected first. The first things to go are the flowers in the lobby and the afternoon snacks."

Once the relative importance of these groups had been rearranged, group heads devised specific revenue goals for each banker in the group. For example, one director said: "The way strategic change affects me is that I might be part of a different business group with different leadership, but most importantly I'll probably get a different set of clients and a different set of revenue targets." While managers focused on devising strategies, bankers were responsible for meeting these targets by bringing in and executing business. One managing director explained how focused goals helped to narrow banker attention, which was a crucial aspect of reducing cognitive uncertainty: "The more you help people focus their attention on specific goals, the better their performance."

One Individual Bank vice president summarized the bank's top-down approach as a response to the business's inherent uncertainty, elaborating on the specific practices that the bank used to reinforce strategic priorities:

> The more complex your business is, the more you need good leadership and strategies. You have to have someone with a vision, someone who decides where the organization is going, what its values are, what kind of organization you are going to be. And then you have to make sure that the values stick. You have to tell people about them, you have to tell them exactly what you expect of them, you have to set clear goals. Each quarter, we tell them exactly which clients to call and exactly how much revenue to bring in. And we train them to do that. We give them marketing skills, presentation skills, leadership skills. You know, you need to give people the tools they need to do their job. Once you have all that in place, you give it bite. You measure people on it. And you reward people really nicely who meet the goals you give them.

This quotation illustrates the internally consistent system that the bank's work practices formed. Internal consistency is important to reducing cognitive uncertainty because it eliminates conflicting information and cues. A managing director summarized how the bank's cognitive-uncertainty reducing practices were designed to support banker decision making: "There is freedom in structure. ... We tell our people what we expect from them – what markets to go into, how much revenue to bring in. And that frees them to worry about what they know best, namely, executing deals." Together these data show how the bankers construed their activities as following an internally consistent conceptual structure that translated top-management's abstract directives into increasingly more concrete guidelines at each lower level of the organization.

The bankers' descriptions of strategy formulation resemble academic accounts from the Carnegie School, an intellectual tradition that has made important contributions to both the management literature and traditional cognitive psychology. March and Simon (1958: 191), for example, depict organizations as means-ends chains that entail: "(1) starting with the general goal to be achieved, (2) discovering a set of means, very generally specified, for accomplishing this goal, (3) taking each of these means, in turn, as a new subgoal and discovering a set of more detailed means for achieving it."

Similarly, Simon (1976: 63) writes about a hierarchy of goals in which a given level is "considered as an end relative to the levels below it and as a means relative to the levels above it. Through the hierarchical structure of ends, behavior attains integration and consistency, for each member of a set of behavior alternatives is then weighted in terms of a comprehensive scale of values – the 'ultimate' ends."

Like the informants at Individual Bank, the Carnegie School construes organizational strategy as a way to reduce the cognitive uncertainty of decision makers, emphasizing an individual's cognitive limitations. For instance:

> It is impossible for the behavior of a single, isolated individual to reach any high degree of rationality. The number of alternatives he must explore is too great, the information he would need to evaluate them so vast that even an approximation to objective rationality is hard to conceive. Individual choice takes place in an environment of "givens" – premises that are accepted by the subject as bases for his choice; and behavior is adaptive only within the limits set by these "givens." (Simon, 1976: 79)

These parallels between Individual Bankers' conceptions and the Carnegie School perspective show how intertwined the Individual Bankers' practical understandings are with a cognitive psychological approach to knowledge.

At Individual Bank, strategy formulation was the first crucial practice for managing cognitive uncertainty. Individual Bank used a top-down process for strategy formulation in which management devised abstract concepts that guided the concrete actions of lower-level bankers. Strategy helped reduce cognitive uncertainty because bankers did not need to make sense of the broader economic environment or attend to idiosyncratic details of each specific deal. They made decisions by following management's abstract standards and they assessed the effectiveness of their performance with reference to these standards.

ROLES

Role definitions were a second practice through which the bank reduced cognitive uncertainty. Like strategies, roles consisted of abstractions that oriented the behavior of general types of employees. Roles were an important concept for bankers at all levels. One vice president said: "What you get paid, what you do, how people treat you, all of this depends on your role here." A banker's role was tied to his or her level in the bank's hierarchy (i.e., analyst, associate, vice president, director, and managing director). Because roles involved hierarchy, different roles conferred differential status. The bankers defined high status as "high social regard, esteem, and respect," "special recognition by your peers," and "heightened importance of the person." A senior title was viewed as desirable because it conferred high status and invited respectful treatment.

Senior bankers consciously made use of the status associated with their official roles when they spoke with clients, introducing themselves using their official title and offering business cards that indicated their title. As one managing director said: "The more senior clients think you are, the less often they'll challenge you." Senior titles thus reduced bankers' cognitive uncertainty by reassuring a client and perhaps preempting the client's probing questions. Mentioning one's title was also viewed as useful for other reasons, as this vice president described: "It helps set expectations. Otherwise things can get very disorienting and discouraging – especially for junior bankers – when clients call with requests they can't handle and it makes them feel and look bad when they cannot respond to a client."

This banker describes how roles reduced cognitive uncertainty by spelling out responsibilities and expectations. The data on Individual Banker roles presented in this section further illustrate the bankers' focus on the individual, the importance of social comparison processes among individuals, and the emotional investment bankers had in such comparisons. This focus on the individual as the principal unit of analysis is also central to cognitive theories. In addition, traditional cognitive theories emphasize the importance of social comparison as an important means to reduce subjective uncertainty (Festinger, 1954).

One important expectation that was made salient to bankers at all levels involved appropriate working hours. Junior bankers were expected to stay until at least 10 or 11 PM every night, even if they did not have pressing work. The more senior the banker, the earlier he or she could go home. As one director said: "As a director, your hours become really manageable. I come to work at nine, leave between five and six at night and rarely have any work during the weekend, perhaps a call here and there." These work norms had an important motivating effect on junior bankers. For example, one associate said: "That is one reason why many of us are willing to work hard in the beginning and establish ourselves, because there is a system here that gives you more privilege as you become more senior." These norms for appropriate working hours, associated with hierarchically organized banker roles, illustrate Individual Bankers' orientation toward abstractions. Bankers did not need to decide their working hours based primarily on the demands of their projects because they could follow the bank's role-based expectations.

Roles also reduced cognitive uncertainty because they provided a limited set of responsibilities for each team member and ensured that each member knew what to expect from others:

> Let's say you meet with a new team for a conference call with the client. You don't have to talk about who does what. As a vice president, I'd start the call and talk about the strategic issues. When it comes to logistics and the daily interactions with the client, that's when the associate comes in. Analysts are typically quiet during the call but take note of all the issues that are relevant for the analyses they have to do afterward. ... And after the meeting, it is clear that the analyst goes off and puts together a book, the associate supervises the analyst and checks the product before I get to see it for mark-ups.

An associate described the role-based division of labor in the following way:

> See my business card says "associate." That's who I am. That is what I do. This means that everything that has to do with managing this deal goes through me, just like everything that has to do with modeling and word processing automatically ends up with Joe [the analyst]. That's how things work around here. ... We have a term here for people like Joe, we call them the "managing analyst."

Role expectations were often enforced informally, through slights or public reprimands in response to violations. The associate quoted in the last excerpt complained about Joe, who had repeatedly neglected his financial modeling tasks and tried to offer input to the associate on issues of deal management, which would normally be a managing director's role. The excerpt also shows how roles were associated with normative expectations among colleagues, such as appropriately deferential demeanor. One associate described this type of experience from the perspective of the person who has unintentionally violated implicit role norms: "A lot of people look at investment banking and think that it is organic and everything. But there is a lot of structure. ... One way you notice this structure is if you unintentionally violate it, overstep your bounds to a vice president or do the job of an analyst. Those are interesting experiences."

One senior Individual Banker was known for his short attention span and temper. He was on the bank's syndicate desk, and other bankers often needed his input for their decisions. When a junior banker approached him in a hurried manner because she needed his judgment for a client call that was taking place in the next few minutes, he sent her away without the information. He explained that there is "etiquette" to observe for how to approach an "officer of the firm" that should be obeyed regardless of how pressing matters appeared to be. In a similar case, an associate left a voice mail for a vice president, asking how a client meeting went that the associate could not attend. The vice president erased this voice-mail without answering it because "he (i.e., the associate) works for me, not I for him." He felt that the associate should have asked the analyst on the deal team for information. These examples show how the abstract, evaluative role concepts informed how Individual Bankers thought, felt, and acted.

Surprisingly, most bankers did not mind when their colleagues acted uncooperatively in situations where role boundaries had been overstepped. Instead, they valued the clear messages such behaviors sent on how to behave. For example, one vice president said:

> Each group has norms and rules on how to behave. At least here you know where you're at with people. In some of the other banks that I have worked for, people only talk about others behind their back. And, of course, you can tell that something is up but you can't quite tell what it is and so you constantly feel like you are walking on eggshells. That's one problem you won't have around here.

Roles at Individual Bank thus reduced the cognitive uncertainty that could arise in the absence of explicit normative expectations.

The examples offered in this section show how role-related considerations often replaced or interfered with task-related considerations. When people felt that their status was threatened – when someone did not show them sufficient deference, for example – they often shifted attention from task-related considerations and focused on rectifying the threat to their identity. Status could also interfere with task completion when higher-status bankers asserted their importance in a way that made poor use of organizational resources. One associate offered the following example of how senior bankers could sometimes disrespect the time of junior bankers:

> I am working with this clueless vice president. You can give her a spread-sheet now and then she turns around and asks: "Where is my spread-sheet?" And when we are in meetings, she just brings herself. We have to carry the books for everyone, and for her we have to bring pens, a pad of paper, we have to tell her secretary about dates that came up during the meeting. When we have a meeting scheduled, she sometimes has people double booked and you have to hang out in front of her office until she is ready to see you. She is an example of someone who has status around here. The people carrying the books for her and hanging out in front of her office are examples of people who don't have status here.

Formal roles at Individual Bank thus represented an abstraction-oriented or deductive approach to organizing experience and dealing with uncertainty. Bankers did not need to refer to the complex details of a concrete situation, but could instead judge the appropriateness of a decision or a behavior based on its consistency with abstract role standards that generalized across situations. This reduced cognitive uncertainty because bankers always had specified responsibilities and predetermined behavioral etiquettes, regardless of the specific type of situation they were in. This approach also had costs, because the focus on abstract roles narrowed the bankers' attention at the same time as it reduced cognitive uncertainty.

Individual Bank's emphasis on roles fits well with traditional cognitive theories. This bank and cognitive psychology construe the relationship between individuals and the social context in similar ways. The traditional cognitive conception of organizations promulgated by the Carnegie School (e.g., March and Simon, 1958; Simon, 1976) borrowed from the structural sociological tradition (e.g., Moreno, 1953; Park, 1955; Linton, 1936) to develop an understanding of how individuals understand themselves with respect to a society conceived in terms of roles and other abstract concepts. Both Individual Bankers and cognitive psychologists construe the behavior of an individual as shaped by his or her individual role in relation to a social network of complementary roles. This perception of how the individual relates to society is not the only possible one, and how a banker or a theorist conceives of the relationship between the individual and society has important consequences. Once an individual banker or a cognitive researcher views the social context as constituted by roles, a predictable set of concerns emerge. For example, both cognitive theory and Individual Bankers are preoccupied with normative expectations and status – issues that were less important in Organization Bank, which, as described in the next chapter, construed the relationship between the individual and social context differently.

STAFFING

Individual Bankers worked on projects that corresponded to their expertise. For example, when the bank received a mandate to sell a healthcare company, it staffed bankers with experience in both the healthcare industry and sell-side assignments. This was an important part of the bank's business model. As one director said, "We sell the knowledge of our superstars." Similarly, one of the bank's strategy reports described how "our brand is tied to our superstars. Ask our clients who Individual Bank is and they will list some of the most influential bankers in the industry." A superstar was someone who had both a relatively senior title and deep expertise in a subject area. For example, one associate said: "Bill is one of our superstars. He is a managing director and knows every single high yield covenant by heart. He is not the most charismatic guy but clients are awed by that kind of crazy expertise." Staffing bankers on the same kind of deal repeatedly helped the bank create such expertise. As one director said, "We emphasize continuity in staffing. We want people to build and capitalize on their expertise." Some of the more senior associates talked about their futile attempts to modify this system. For example, one fourth-year associate said: "Initially, when I came here I wanted to see different kinds of industries but I soon realized that the ticket to success is specialization and so I picked an industry and kept working on deals in that industry." A third-year associate said: "The expert mindset is so much part of the system that trying to work against it is like swimming upstream. I really wanted to stay broad and kept fighting to be placed on deals in different industries but invariably when something in the defense sector came up it was like: 'Joe, we really need you on this.'"

In what they called "pitch books," the presentations with which bankers solicited client business, Individual Bank emphasized the expertise of specific bankers. As a vice president said, "our pitch books always highlight banker biographies. You get the deal if you have individuals with strong expertise." And most clients did believe that having specialized senior bankers on their deal was desirable, because they expected that the most senior bankers had accumulated the greatest amount of knowledge. One client said: "If you have done this type of deal so many times, you know about things and little tricks that someone who is new doesn't." For other clients, having specialized senior bankers on the deal team meant reassurance that the bank was committed to serving the company well. Another client said: "The risk in going with a large bank is that if you are a smaller company, you'll end up with the b-team – a bunch of MBAs who are fresh out of school and who have never done work in our industry before."

The bank's superstars were also regularly featured in industry publications for both investment banking and the client industry they focused on, where they commented on new developments. These superstars were referred to as "public personalities" within the bank. This publicity was designed to strengthen bonds with existing clients, reassuring them that they were working with the most knowledgeable people in the industry. It also created the bank's reputation for excellence in that industry, and it attracted new clients. As one director said:

> One of the best marketing opportunities is to your existing clients. You are up to speed on the client and the industry and you ideally have already proven yourself. A column in a trade magazine or a blurb in a newspaper is a great reason to call on them and to feel them out for new opportunities. . . . And it is great for them because it helps them justify their choice of investment bankers to their boss: "See, Harris, who I brought on board to help us, is a recognized expert."

A new client, a biotech CEO, called Individual Bank after he read an interview with Gary, a biotech expert, and said: "You don't even have to pitch to me. Just tell me that Gary works on this and I'll give you my business." The staffer who received this call said that it was "typical. We always get at least one or two calls out of an industry article. It is great business." As a managing director said, "This kind of public dialogue is crucial for us to establish thought leadership in the industry. At some level we are the sum of the expertise of our superstars." This comment suggests that a bank only knows what is in the heads of its individual bankers, which is how cognitive theory construes organizational knowledge (Simon, 1991).

Individual Bank's staffing practice – cultivating superstars and assigning expert bankers to deal teams in their area – reduced cognitive uncertainty for various reasons. For one, bankers only had to master a limited domain of knowledge. As one vice president said, "This business is so complex and so dynamic that you just have to specialize. It is impossible for one person to be an expert at more than one small area." A director noted: "The client is buying *my* expertise. I am not only expected to read out of a book that the team has produced. I am supposed to have answers and to speak with confidence and authority. You can only do that if you can draw on a deep knowledge base." This excerpt also illustrates how Individual Bank's staffing approach reduced cognitive uncertainty by enhancing bankers' confidence and ability to meet client expectations. Such confidence was important as bankers competed for business.

Clients also valued bankers with specialized knowledge about their industry and their problems. One vice president uneasily remembered a client meeting that focused on his expertise:

> It was a really unpleasant and uncomfortable meeting. The client kept grilling me on details about the industry that I had no clue about. I knew what kinds of deals had been done at which multiples, who the likely buyers were, and so on. That's the stuff that really matters. But they wanted me to have really detailed knowledge like they wanted me to know the market strategy of competitor X, the anticipated market response to product Y, what I thought about the new developments of another competitor. And I tried to steer the topic back to issues that I was knowledgeable about, the banking issues, but I had lost all control over the meeting. It was impossible to establish credibility after that. Needless to say, we didn't get the deal.

This quotation shows how clients interpreted bankers' lack of specialized expertise as a weakness. This vice president experienced cognitive uncertainty because he sensed the client's skepticism, which undermined the superstar personality he wanted to project, and because he could not anticipate where the meeting was going.

Individual Bank's staffing approach is consistent with cognitive theories that locate expertise in the minds of particular individuals (e.g., Chase and Simon, 1973). The bank's notion of the superstar, which focused on both seniority and specialization, reflects the cognitive view that expert performance results from many years of deliberate practice (Ericsson and Lehmann, 1996). Superstars were either directors or managing directors, titles that were usually reached after about ten years of relevant experience. The bank's emphasis on specialization also corresponds to the cognitive finding that expertise is tied to a relatively narrow domain of knowledge (Ericsson and Lehmann, 1996). Finally, consistent with cognitive theories, the bank's staffing practices assumed that the knowledge bankers gained in one situation was transferable to similar situations – a claim that sociocultural theorists dispute (e.g., Anderson et al., 1996, 1997; Brown et al., 1989; Greeno, 1997).

FEEDBACK

Individual Bankers were evaluated annually using a 360-degree feedback process (Burton, 1998). In this process, the focal individual was reviewed "from all sides," with input from superiors, subordinates, peers, and both internal and external clients. As the first step in the process, bankers received a list of all people with whom they had worked during the previous year. Each banker was supposed to indicate those individuals with whom he or she had significant interactions. Those individuals would then fill out a review on the focal banker. In addition to completing reviews for others they had worked with, bankers filled out a self-evaluation form. This initial part of the annual evaluation process was standard practice in the industry. Organization Bank used similar procedures.

The banks differed, however, in how they selected criteria for the evaluation. Organization Bank determined criteria mostly inductively, based on interviews with bankers at all levels. An Individual Bank human resource specialist described his bank's more deductive approach:

> There are certain types of competencies that we want our people to have, and the review reflects these competencies. I guess some of these are generic, and you'll find them on the review of every investment bank. I cannot imagine that there is anyone out there who doesn't have some version of teamwork, selling, leadership, and quantitative ability. The more specific behaviors, we came up with in consultation with management to make sure that they reflect our strategy. This year, for example, we included something on global perspective and also something on diversity to reinforce our strategy.

This quotation illustrates how the review was based on categories that were relatively abstract and tied to the bank's strategy – which was itself based on abstract principles, as described above. Individual Bank cultivated in individuals the habit of categorizing situations in relatively abstract ways, which contrasts to the more concrete orientation that Organization Bank fostered.

Another human resource specialist emphasized the importance of internal consistency between the annual review criteria and the bank's other practices: "The review is critical for sending a message to bankers about what we want them to do. And it is important that this message is aligned with all the other messages we are sending with our strategy, with training, with money. They all have to be aligned, otherwise people get confused."

The review process was thus another way of reducing cognitive uncertainty because it helped bankers focus their attention on a limited number of behaviors that were important to the bank. As the quotation suggests, internal consistency was important at Individual Bank. Because bankers evaluated the effectiveness of their behaviors not primarily with respect to concrete situations but instead with respect to abstract concepts conveyed through strategy, roles, feedback, and other practices, Individual Bankers attended closely to internal consistency between their behavior and the bank's standards. Internal consistency among concepts is also an important idea in cognitive theory, which focuses on the relations among representations. Prawat (1996), for example, observes that, according to cognitive theories, "valid or correct ideas cohere. They fit together like the pieces of a puzzle," and he claims that such coherence is a central criterion for judging ideas' validity.

Individual Bank also relied relatively more on quantitative assessments in its evaluation and feedback process. For each review criterion, such as "leadership," the form provided a scale consisting of three boxes, which were labeled "area for development," "meets standards," "exceeds standards." The space for comments was rarely used. One human resources specialist explained this by saying, "I guess bankers have too much to do to write anything. We are happy when they give us numeric rankings." A managing director commented on the design of the review form:

> I think our competitors are more sophisticated on this. They rank people on more items and make finer distinctions, letting you rate someone on a scale between one and six, for example. Here you either meet the standard or you don't. It's that simple. I think people here are uncomfortable with qualitative assessments. Even with this simple system, you'd think that people take the numbers as a rough guide and look more at what people actually said about a banker. What you find instead is that in review meetings, you hear people make distinctions between someone who averaged 2.7 on an item, as compared to someone who averaged 2.2 on an item, as if this difference reflected some kind of reality.

This excerpt illustrates the Individual Bankers' orientation toward abstract concepts, such as those conveyed by numerical ratings. It also shows that some Individual Bankers recognized potential problems with such an orientation, including mistaking an abstraction for the more complex reality it is designed to summarize.

The banks also differed in how they used the information collected in the review. At Individual Bank, the head of the department provided feedback to all bankers, sometimes together with the department's chief operating officer. One human resource specialist explained this choice: "These things need to come from above to make an impression on bankers." A vice president described the structure of the typical review meeting: "They tell you in one sentence each what your strengths and weaknesses are. . . . If there are major problems, they might make suggestions for improvement. For example, some bankers were sent to remedial corporate finance training."

Another vice president showed us a sheet that he had received during the review. Under "strengths" the sheet said: "Peter is well respected for his diligence and his quantitative abilities." As a "weakness" it listed: "Peter needs to develop more presence in client meetings and pursue new business opportunities more aggressively." The suggestion Peter received was: "Work with a marketing skills coach." A "strength" or "weakness," as represented on this form, provides an abstract summary of how the banker behaved across situations. This formulation encouraged bankers to construe their performance in abstract ways, in terms of general traits.

Most Individual Bankers valued the review process because it reduced cognitive uncertainty. Peter commented on his review: "There is very little ambiguity here, which is good in a way. It's very clear cut: here is what we want you to focus on and here is how." Another vice president said: "I like our system because it does not leave you hanging, letting you figure things out for yourself. You get clear and specific guidance." Even though this guidance was perceived as helpful by the bankers, it was still fairly general and did not take the situation of particular bankers into account. Associates who scored low on analytic capabilities, for example, were all given corporate finance training. Associates who were lacking certain types of knowledge were all told to seek out projects that provided this knowledge.

For senior bankers, the evaluation system mattered much less. Feedback occurred, but the annual evaluation process was less important than the revenue individuals generated. According to one vice president: "People still give you your yearly feedback. It just becomes less important. I would just be stunned to see them fire a major rainmaker just because he wasn't popular. We have lots of big, abrasive egos around here who get away with pissing people off because they bring in revenues."

The feedback process at Individual Bank reduced uncertainty because bankers were oriented toward relatively few – and, with seniority, increasingly fewer – evaluation categories. Moreover, bankers preferred to construe these categories in quantitative ways, avoiding messy qualitative data. Like the other practices the bank used, such as strategy formulations and role definitions, the review process reduced cognitive uncertainty by pointing bankers to an internally consistent system of abstract concepts.

TRAINING

Individual Bank's training practices also reduced cognitive uncertainty. The Individual Bank human resources department was responsible for organizing training. Outsourcing training to human resources reduced bankers' cognitive uncertainty by narrowing the kinds of issues bankers had to focus on. One Individual Bank managing director sneered at the Organization Bankers' practice of having bankers conduct banker training:

> Western society thrives on specialization. I can do all the things I need to do because I don't have to worry about how the computer, the phone, the TV function. I let others worry about the intricacies of these instruments so that I can just push the button. The same principle applies here. Bankers have their heads full with execution. We don't know anything about training. That's the way it is supposed to be. We let the training department worry about training.

As described in the next chapter, Organization Bankers viewed training as inextricable from doing. In contrast, the Individual Bankers felt that training could be separated from doing and requires the intervention of experts. As one Individual Bank director said, "When we have a performance problem, we don't have the time or knowledge required to deal with it. What I do in these situations is I contact HR to get the banker some training." At Individual Bank, people conceived of learning as something that should take place separately, in a classroom setting. A similar separation between practical and abstract ways of knowing appeared in Individual Bank's strategy formulation practices, as described above.

The human resources staff selected training programs, vendors, and content based on "best industry practice." This was an abstract standard that did not take Individual Bank's specific needs into account. One critic of this approach at Individual Bank said, cynically:

> The way we are selecting training programs and vendors is very simple: We do whatever the Joneses are doing. Why go through the messy

process and figure out what bankers actually need to know when you can just do whatever [a prominent consulting firm and investment bank] are doing? Even if the program is completely wrong for us, who would fire you for doing what they are doing?

This critic accused the training staff of illegitimately simplifying their decision making by ignoring the fit of the training product. Most Individual Bankers approved of the "best practices" approach to training, however, and used it themselves. As one vice president said: "There is a reason why these things are called best practices. You'd be stupid to dismiss the collective expertise of an entire industry." The best practices approach reveals Individual Bankers' belief that knowledge can often be transferred unproblematically from one type of context to another, a belief that cognitive psychologists would agree with.

At both banks, bankers felt too pressed for time to attend training. Even if they attended, they stepped out frequently to make calls. Realizing this difficulty, Individual Bank's management made some courses mandatory. Among the mandatory courses, bankers felt that two were particularly helpful. One course used the Myers-Briggs inventory to help bankers interact with colleagues and clients. With reference to this tool, one banker said:

> I am just amazed how accurate this is. I can look at anyone I am working with and it is very clear where that person falls. Having a tool like this can really help you make difficult decisions. When I have to staff people on a project that requires difficult communication and delicate handling of the client, I would probably not go with an "I" [introvert].

Another banker said: "I wonder whether 'I's' [introverts] should be in our group in the first place. I think they'd be happier in something like structured finance, where they do heavy analytics and don't need to be in constant client contact."

These Individual Bankers accepted the Myers-Briggs categories as accurate descriptions of individual people. The categories then reduced cognitive uncertainty because they narrowed the dimensions along which bankers could classify another person and because each category was associated with an appropriate way to treat an individual.

The other popular training course at Individual Bank helped bankers classify subordinates into a two-by-two matrix. One axis represented the extent to which the subordinate was motivated or not, and the other axis represented the extent to which the subordinate had the requisite knowledge to complete the task. Once the subordinate was classified, the leader could apply a predetermined set of techniques. One vice president explained how this approach reduced uncertainty: "It takes the guesswork out of working with junior people. All you need to remember is to ask yourself two simple questions and the rest falls into place." Both courses also offered detailed checklists that the bankers could use on their jobs, which were a much-appreciated aid. One trainer explained how these materials could help reduce bankers' cognitive uncertainty by simplifying their decision making: "We put a lot of effort into the design of the training material, in particular those aspects that the bankers can use on the job. We want this material to give very explicit advice. I mean that is the whole purpose of the material and the course, to simplify your daily decisions."

It makes sense that these two training courses would be so popular with Individual Bankers. As we have seen, the bankers tended to construe people using relatively abstract categories. They also believed that their abstract categories for classifying people accurately predicted behavior. As a result, they tended to ignore the situational factors that Organization Bankers attended to and that sociocultural theories claim are important for understanding behavior.

Training courses were less popular at Individual Bank when they did not offer practical guidelines, when they raised more questions than they answered, or when they either were internally inconsistent or contradicted something that the bankers had learned in another course. For example, one director complained about a forum of "leading thinkers" designed to introduce bankers to provocative ideas in the social sciences: 'I just don't have the time and patience for this type of pontification. If there is no take-away that I can use, I am just not interested.' A vice president agreed: "Good training is supposed to help you answer questions. But most of these so-called thinkers congratulate themselves on raising new questions so that you can see what complex people they are." Another vice president complained about the inconsistency across marketing courses: "The last time I took a course, it told me to drill into clients to make them 'feel the pain' [of their organizational problem]. But this consultant is telling us that this approach is completely wrong and insensitive. The least they [i.e., human resources] can do is to make sure that each course has the same message." These excerpts show how Individual Bankers resisted training experiences that broadened their range of attention beyond what was relevant to their organizational role, as well as ones that made situations seem complex and asked them to embrace inconsistencies.

A few internal critics of Individual Bank's approach to training noted its tendency to oversimplify situations. For example, one director commented on the Meyers-Briggs course with some skepticism: "I think this is getting somewhat out of hand. I appreciate the beauty of having a magic formula for figuring people out but the problem is that this formula doesn't exist." Another director said, with disdain: "Instead of fretting about whether the client is an I or an E, they would be better advised to listen to what the client is saying." Others criticized the cookie-cutter strategies for management taught in some courses. One informant described how her manager had participated in a leadership course where she learned that her usual "I disagree with you" might alienate colleagues and was not conducive to gaining their cooperation. The trainers helped the manager to develop a more cooperative leadership style which, in practice, meant that she now replaced the words "I disagree with you" with "help me understand this." The informant said that this did not have the desired effect, because the managers' subordinates now simply decoded the latter as meaning the former: "How stupid does she think we are? She leans forward with that fake smile on her face and her hands on the table like one of these baboons in the zoo and thinks that this will make me feel all warm and fuzzy toward her."

Individual Bank's clients had often learned the same material in their internal training courses, and they sometimes felt manipulated when the banker interjected such utterances as: "How does this situation make you feel?" One CEO commented after a meeting: "I know exactly what they are doing. I took the same course. I wish they would pay as much attention to what I am telling them." Another client complained: "These cookbook strategies worry me. When you hire an advisor you expect someone who has the ability to think for themselves, not just mechanically apply some kind of recipe." Other clients were more complimentary, however. One said, "I think it is fabulous that they are taking training so seriously. That tells me they invest in their human capital." Another client remarked, "I like it that they have a consistent approach, that you can count on the quality of their bankers."

Individual Bank's training practices fit well with traditional cognitive theory, but they also embodied some aspects of sociocultural theories. Like Organization Bank and most professional service firms, Individual Bank relied heavily on apprenticeship methods of training. At least implicitly, then, Individual Bankers believed that engagement in practice could be an important source of learning. Individual Bankers also empasized the trajectory from "peripheral" to more central participation described by Lave and Wenger (1991). In fact, Individual Bank encouraged peripheral participation by new bankers much more than Organization Bank, which threw new bankers into the middle of deals from the beginning. This difference is described in more detail in Chapters 5 and 6.

At the same time, Individual Bank's assignment of training responsibilities to the human resources department, its adoption of industry best practices, and its focus on classroom training all embodied the separation between learning and doing and between abstract and practical ways of knowing that characterize traditional cognitive approaches. As Lave (2003: 12) argues, traditional cognitive psychology "involves two theoretical claims that are in question here: One is that actors' relations with knowledge-in-activity are static and do not change except when subject to special periods of 'learning' or 'development.' The other is that institutional arrangements for inculcating knowledge *are* the necessary, special circumstances for learning, separate from everyday practices." She claims that this cognitive view is based on an epistemology that locates "knowledge as a collection of real entities, located in heads, and of learning as a process of internalizing them." Individual Bankers shared this view – as revealed, for example, by their interest in learning general principles that they could "take with them" from the classroom to their jobs.

Cognitive psychology's emphasis on abstract knowledge mentally represented by individuals has also informed theories of "professionalism" that carry weight at Individual Bank. According to theories of professionalism, the application of general principles is the hallmark of what it means to be a professional. In his article "Who is a professional?" Nanda (2005: 2) defines professionals by what they do, including diagnosis and inference: "Diagnosis categorizes and removes the extraneous qualities of an object being studied. It is a process of departicularizing, of removing the idiosyncratic aspects of an object to enable a service provider to focus undistracted on the 'problem' it presents. . . . Inference is the process of converting an analysis of the problem 'type' into a prescribed 'solution.'" This quotation captures the importance of abstract knowledge that we observed at Individual Bank.

This chapter has described how Individual Bank reduced cognitive uncertainty by orienting bankers toward abstractions. Five central practices for reducing uncertainty – strategy formulation, role definition, training, staffing, and feedback – encouraged Individual Bankers to attend to abstract concepts and guidelines as they conceptualized themselves, interacted with others, and did their work. The abstract vision that was central to the bank's strategy freed bankers from thinking about complexities of the economic environment and particular client situations. Roles provided abstract principles that bankers could use to make such decisions as how they should contribute to a deal and how many hours they should work. By staffing individuals consistently on the same types of deals, bankers became specialists in types of transactions and learned relatively standard problem solving procedures that applied well to those situations. The bank's feedback system classified bankers into abstract categories – such as "weak in client contact" – that were associated with generic recommendations for improvement – such as "take presentation skills class." Finally, training gave bankers tools for classifying situations and people, using categories that suggested relatively generic courses of action – "don't use an introvert on client-intensive deals." The abstract categories embedded in all these Individual Bank practices reduced cognitive uncertainty because bankers could respond to new situations using these familiar concepts. Abstractions apply across specific situations, and so Individual Bankers did not need to explore concrete aspects of unique situations, which allowed them to do their work more efficiently.

3

Practices That Amplified Cognitive Uncertainty at Organization Bank

Organization Bank took a different approach to managing cognitive uncertainty. When asked the same open-ended question about factors that
were critical for a bank's performance, Organization Bankers said that
banks fail when "people think of themselves as experts and don't realize
that their knowledge doesn't apply to a new situation," that "bankers
develop these recipes for how to do things and forget that each situation
is different," and that "people put too much faith into what they think to
be true." Out of forty-two senior bankers interviewed, thirty-seven made
reference to practices that involve uncertainty amplification. They said that
banks succeed when they "continuously remind people of how little they
know" and "create the 'insecure overachiever,' someone who compulsively
doubts what they know all the time." Because Organization Bank believed
that general concepts could encourage a dangerous sense of cognitive
certainty, it discouraged the abstract strategies, roles, and criteria that were
encouraged at Individual Bank. Furthermore, Organization Bank actively
created cognitive uncertainty, counteracting people's tendency to rely on
abstract concepts by forcing bankers to attend to a broad range of concrete
information and denying them abstract concepts to organize that information. None of the Individual Bankers mentioned anything resembling
cognitive uncertainty amplification in their responses, and none of the
Organization Bankers mentioned anything like cognitive uncertainty
reduction.

This chapter describes how Organization Bank implemented its counterintuitive program of cognitive uncertainty amplification, exploring the
same five practices of strategy formulation, role definition, training, staffing, and feedback. At Organization Bank, these practices intentionally
amplified uncertainty, overwhelming bankers with cognitive demands so
that they would use organizational resources to address problems and

putting them in unfamiliar situations so that they would not get comfortable with general strategies. We describe Organization Bank's uncertainty-amplification practices in relatively more detail because they are less familiar than Individual Bank's uncertainty-reduction strategies.

In contrast to Individual Bank, senior Organization Bankers were not primarily strategists and managers. They did not promulgate abstract visions designed to reduce cognitive uncertainty. Instead of giving subordinates abstract principles that applied across situations, they established and maintained an unusual set of practices that reminded bankers of the uncertainty present in every situation and helped bankers arrive at unique answers for each specific problem. As one group leader explained: "I don't manage people. I am a believer in process. I make sure that people get the facts and they can then manage themselves." This theme was echoed by a vice president, who said about the group leader: "Joe is where he is not because of some kind of management skill – we actually do not have managers around here, just so you know – but because he is just a terrific banker. He is just masterful with clients. That's why people bring him in on difficult deals. So he still deals with clients all day."

As this vice president says, very senior Organization Bankers had both management and deal responsibilities. Relative to the more specialized Individual Bankers, this expanded each banker's decision range and business perspective and thereby introduced more cognitive uncertainty. Even the most senior professionals remained in client contact and, as a result, experienced the business through concrete transactions as well as abstract trends.

Organization Bankers did not expect their leaders to formulate strategies or visions, and they were skeptical about the usefulness of such abstract concepts. At one point during our fieldwork a consulting firm pitched to the group's leadership, urging them to put more explicit goals and strategies in place. A vice president responded during the meeting:

> Strategies, goals, visions, and that stuff don't work here. Our business is too complex for that. You have to take one little step at a time and then see where it gets you before you take the next one. . . . Sure, we have leadership. It kind of works by vacuum. People do what needs to get done. And Joe [the group leader] leaves you alone. Unless you are violating some really basic principles, like lying, cheating, stealing – that

kind or stuff. Then he comes down on you like a ton of bricks and you are out of here.

This excerpt shows how senior bankers refrained from dictating general principles that other bankers could then apply. Instead, senior bankers reinforced stepwise processes through which bankers attended to specific actions and responses and let answers to problems unfold. The vice president here speaks like a sociocultural theorist. Suchman (1987: 52), for example, argues that abstract knowledge, like plans and strategies, are too vague to guide behavior and that more effective decision making requires contextual sensitivity and willingness to readjust: "It is frequently only on acting in a present situation that its possibilities become clear, and we often do not know ahead of time, or at least not with any specificity, what future state we desire to bring about."

Two examples of such stepwise processes at Organization Bank were "probabilistic decision making" and "due diligence." Both of these notions acknowledged uncertainty as an inevitable part of the business. They were not designed to reduce cognitive uncertainty, but instead provided ways in which bankers could work with uncertainty. One managing director reflected on how the practice of probabilistic decision making became culturally shared:

> If there is one thing that comes from the top, it is the constant awareness that all the decisions we make are probabilistic ones. That is not just a belief that is communicated, but something that is ingrained in behaviors. Most of us run around with our yellow pads and in meetings keep calculating the odds that certain outcomes will occur.

A director described how senior bankers encouraged due diligence in other bankers:

> In my interactions with management, I need to be prepared to answer a barrage of questions, each one drilling deeper on the previous one. I think this is actually the way they lead. They don't tell you what to do but make sure that you have done your due diligence. . . . You'll never have all the answers when you have to make a decision. But at least you know what risks you are taking.

As this director suggests, Organization Bankers carefully gathered and analyzed relevant information because senior bankers routinely asked for such analyses. A vice president outlined the stepwise nature of this approach: "It is actually an iterative process. Due diligence is like a conversation with the facts. You poke for facts, go away and do some calculations, see that you don't have all the answers and then poke some more until very gradually you see a bit more of the picture."

These passages show that Organization Bank management had influence over lower level bankers in a very different way than Individual Bank management. Senior Individual Bankers circulated abstract concepts for subordinates to internalize and act on. They relied primarily on the types of abstract mental concepts that are foregrounded by cognitive theory – strategies, scripts, roles, and procedures. In contrast, senior Organization Bankers used artifacts and activities – such as using yellow pads to calculate odds and probing questions – to shape bankers' behaviors. They did not simply give bankers an abstract principle – "remember that our business is uncertain" – but instead structured the task environment so that it continuously reminded bankers of this fact.

The last passage above also shows that Organization Bankers thought of traditionally intramental processes like checking the facts as a "conversation" between the facts and the person. Like sociocultural researchers (e.g., Barab and Plucker, 2002; Gibson, 1977), these bankers construed cognition as a more situated process. They created interactions between people, objects, and activities in order to achieve goals that Individual Bankers achieved through the transfer of mental entities from one individual mind to another. Organization Bank thus enacted sociocultural theory's emphasis on the interdependence between a person and the social and material environment. Lave (1988: 1) accurately describes Organization Bank's more situated approach: "'Cognition' observed in everyday practice is distributed – stretched over, not divided among – mind, body, activity, and culturally organized settings which include other actors." Lave's description, of course, can also be used to understand the Individual Bank context. But we argue that cognition can be more or less distributed, depending on the extent to which actors note and effectively utilize the cognitive contributions of the social environment.

Like Individual Bank, Organization Bank had to manage chronic uncertainty. Individual Bank used a deductive process in which abstract principles framed bankers' understandings of particular situations. Organization Bank, in contrast, used what Peirce (1934) called an "abductive" process. Like induction, abduction orients first toward concrete information before arriving at more general understandings. Induction encodes concrete information for the purpose of building or retrieving an abstract concept from memory (Brewer and Harasty Feinstein, 1999), and as a result inductive processes only represent what is immanent in the concrete data without arriving at new understandings. Deduction is also unlikely to yield new insights because it merely generalizes existing principles to new situations. Abduction, in contrast, involves creative inference to a new explanation.

Organization Bankers used distributed cognitive processes to arrive, abductively, at new courses of action. Through ongoing observation and interactions among bankers, new understandings emerged. The following example illustrates how lower-level bankers took action and then collectively examined the consequences to guide their next steps – instead of deciding on a plan and then deductively acting on it. At one point, a vice president explained how he had encountered a problem with a client in the health care industry: "The client just kept asking us these really specific questions about the industry and wouldn't even get to the finance part." Because the banker did not know what to do, he consulted with colleagues. He explained how, in these conversations, bankers compared their experiences and discovered common experiences: "As it turned out, we all had the same experience. The clients wanted industry knowledge and none of us could offer that. So we turned adversity into opportunity and only days later had the healthcare group up and running."

The bankers did not understand the clients' request for industry knowledge because they had previously been judged on their financial expertise. But once they discovered that clients wanted domain-specific knowledge in addition to financial expertise, they created a group that collected such knowledge. Other Organization Bankers could then draw on the resulting industry-specific knowledge as needed. The bankers thus transcended their previous mindsets and were able to develop new responses.

Bankers at all levels were assigned to make contributions to this new group while continuing to work on other assignments. For example, analysts compiled databases with industry-specific deal comparisons and created a basic set of statistics and graphs that summarized industry trends. Associates checked and guided this work. More senior bankers regularly spoke with clients and industry experts throughout the firm to understand the unique dynamics of the industry. Marketing experts devised products and presentation templates that capitalized on the opportunities that were discovered in this way.

During weekly conversations at the department's staff meeting, members of the group discussed their new initiatives and the preliminary responses from clients and colleagues in other departments. A managing director mentioned the course corrections that resulted from such conversations: "We have these ongoing conversations because whenever you do something new and respond to a new kind of environment, you don't get it right the first time, and you have to adjust what you do a little every time." The bankers' experimentation was motivated by cognitive uncertainty, the sense that whatever one does can probably be improved upon. As noted above, socioculturalists also emphasize how action in a situation can become a resource that informs the next step to take (Suchman, 1987). Another Organization Bank managing director described one such course correction:

> I think we initially overemphasized the infrastructure, the databases and products and templates and what not. But clients wanted to be able to talk to *people* who had experience with their competitors or who were following their market segment. So we put more emphasis on a process that invited experts from these different areas of the firm to each client meeting. In other words, industry focus partly meant moving away from the product focus that we had, where it was a merger banker sitting in the meeting, armed with [industry-specific] knowledge.

These quotations illustrate the iterative nature of abductive inference. Bankers used concrete information to arrive at one potential solution, which they then tested by gathering more information; then they revised their actions, and gathered more information, and so on.

These iterations differ from the "one-shot" planning process used by Individual Bankers. Individual Bankers differentiated between the planning and the execution stages of a project. During the planning stage, top management conducted relatively comprehensive data collection. During the execution stage, data collection was minimal and consisted mostly of monitoring the planned state against the actual state of the project. In addition, management was responsible for planning and strategy formulation, while lower-level bankers were responsible for execution. This dualistic split between the abstract and the practical was characteristic of Individual Bank and also of cognitive theory, as described in Chapter 2. In contrast, at Organization Bank, the planning stage and the execution stage were interwoven. Both stages were conducted by the same group of people, and planning and execution went hand in hand as bankers gathered more information and tinkered with the solutions they were implementing. Like socioculturalists, the Organization Bankers treated plans as resources for action, as something that is "located in the larger context of some ongoing practical activity . . . [and is] part of the subject matter to be investigated" (Suchman, 1987: 49), not an abstract entity that underlies and guides action.

Organization Bankers believed that, under conditions of uncertainty, foregrounding the concrete ensured that information was more likely to be reliable and productive. The bankers talked with each other throughout the planning and execution of deals, comparing concrete observations ("what happened with my health care client"). From this comparison, a set of higher-order patterns ("opportunities in the health care industry") became salient that integrated the lower-level details, something similar to the magical transformation described by organizational research on distributed cognition (Weick and Roberts, 1993). As one vice president said, "Whenever people here need to make decisions, we get input from others to see whether they see the same facts and interpret them in the same way.... In a business as complex as ours there is just too much noise to do it any other way.... [There is no other way] to make sure that what you are acting on is a trend, not a fluke." According to the bankers, information is reliable when several bankers independently observe similar situations – valid because bankers interpreted the facts in the same way, and general because bankers could discard the irrelevant noise associated with any particular case. This process is abductive because the bankers did not start out with general information but instead arrived at a new, more general understanding through a collaborative process.

The industry-specific group was not planned by top management and executed by lower-level bankers, but instead *emerged* as a localized solution to a problem that lower-level bankers recognized and spoke about. Describing the emergent nature of the bank's strategy, one banker said, after Organization Bank completed a number of high-profile transactions in the industry, "we looked back and saw: 'Gee, we have a health care strategy.' " This generalization-after-the-fact approach differed from the forward-looking strategic planning process at Individual Bank. At Individual Bank, general strategy came first and then was implemented. At Organization Bank, details came first and then provisional strategies emerged. Organization Bank's approach illustrates the generative power of absences. The absence of organizational guidelines amplified bankers' cognitive uncertainty and catalyzed a collaborative problem-solving process. At Organization Bank, as described in sociocultural theory, absences and erasures could be constitutive (e.g., Latour and Woolgar, 1979). Organization Bankers became more creative because they oriented toward concrete instead of abstract information and relied on interactions with organizational resources – thus enacting the more abductive, situated processes described by sociocultural theories instead of relying primarily on their own minds and acting like individual-centered cognitive theorists.

After reading a version of the above paragraphs, an Organization Bank managing director, who was part of the health care group, explained further:

> You have to understand that at the time bankers still had a different mindset because the environment was different. If you didn't get a deal, it was typically because the client had a better relationship with another bank. Among all the things that a client could say to you about why you are not getting a deal, "industry knowledge" just didn't register for bankers because it just wasn't something that bankers thought they had to have or that they were competing on. People literally did not hear those words.

This explains why bankers had difficulty understanding readily available information (e.g., "we would like you to have industry knowledge") – because it did not fit their preexisting notions. A vice president who also participated in the group and read our manuscript explained how conversations were crucial to the abductive process:

> You really have to emphasize the conversations. Even though every one of us heard "industry knowledge," we didn't really understand the significance of this until we talked to others who had the same experience. Before I had these conversations, I thought that this was about me, that the client thought I wasn't competent enough and then I went off on that tangent. And I think, no actually I know, that others felt the same way. Only when we kept talking did we recognize that this was an institutional kind of thing. This was about how deals had been done for decades and now as the environment was changing we had to find a different way of doing deals.

These bankers understood that a genuinely new aspect of the environment is difficult to recognize by an individual expert in isolation. Like sociocultural theorists, they appreciated that social interactions, like the conversations among bankers, influence individuals' perception and cognition (e.g., Cole, 1996; Rogoff and Lave, 1999; Wertsch, 1991). Because of the social tools that can emerge during interactions – such as the right language and appropriate behaviors – and the social validation of others' impressions, participants in such conversations are able to perceive aspects of the environment that they previously did not see. In our example, interactions helped the bankers more deeply understand the words "we want you to have industry knowledge." The managing director also said: "And now, years later, everyone here and in other firms understands the importance of industry knowledge and knows how to convey to the client that you have such knowledge." This insight was made possible by abductive processes that sensitized Organization Bankers' perceptions ("only when we kept talking did we recognize that this was an institutional thing"). Instead of transferring abstract social concepts to bankers, Organization Bank's practices sensitized the perceptual and cognitive system in ways described by sociocultural researchers (Gibson, 1986; John-Steiner and Mahn, 1996; Wertsch and Stone, 1985).

Individual Bank was among the competitors that imitated Organization Bank's industry focus groups. But Individual Bank adopted the practice in a very different way, reflecting its emphasis on uncertainty reduction. As one Individual Bank vice president described, they implemented this approach as a top-down strategy initiated by management: "I think we adopted this because management recognized that it was a best practice." Individual Bankers adopted the notion of an industry focus group when it was circulated in the industry as a general practice that could work across different banks and situations, but they were not able to develop such ideas on their own.

At Organization Bank, the interactions that led to the formation of the health care group consisted of a joint discovery process among peers in which puzzles and contradictions had to be continuously reconciled and bankers adjusted their perspectives gradually. Sociocultural theorists also consider inner contradictions as an important source of development for a system such as an organization (e.g., Engeström, 2003). In contrast, at Individual Bank, lower-level bankers simply adopted a notion that was transferred to them by top management without going through a gradual transformation in their understanding. They did not have to wrestle with difficult-to-understand demands from clients, discover what aspects of their personal experience were widely shared, or devise an appropriate solution through trial and error. As Engeström (2003: 71) notes, if abstractions are imposed "'top-down,' they eliminate multivoicedness" and thereby quell the bottom-up processes that spurred change at Organization Bank. Our analysis shows that the transformative potential of contradictions was relatively more developed at Organization Bank because practitioners implicitly recognized and capitalized on this potential.

This difference in how bankers arrive at new understandings has important implications. Damon (1984) found that transformational learning, in which people have to give up existing notions, is more likely to result from interactions with peers, as in the process that took place at Organization Bank. Interactions with more experienced participants – or directives from superiors, as at Individual Bank – are more likely to add a new type of concept or skill to an existing repertoire. This is consistent with the argument that we make in Chapters 5 and 6, where we describe how junior Individual Bankers learned by adopting and internalizing organizational skills and concepts, while junior Organization Bankers learned to suspend abstract concepts and think in a fundamentally different way. The health care group example shows that Organization Bank accomplished this by opening bankers to the contradictions and uncertainties that emerge in concrete situations.

Organization Bank's emphasis on emergent strategy encouraged an open mindset in bankers. This fit with the bank's more fluid organizational structures. Organization Bankers did not view groups like the health care focus group as organizational structures that involved formal reporting relationships. They often referred to such groups as "efforts," "initiatives," or "projects," implying their temporary status. As one managing director said about the health care group:

> We don't really think about this as a formal group. It's more like a project. Some of us focusing some of our time on creating information that we can disseminate to others and that we can all use. Once everyone has a general awareness about the issues we need to attend to in the industry, the project will fade out because it is now part of the collective consciousness.

In fact, about fifteen months after the creation of the group only a few bankers continued to spend time on the effort. An analyst kept the database up to date and deal teams contributed their presentations to the deal library for others to use, but no additional effort was required. This example shows that, unlike Individual Bank's structures, Organization Bank's strategy and organization did not direct the bankers' attention away from a messy environment and did not focus them on abstract structures and standards. Instead, structures such as the health care group were catalysts that encouraged bankers to engage jointly with an uncertain environment. They functioned as perceptual sensitization devices (Gibson, 1986; Wertsch and Stone, 1985) – as the terms "awareness," "attend to," and "consciousness" in the excerpt indicate – and therefore were a critical aspect of the bank's uncertainty amplification process.

During our fieldwork, various groups at Individual Bank had been dismantled because a new manager brought in a new leadership team and a new strategy. This restructuring created substantial political strife. Incumbents refused to relinquish power and reassured their teams that they would fight to keep the groups together. When groups faded away at

Organization Bank, in contrast, such responses did not occur – although it is possible that some did occur but were more clandestine because of the bank's lower tolerance for such responses. When asked about his response to the health care group's diminishing importance, one managing director who had spent a lot of time on the health care effort said:

> I don't really think about it much. People here are used to working on multiple projects at the same time and most of our projects last for relatively short periods of time. If you see yourself as contributing to just another project, you don't really develop the same kind of identification and attachment that you might develop if you were the leader of a new group that is yours to build from scratch and if you had others in the group who identify with that group and feel loyal toward it and see their future staked on the group's success.

This managing director illustrates one of our central arguments, namely, that different ways of construing the self have distinct implications for how people think, feel, and act. He contrasts two ways in which bankers can construe the self. The first way, prevalent at Individual Bank, involves relatively abstract social identities in which bankers perceive themselves as group members or role occupants (e.g., "I am a health care expert"). Cognitive and organizational researchers also conceptualize identities in these abstract terms (e.g., Haslam, 2004). Such social identities are abstract because they generalize across the different projects bankers work on and the different situations they find themselves in. The Individual Bankers viewed this type of social identity in positive terms, claiming that attachment to such identities motivates participants and guides decisions. In contrast, the Organization Bank managing director believed that social identities of this sort could focus employees on the personally relevant issues, such as their careers, that potentially conflict with the task-relevant aspects of the situations they encounter. The Organization Bank managing director thus favored the second type of self-construal in which bankers think of themselves in terms of participating in an activity (e.g., "contributing") in which the self is a way of doing and not a way of being.

This view is congenial with sociocultural theories that also construe group membership as a process of participation (e.g., Sfard, 1998). On this account, the self is defined in relation to the multitude of specific projects that a person participates in. Because the self is spread out over multiple, relatively short-lived projects, Organization Bankers' attachments to each particular project were less extreme. The managing director believed that the bank's work practices facilitated such an activity-based self-construal, while Individual Bank's practices encouraged a more abstract self-construal. Organization Bankers deliberately designed their work practices in order to create the second kind of self-construal. Thus, they chose to enact a more sociocultural version of self because they believed that it facilitates better performance.

From a cognitive perspective, Organization Bank's resistance to abstract strategies and identities is puzzling. Many psychologists have found that, once social concepts, norms, and behaviors have been established, participants act to maintain and protect these familiar standards (e.g., Hardin and Higgins, 1996). Cognitive psychologists argue that this institutionalization of abstract concepts happens automatically, without people's awareness or intention and without any prompting from a social institution, and that it reflects universal psychological principles. People integrate abstract norms and standards into their self-concept, as part of an identity, and use them to regulate their behavior (Higgins, 1996; Hardin and Higgins, 1996). This certainly happened at Individual Bank, very much as cognitive psychologists have described. Organization Bank's work practices, however, actively worked against these self-processes and achieved outcomes that are puzzling from a cognitive point of view. The bank highlighted the temporary nature of projects and spread people's efforts across domains so as to minimize bankers' attachment to and self-construction in terms of any given domain.

The strategy at Organization Bank thus was formulated to amplify banker uncertainty through the withholding and undermining of the abstract guidelines that Individual Bank's top management provided. Without management directives, Organization Bankers were forced to ask others for help when they were faced with new and difficult-to-understand situations. They were forced to reason abductively – to attend closely to the details of unfamiliar situations, to develop new ideas tailored to those situations, to try out solutions, to gather more data, and to modify their solutions in an overlapping process of planning and implementation. New understandings and temporary solutions, such as the health care group, were continuously refined through the same situated, iterative problem-solving process.

"Strategy" at Organization Bank thus did not correspond to the top-down, means-ends chains and the logic of internal consistency that cognitive organizational theorists use (e.g., March and Simon, 1958; Simon, 1976) and that Individual Bank enacted. Strategies bubbled up based on the local interactions of people at lower levels in the hierarchy based on what the situation demanded instead of being guided by organizational charts and other abstract plans and directives. In contrast to what the superstar-oriented Individual Bank set out to accomplish, the goal at Organization Bank was not "for the behavior of a single, isolated individual to reach a high degree of rationality," as Simon (1976: 79) argues, but for the organization, as a whole, to develop a way of acting that was constantly subject to collective revision and adjustment.

ROLES

Organization Bank deemphasized roles. Business cards only mentioned a banker's name and contact information and provided no title. Likewise, bankers rarely introduced themselves by title. One vice president said: "We don't use titles because they fixate the client on the banker and the banker's status. What we want the client to focus on are the resources of this organization." This statement indicates how a reduced emphasis on titles signaled to clients that individual experts were less important than the bank's distributed cognitive processes. A senior associate said:

> Titles are industry norms that we follow for formality's sake but they don't mean anything here. . . . When I introduce myself or others to the client, I just tell the client: "My name is Tim and I hope that you will rely on me for helping you call buyers. Here is Melissa and she will manage the data room for you."

Tim came to think this way because the bank's practices instilled a distance from taken-for-granted notions, such as titles, which was the desired effect of the bank's uncertainty amplification. Another senior associate said: "I don't even know what that means to say 'I am an associate.' That has no information value for the client. All the client wants to know is who is doing what for me." Abstract role conceptions thus were less meaningful at Organization Bank than at Individual Bank. The Organization Bankers oriented instead toward concrete, situation-specific information about what they and others could do for clients in specific situations.

Bankers in a comparable role had similar basic tasks at both banks. But Organization Bankers up to the director level could also be assigned additional tasks that typically would be the responsibility of a more senior banker. For example, one associate said: "I sometimes lead small deals, which at other banks is left to vice presidents." Another associate explained with some exasperation how this more fluid relationship between roles and tasks amplified uncertainty: "I have been here for four years now and I am still on edge with every new project because the one thing I can count on is that there will be surprises about what I have to do." Unlike the Individual Bankers, the Organization Bankers could not just walk into a meeting and rely on a generally applicable set of expectations about who was responsible for what. This uncertainty sometimes created conflict among bankers. The most frequent source of conflict was that junior bankers were hoping to assume more responsibility than senior bankers were willing to give. For example, a vice president reported about a recent run-in with an analyst after a client meeting: "I could tell that she was pouting during the meeting and when I asked her after the meeting what happened, she said in this very accusatory tone: 'You treated me like an analyst.' She was almost in tears! I think she was hoping to get more responsibility because it is a small deal."

The Individual Bankers knew of these practices at Organization Bank and commented on them with a mixture of dismay and admiration. For example, one Individual Banker said: "Some of these kids [i.e., Organization Bank team members] are thrown on kinds of deals that they have never seen before in their life. And for most of the time, the undergrads are running the show. But somehow they keep pulling it off."

As roles receded into the background, Organization Bankers organized around the demands of the task, deemphasizing relative status. In contrast to the Individual Bank vice president quoted previously, who ignored a request for information from a subordinate, Organization Bankers passed on whatever new information they received to all other team members. One competitor remarked with respect about this aspect of Organization Bank's culture: "Communication is the big bottleneck for everyone in the industry. You just can't get people to talk. There are issues of hierarchy, competition between departments or even between people within the same department. . . . I don't know how they [the Organization Bankers] do it."

Organizing around the task sometimes implied overstepping role and status boundaries that were rigid in other organizations. In one case we observed, secretaries helped junior bankers with basic spreadsheet analyses. Another junior Organization Banker described his experiences with document duplication:

> All they need to do is copy the books for me and dump them on my desk in time. That means that I would have to hang around until the early morning hours, rush home, shower, order a car, and catch my flight without having slept. But so often Josh [low-level worker in document processing] and others just saved my life. They check the books for me so that I can go home and get some sleep. They order the car for me and put the books in the car. And then they even give me a wake-up call.

The Individual Bankers agreed that similar situations were unlikely to occur at Individual Bank. One Individual Banker complained: "I just don't know why we cannot whip our secretaries into that kind of a shape. Mine doesn't even know my name and is too busy surfing bradpitt.com to learn it."

In contrast to the previous examples, in which Organization Bank employees might have taken on more responsibility because this would identify them with a more prestigious role (e.g., secretaries acting as junior bankers and junior bankers acting as more senior bankers), the document duplicating example illustrates how employees at all levels also took on relatively menial tasks that were not part of an official role description. While taking on extra responsibility can signal social identification (e.g., Van Knippenberg and Ellemers, 2003), the Organization Bankers explained these behaviors as task-orientation, which one vice president defined as follows: "You just do what needs to get done and don't think about it much." Another vice president elaborated:

> It's just not about positions and egos here. It is just about getting the work done. There is not ... this intense desire to be "a good citizen." I have seen companies like that and they often have a lot of politicking, which you don't see that much around here. You know, people who are toeing the company line better than others, doing things to look "appropriate" and "successful" and "like a good team player." I think that people in organizations who have these kinds of cultures are just not busy enough.... You just don't have the time for that here.

This statement indicates that Organization Bankers were less likely than Individual Bankers to invoke abstract group norms and social identities as explanations for their hard work. In fact, they believed that such abstract norms could be counterproductive.

The concept of task-orientation shows another important aspect of Organization Bank's practices. The bank did not block bankers from internalizing and applying abstract identity and role concepts simply by telling them not to. It actually *forced* the bankers to behave differently. Organization Bank counteracted political behavior and other distractions by creating a constant crisis mentality that required the bankers to remain focused on the task at hand. A similar behavior can be observed in crises and disasters in society at large. When people are faced with overwhelming challenges they often abandon familiar scripts and self-concepts and they come together to address the task at hand. Organization Bank forced bankers to communicate with each other, to avoid politics, and to attend to the details of a problem by withholding abstract concepts and directives that could guide their understanding. By creating constant crises and withholding abstract norms, Organization Bank amplified cognitive uncertainty and produced the desired banker behaviors.

For junior bankers especially, the uncertainty created by the absence of norms and roles was difficult. One incoming associate said that the bank was "a very confusing place to figure out in terms of what the norms are." Another newcomer complained that he could not even find out what constituted acceptable work hours:

> I know that this ain't going to be eight-hour days. But, I mean, can you at least give me some guidelines beyond that? Sometimes people work around the clock for weeks in a row, seven days a week. But then people also sometimes come to work at 1:00 PM, go to the gym during all hours of the day, sometimes they don't show up at all because they just decided that they had been working too hard and are taking a day off, and then there is this warehouse sale when people are just out the door and come back later with huge shopping bags, walking right by Joe [the head of the department].

When associates asked senior colleagues about norms for such things as acceptable work hours, they usually heard that "it all depends on the deal. When there is work, you get it done, if not, get out of here." This rule also applied to senior bankers, and even managing directors often worked until late at night. The answer did not satisfy the associates, however, because it failed to reduce their cognitive uncertainty: "They are basically saying: you go figure it out for yourself. So I never really know what to do," one associate complained.

In this case and others, Organization Bank prioritized the concrete demands of specific situations. This differed from the more abstract norms at Individual Bank where, for example, bankers followed the norm of staying late every night even when they did not have pressing work. In a related example, Organization Bankers explained their uniformly cheap watches as sensitivity to clients. One associate explained: "Imagine how a client feels who is older than you, more senior than you, but earns considerably less. And here you are flashing your Rolex." This differed from the Individual Bankers, who chose watches to signal the identity attributes associated with their organizational roles. Individual Bank traders mostly wore Rolex watches, but the investment bankers wore watches that they considered more "sophisticated," "elegant," and "original," such as Patek Philipp, Audemars Piguet, and Franck Muller.

Individual Bank and Organization Bank thus differed in how they implicitly construed the relationship between the individual and the bank. At Individual Bank, each individual owned a role. The bank could be conceived of as an aggregation of these individual roles. Each role was integrated with other roles through abstractions, such as strategies, norms, and behavioral expectations. When the Individual Bankers stepped into a meeting, analysts, associates, vice presidents, and directors each knew in advance what to do and how to relate to incumbents of the other roles. This focus on the individual knower and his or her abstract knowledge is consistent with cognitive theory. At Organization Bank, in contrast, the system was in the foreground in a way that enacted sociocultural theory. The individual was integrated into the social context not through preexisting abstract structures but by following the cues in a concrete task situation. This is consistent with the sociocultural notion that "people organize themselves to attend to and give meaning to figural concerns against the ground of ongoing social interactions" (Lave, 2003: 19).

STAFFING

Organization Bankers were staffed based on availability rather than expertise. Client requests for a specific banker were usually declined with the comment "our bankers are fungible." When one banker went on vacation or was overloaded, other bankers substituted seamlessly. This staffing procedure produced good results for clients, but it also created stress for bankers. Unexpected substitutions onto unfamiliar projects created persistent cognitive uncertainty for bankers at all levels. As one vice president commented about this staffing practice, "it is truly humbling; you never feel like you have all the answers." A fourth-year associate explained that this staffing practice caused cognitive uncertainty because he regularly confronted unfamiliar tasks and unclear client expectations:

> I have been staffed on this sell-side project. This is the bread and butter of our department and the client probably expects that I have done hundreds of these. But I haven't. . . . So first I need to figure out what needs to get done before the first meeting. . . . I also don't know what to expect from the meeting, what kinds of concerns or objections clients typically have.

Even bankers who had been with the bank for years continued to be placed on projects for which they lacked experience.

One director justified the cognitive uncertainty that this practice induced in bankers in terms of the positive cognitive effects: "One of the reasons why we staff bankers fungibly is to keep them on their toes, to think in fresh ways." A managing director stressed that bankers who experienced cognitive uncertainty were more likely to draw on the organization's resources. "When we don't know something, we have more of an incentive to make good use of our colleagues." The fungible staffing also created knowledge overlap in Organization Bankers. For example, instead of one banker having all the health care industry expertise, this knowledge was spread out across various bankers. As a result, the bank was less vulnerable to knowledge gaps that could result from attrition.

Organization Bank employed fungible staffing quite strictly up to the director level, where bankers began to develop some expertise. To encourage fresh thinking and collaboration, however, senior bankers regularly had to switch from one area of expertise to another by taking on special projects, helping to get a new group started, or assuming international responsibilities. Individual Bankers who knew about Organization Bank's fungible staffing believed that it did a "disservice" to Organization Bank and its clients because experts were more marketable. In contrast, the Organization Bankers believed that this practice kept their career options open. As one managing director said: "My expertise is not in a particular area that is likely to change quickly anyway. What I can bring to other organizations, besides finance knowledge, is a way of working with others to solve problems." Another managing director said:

> The facts speak for themselves. People who leave here can do what they want. They can assume leadership positions in other organizations or in government. They go to other banks, hedge funds, private equity firms. They form rock bands or open their own stores. . . . I actually think that you learn most about who we are as an organization by looking at where our people go and what they do there.

During their tenure at the bank Organization Bankers also cultivated a low profile. It was the bank's policy that individual bankers should not talk to the press. One director explained the rationale: "It is misleading for clients. Our clients are not served by individual bankers. They have access to the resources of the entire organization." When asked why it was not important to establish more public leadership in the field, one vice president said: "There are different ways of doing this. Some organizations do this by showing off their really smart people. We do this by showing off our innovative products and transactions: [lists the bank's proprietary finance products]. In all of these we were first to market."

Some Individual Bankers claimed that the Organization Bankers did not use the public personality strategy because their bankers were "bland" and "without personality." These Individual Bankers may have been motivated by resentment at Organization Bank's success. It is true, however, that Organization Bankers who achieved some prominence after they had left the bank were often described as "humble," "self-effacing," or "neutral."

Fungible staffing, then, produced cognitive uncertainty that caused bankers to make good use of the bank's resources, signaled to clients that they were served by the bank as a whole, and discouraged egocentric dispositions in bankers – who became organizational resources instead of flamboyant superstars. The fungible approach to staffing also meant that the bank could staff fewer, and more junior, bankers on deal teams for comparable transactions, as compared to Individual Bank.

Because expert-based investment banking was the norm at the time, clients often were surprised by the fungible-banker approach and slow to recognize its benefits. Organization Bank's client presentations did not feature banker biographies, but instead focused on the bank's resources, and clients sometimes complained. In one pitch meeting, which we described above, the CEO looked skeptically at the young Organization Banker team, grabbed the presentation book wordlessly from the analyst who was carrying it, and flipped through it to find the banker biographies. When he did not find any, he exploded at the team:

> What is this? The high school science project team? I have a grand-daughter who is older than you are.... My ass is on the line here and this is the best that you can come up with? You know what this is [pointing to a stack of business cards in front of him]? These are business cards from other bankers I am dealing with [reading off the name of the bank and the bankers' title]: ... head of investment banking, ... head of sales and trading, ... head of global corporate finance. These banks send in their superstars, their most experienced bankers. I want the same kind of attention from Organization Bank.

This client's reaction was not unusual. Organization Bankers often received tough questions about their experience, and they sometimes met with outright hostility. These contentious client interactions certainly caused cognitive uncertainty and discomfort for the bankers, but Organization Bank insisted on its fungible staffing practice and continued to thrive. Organization Bankers maintained that fungible staffing – which increased cognitive uncertainty by forcing bankers into unfamiliar situations – made the bank better by forcing bankers to avoid abstract, scripted responses and to draw on the resources of the organization.

Organization Bank's fungible staffing practices enacted the tenets of sociocultural approaches to "distributed" or "situated" cognition (Lave, 1988; Hutchins, 1991, 1995). These practices implied that a task could be completed best through a situation-specific combination of heterogeneous resources, not by the mental representations and skills of an expert. Whatever one banker did not know could be obtained from other bankers or from tools such as templates developed for prior presentations. This approach may be difficult to understand from the perspective of cognitive theory, which locates expertise primarily in the individual, but Organization Bankers consistently solved client problems using this approach.

FEEDBACK

Like Individual Bank, Organization Bank had a 360-degree feedback process. Organization Bankers filled out a form every year requesting feedback from colleagues with whom they had interacted frequently. Bankers also filled out a self-evaluation form. In contrast to the Individual Bank process, however, the Organization Bankers determined their review criteria abductively, through interviews with bankers at all levels. In these annual interviews, bankers were asked to give examples of situations in which a banker excelled and in which a banker performed poorly. The bankers who collected this information coded it and developed general categories for evaluating banker behavior. Under each category, they also collected a list of specific behaviors that counted as evidence of that category. (Unfortunately, we cannot offer examples because the bank asked us not to publish this information.) Compared to Individual Bank's review form, the Organization Bank form required bankers to supply more qualitative information, asking them to include concrete examples and narratives. The qualitative nature of the review process amplified cognitive uncertainty because bankers had to attend to more and more complex information. They did not, for example, only have to think of themselves and others in terms of simple categories such as "leadership." They also had to consider how "leadership" manifested itself in specific situations. This encouraged them to notice variability and conflict across situations because sometimes the same behavior can count as successful leadership in one situation but not in another.

The interviews through which Organization Bank developed its evaluation criteria happened regularly, every year. As one associate explained, "we repeat the interviews about every year so that the form keeps up with the market." The yearly changes in the review form were relatively modest. In one year, for example, two categories were removed from the form, one new category was added, and about eight specific behaviors were added to the existing categories. Despite these relatively modest annual changes, bankers worried that they could not anticipate the review categories. They complained that they could be judged by a new review form at the end of a year without knowing throughout the year whether there would be a new review form and what categories it might contain. This created cognitive uncertainty that junior bankers experienced as "unnerving." Some junior bankers felt that the logic behind this process was "incomprehensible," or that the process constituted "bad management." One associate said: "In every management course you learn that you have to tell people what you expect of them up front." These junior Organization Bankers expected a review process more like that of Individual Bank. They envisioned review criteria as abstract standards that they could keep in mind as they approached each new situation.

Senior Organization Bankers saw the review differently. One director responded to the above complaints:

> They [the associates] have the wrong picture of what we are trying to accomplish with this. This is not really a management tool. We don't have managers here and there is no manager reviewing bankers. There are no one-size-fits-all goals that anyone is measured on. This is more of a discipline that says: "the views of the people you work with and that you work for are important, so try to find out what they value and behave accordingly."

This director portrayed the review process as a sensitizing device that alerted bankers to their colleagues' perspectives and to the variability in standards across situations. One vice president emphasized the collective conversation aspect over the evaluation aspect: "I actually think that the yearly collective reflection about what matters now [i.e., the interviews] is at least as valuable as the actual form that comes out of it. I see the form as a kind of memorandum that documents our conversation." Another vice president agreed: "It is a way to force everyone to constantly think about what they are doing and why and to learn from each other." Senior bankers thus valued the ongoing reflection encouraged by the evaluation process and the heightened attention it fostered. Like sociocultural researchers, the Organization Bankers appreciated how social interactions can catalyze higher-order thinking in individuals. They were thus more likely to use business practices that promoted conversations than were Individual Bankers.

As the director said, there were no managers to conduct the review. Bankers were not reviewed by the department's leadership, but by a more senior banker with whom they had worked extensively. This was designed to create a more collaborative and less hierarchical atmosphere during the review meeting. Because the reviewer had witnessed many of the situations that were referred to during the review, he or she was better positioned to help the focal banker understand the evaluative comments.

Nevertheless, most of the informants did not feel that a joint sense-making process took place during the review. For example, the following conversation pertained to a vice president's review process:

> VICE PRESIDENT: It mostly consisted of him [a director] reading from what people wrote about me and that's about it.
> RESEARCHER: Did he interpret this information for you?
> VICE PRESIDENT: No, that's not the style around here. It's, here are all the facts you can handle. Deal with it. .... I had to make sense of this myself.
> RESEARCHER: Did you receive a quantitative score?
> VICE PRESIDENT, LAUGHING: God, no! That would make things too easy, wouldn't it?
> RESEARCHER: Any suggestions for improvement?
> VICE PRESIDENT: No.

The director thus left it to the vice president to process the review information herself. More junior bankers often complained about the resulting uncertainty and pressed for "specific takeaways" and "actionable suggestions." One managing director responded to such requests: "I just don't see the point in creating an illusory world of certainty. People have to learn to be comfortable with incomplete information, to sift through lots of data and figure out for themselves what matters and what doesn't. .... That's at the heart of being a great banker."

Specific recommendations were rare also because Organization Bank relied on other feedback mechanisms. For example, senior Individual Bankers were reviewed quarterly against revenue goals. In contrast, one director listed the many dimensions on which Organization Bankers received regular – often weekly – information:

> Revenues here are important. So you'll hear about that, including what you brought in and what you missed. But we also measure people on a gazillion other dimensions that have to do with cost and that our

competitors don't measure people on: how much junior-banker time you use up on a deal, the cost of producing client books, including whether you used expensive color copies or not. And then you have to write down on a weekly basis how much time you allocate to different industries and types of projects.

Senior Organization Bankers received information that was relevant to their decisions in more detail, more frequently, and on more dimensions than their Individual Bank counterparts. Instead of receiving specific quantitative revenue goals, senior Organization Bankers were given a broader set of information and trusted to respond appropriately. They had to figure out for themselves which client projects to pursue and how many resources to devote to a given project. As a managing director explained: "We do not tell people what goals they should achieve, because the person closest to the situation knows best what is possible. We just constantly feed people with all available information." Thus, the bank favored situation-specific information as opposed to a more deductive application of abstract guidelines to a situation. The chief operating officer elaborated on the reasons the bank refrained from giving bankers guidelines:

> Whenever you give people criteria, they work up to them and lose sight of the big picture. If you only reward people for the revenues they bring in by year end, you are bound to create "people eaters." People start allocating resources to deals that could be used more productively on other deals. . . . So you can't make people only focus on one thing and only at one point in time. They have to look at everything and they have to do that constantly. It keeps you on your toes.

This ongoing feedback process amplified cognitive uncertainty because bankers had to attend to more information without explicit decision guidelines. As one vice president commented: "Sometimes I do wish there was more guidance. Slugging through this stuff can be over whelming and continues to be a source of endless frustration and even aversion but, hey, it also does its job and keeps everyone from becoming complacent."

Organization Bank thus conducted its annual reviews differently than did Individual Bank, and it also used task processes – such as weekly reports about how many resources bankers had used and how many deals they had lost to the competition – to create a feedback-rich environment. This constant, situation-specific feedback was more concrete and timely, and it could therefore guide banker behavior in more focused and productive ways than abstract review categories. Even Organization Bank's annual review process contained the type of comprehensive, contradictory information that the bank's cognitive-uncertainty amplification process thrived on.

TRAINING

Organization Bank used training reluctantly and only as part of a broader system of guiding banker behavior. The bankers believed that performance problems could not be addressed by training alone. For example, at one point, the bank incurred a heavy loss in a particular department. It was rumored that the loss came about because some professionals had used their habitual strategies without noticing the rapidly changing environment. The managing director of a different department explained how this situation repeated the dynamics of earlier losses: "Our most catastrophic problems came about because people thought they were the experts. They thought they knew what was going on even though the market had changed." He continued, referring to his own department's work practices: "What we do around here has to do with dispelling these illusions." His department conducted an internal study, in the form of interviews and focus groups, to determine whether it was prone to similar problems. The findings of the study concluded: "It is in the nature of experts to become overconfident. . . . Training and incentives are not sufficient to keep overconfidence in check. . . . Checks must be designed into the work process." Training was therefore only one aspect of a larger set of practices that continuously reminded bankers of uncertainty and urged them to treat each situation as relatively unique.

While the Individual Bankers cooperated willingly with the HR department, and even sought out its help, one Organization Bank vice president said that they had "fired" the HR department by relegating them to unimportant tasks. "They are training secretaries on how to work the phones, but the bankers don't see value in what they are offering so we are not using them." During a presentation at a staff meeting, one senior banker formally announced the department's decision to discontinue formal banker training, partly because "recipes are dangerous in our business." The training department tried to fight back, justifying its structured approach to training by circulating a white paper which warned that the "high uncertainty that our professionals experience on a continuous basis is unusual by industry standards . . . and is likely to eventually result in attrition. . . . It is likely to damage our ability to attract the strongest talent."

Shortly thereafter, however, the Organization Bankers felt pressured to reevaluate their approach to training because shareholders were increasingly demanding training, viewing it as evidence of a firm's appropriate investment in human capital. Dissatisfied with the training content offered by the HR department, a group of bankers took responsibility for researching existing approaches to training and introducing them to colleagues. After a few months of talking to other professional service firms and a variety of outside training providers, the bankers invited various providers to "pitch" to a larger group of bankers. One of the providers included a consulting firm that used the Myers-Briggs Inventory, which the Individual Bankers found useful. The group had chosen this supplier because it was praised by a highly esteemed consulting firm. An associate described this pitch meeting:

> It was a disaster. People here just have no patience for these generic approaches. And some of these vendors are apparently used by reputable firms. Perhaps they are more intellectual than we are. I do not see anything useful in trying to figure out whether someone is an I [introvert] or an E [extrovert]. I don't even recall what all these terms are.

Other attendees agreed, including a vice president who simply said: "I don't see how any of that helps me do my job better." Organization Bankers saw the vendors' material as too abstract, too divorced from their practical engagement in their work. Other bankers simply thought that this approach was "hokey." For example, one vice president mocked the bankers who had selected the Meyers-Briggs consultant: "I think they have spent too much time in the New Age section of the book store." It is interesting to note that at first the Organization Bank team responsible for scouting out training vendors did precisely what Individual Bank typically did – look at best industry practices with the hope of adopting a working recipe. Although the Individual Bankers generally respected this approach, however, Organization Bank's "culture rejected it as too generic," as one vice president said.

Thus, the Organization Bankers responded negatively to the material that the Individual Bankers found most helpful. In fact, they criticized the Meyers-Briggs for the very feature that made Individual Bankers to appreciate it, namely its abstract categories for classifying other people. The two banks' different attitudes toward abstract classification schemes illustrate one important aspect of our argument. We argue that, when people experience different types of cognitive uncertainty, they develop different tacit beliefs about what the world is like and what types of information are useful. Because of Individual Bank's uncertainty-reduction practices, bankers only encountered transient uncertainty and therefore experienced the world as relatively predictable. They consequently oriented toward the enduring, more abstract properties of people and situations, and they built taxonomies to aid prediction. Thus, such classification devices as the Meyers-Briggs were welcome aids. In contrast, because of Organization Bank's cognitive-uncertainty amplification practices, Organization Bankers experienced persistent cognitive uncertainty and therefore viewed the world as relatively unpredictable. They consequently oriented more toward concrete information and tried to understand the unique dynamics of situations (cf., Chiu et al., 1997; Whitehead, 1938). For this purpose, the Meyers-Briggs was not considered helpful. Even though bankers at the two banks were engaging in the same types of tasks, they perceived these tasks very differently because of the different uncertainty-management practices that the banks had developed.

To reconcile shareholder wishes with the bankers' own preferences, Organization Bank offered two types of training. The first was a series of informal sessions. The content of each session was determined by interviews that a team of bankers did with colleagues. Interview questions included: What have you recently learned that you consider new and important? What kinds of problems have you been struggling with recently? The bankers encouraged interviewees to give detailed examples that could become case studies. Consulting with other bankers, the team picked the most pressing problems and the most promising insights as material for training sessions. This approach was abductive because the content of training courses was not determined by a curriculum of general principles but instead derived from the specific problems that bankers encountered.

Two senior bankers took responsibility for each training session. In contrast to the consultants at Individual Bank, the Organization Bankers merely prepared case studies for discussion and did not recommend a script or a solution because they believed that "there is no right answer. We just want to keep people on their toes ... and remind ourselves how complex our trade is." This approach would have been highly aversive to the Individual Bankers, who required unambiguous answers. One Organization Bank managing director said about the session he was preparing: "There really is not much for me to prepare. My main job is to facilitate this, to draw out different ideas, get people to challenge one another." In building these training sessions, Organization Bankers were following a more sociocultural approach to designing learning environments. When educational scholars build learning settings in line with sociocultural theories, they often do not cast the instructor as a conveyer of knowledge but as a facilitator of interactive processes (e.g., Palincsar, 1998).

The typical Organization Bank training session evolved into a discussion of the contradictory facts and demands to which bankers had to respond. In one session, bankers discussed situations in which they had to notice and act on specific contradictions: "We want to make swift, practical decisions and carefully analyze all available information." One director explained the usefulness of this exercise: "Many people who come here are quant jocks who have learned to think in a very logical way. But reality is not like logic. We are reminding ourselves that there can be contradictions and that we have to deal with them."

A vice president said: "It is human nature to be intolerant of any kind of vagueness or inconsistency. Here you learn not to like complexity, which I don't think is possible, but at least to notice, accept, and work with it." These examples show how training at Organization Bank further amplified bankers' cognitive uncertainty, which made them aware of contradictions that occurred in their regular business practices, and withheld recipes for dealing with such contradictions, which directed them toward the details of specific contexts and away from abstract categories.

A second set of courses was offered to bankers who had done a particular type of work, such as supervise analysts and interact with clients about logistical issues, and who were now expected to do a different kind of work, such as counsel clients on strategic issues and revenue opportunities. Organization Bankers had a word for the inflexibility that comes from doing the same type of work repeatedly: "associanitis." The illness metaphor suggests that inflexibility is a problem. But this particular illness metaphor also located the cause for the illness not in the afflicted individual, but in the person's history of participation in the organization – in this case their work as an associate, which sometimes restricted a banker to repetitive work.

The training meant to cure associanitis had two aspects. One aspect resembled the bank's informal training sessions, with participants working on cases that had been culled from prior interviews with bankers. In addition to discussing cases, the bankers role-played and gave one another feedback, learning through participation and interacting with others. A director described the second aspect of the training: "It is a time to look backward and to look forward. To put what you are doing into a context." In practice, this meant that panels of bankers who had made the transition out of associanitis reflected on their previous difficulties, why they occurred, and how these difficulties disappeared. One managing director explained the rationale behind the training as a form of consciousness raising:

> These habits have developed in people on a daily basis over a period of years. We don't think that this can be undone by a single training session. But what the training can do is help people to see themselves in context. To realize that these particular shortcomings are not their fault because everyone else who did the same kind of work has the same kind of problems. That gets people to relax and focus on their new tasks.

The managing director suggests here that training can give people insight into the social mechanisms through which they become who they are. Training could, for example, help associates understand that they developed associanitis because of the kinds of practices that the bank imposed on them, not because of their personal incompetence.

Organization Bank thus attempted in a practical context the developmental analysis that socioculturalists consider critical for understanding the social formation of psychological processes (Vygotsky, 1978; Wertsch, 1991). Like socioculturalists (e.g., Cole, 1996; Scribner, 1999), the bank argued that people are formed by the specific activities in which they engage. This differed from the Individual Bankers' idea that people behave in consistent ways because of inner predispositions that are relatively context independent. As we elaborate in Chapters 5 and 6, these different forms of self-interpretation that the banks facilitated had differential consequences. The Organization Bank training counteracted the self-focus that could arise when people seek to explain the difficulties they are having by citing their own qualities. This was confirmed by various participants during the training. For example, the following conversation took place toward the end of training.

> VICE PRESIDENT: The last few months [at work] had been really stressful because I thought that I might not be up to these new responsibilities.
> RESEARCHER: So you felt stressed because you had to work extra hard?
> VICE PRESIDENT: That too. But mostly because I kept observing myself in every situation and obsessing about whether what I did was OK.
> RESEARCHER: And training did something to change this?
> VICE PRESIDENT: We'll see but it was a real insight for me to see that this is not me. We all have the same experiences. So let's just get on with work.

One could interpret this training as the opposite of an approach based on abstract classification. Instead of learning to think about oneself and others in terms of personality traits, the training focused people away from their own attributes and skills. It let them recognize that what they misperceived as being caused by their own traits was instead caused by repeatedly participating in a social context in specific ways.

Conventional organizational research considers organizational socialization activities, such as training, as ways to reduce participants' cognitive uncertainty. These activities are designed to convey concepts and knowledge that help participants understand and respond to the situations they encounter (e.g., Chao et al., 1994). Individual Bank followed this approach, but Organization Bank did not. Organization Bank was skeptical, fearing that such an approach might lead bankers to search for and adopt simplistic "recipes." It consequently designed its training to amplify cognitive uncertainty, to make participants more aware of the contradictions and complexities they encountered and less likely to rely on generic concepts.

There are at least two points of convergence between Organization Bank's training practices and sociocultural theories of learning. First, like Organization Bank, sociocultural approaches consider learning to be contextualized. Lave (2003: 6), for example, writes that, in a "theory of situated activity, 'decontextualized learning activity' is a contradiction in terms." Like Organization Bank, sociocultural approaches are skeptical of decontextualized, classroom-based approaches to learning. Second, sociocultural approaches emphasize that a learner's accomplishments depend on the affordances of the social context (e.g., Barab and Plucker, 2002). In contrast, traditional cognitive theory considers classroom-based learning a useful practice and treats the learner's mind as more important than the social context in explaining cognitive accomplishments.

Organization Bank's training practices amplified cognitive uncertainty by extending the range of information bankers attended to and by withholding abstract concepts, sometimes even counteracting the formation of such concepts, thus forcing bankers to attend to the unexpected details of new situations. These practices forced bankers to compare action choices against the specific details of concrete situations, not against abstract standards imported from outside the situation. Underlying these practices was a different approach to performance based on the belief that one can optimize organizational performance simply by making sure that participants constantly monitor the specifics of the processes that they have influence over and forcing them to resist abstract planning, strategies, and reference standards.

INDIVIDUAL-CENTERED AND SOCIOCENTRIC
THEORIES IN PRACTICE

Our description of the two banks' distinct uncertainty-management practices, in Chapters 2 and 3, shows how the banks enacted different cognitive theories. Individual Bank relied primarily on the minds of its individual superstars, enacting the type of cognition described by traditional cognitive theory. This was reflected in the frequent references Individual Bankers made to individual bankers and their "brains." Individual Bankers said things like, "He is the brain behind the derivatives effort," "We are the best bank because we have the best brains in the industry," and "Our assets do ride the elevator every night." Similarly, in client meetings individual bankers stressed both their professional expertise and their personal attributes. As described above, Individual Bankers included their biographies in pitch books and attracted clients through publicity efforts that showcased their personal expertise. Highlighting his personality, one vice president told his client: "You want me by your side because I am known to fight for the last cent." Even though Individual Bankers were supported by organizational resources, such as input from other departments, they were expected to have the answers to a client's situation when asked. The uncertain environment could overwhelm individual decision makers and impede their effectiveness, so Individual Bank developed the practices described in Chapter 2 to reduce cognitive uncertainty for its individual bankers.

This bank's reliance on the knowledge of individual bankers was also shown in the detrimental effects of banker attrition. When one superstar left, clients and colleagues often followed because they believed that the bank could not fill the resulting knowledge gap. One associate explained: "When Mike leaves, he takes along a huge chunk of our industry expertise. I do not believe that we can hold our position in the league tables without him." On several occasions, the remaining bankers' nervousness about a superstar's departure was fueled by speculations in the financial press about the resulting vulnerability of a given department. Some of these speculations heralded bad news to come. For example, when two senior bankers left during the observation period, the bank had to exit a lucrative market and shut down a business group.

Organization Bank did not primarily rely on particular bankers' knowledge. Bankers instead combined their own knowledge with the resources of the organization. In each specific client situation, a banker was responsible for finding the best combination of resources to solve the problem, not for coming up with an answer by himself or herself. This reliance on inter-actions enacts the systemic emphasis of sociocultural theories of cognition, which focus on combinations of heterogeneous resources that together facilitate cognitive accomplishments. As one director said: "I can confi-dently say that this is the only place . . . where it is as natural for people to talk to their colleagues as it is to take the next breath." Another director said: "Individual bankers here know that they do not and are not supposed to have all the answers." Similarly, a managing director explained: "Even very junior bankers can take on very complicated projects because they have access to the firm's resources." This systemic approach to cognition was reflected in Organization Bankers' descriptions of themselves as merely gathering information, while they attributed thinking to the or-ganization as a whole: "We are the arms and the legs of this organ-ization. . . . We access for you the resources of [Organization Bank]." In another example, a director told a client who was complaining about the young and inexperienced Organization Banker team:

> Think of it [i.e., the deal process] like one of these sausage machines. I think of myself as putting things into the machine. Once this machine is set in motion, it inexorably grinds toward the end. This means that when you hire [Organization Bank] there is no stopping – your deal will get done, independently of what any one of us does or doesn't do.

When Organization Bank lost senior bankers, it remained relatively unaf-fected. The bank did not have to leave markets or rebuild departments. The bank's internal data and an industry survey showed that clients and colleagues rarely followed departing bankers. One client explained: "I have seen how this machine operates. It is more like an ant hill or like a dragon. When one head gets cut off, seven other heads fill that place without a hitch."

As will be described in Chapters 5 and 6, the bankers' propensity to draw on organizational resources did not emerge from preexisting pref-erences for teamwork or collaboration. In fact, just like junior Individual Bankers, incoming Organization Bankers would have preferred to com-plete their tasks independently. Organization Bank's cognitive uncertainty amplification practices did not permit this, however. By amplifying cog-nitive uncertainty, the bank forced overwhelmed bankers to draw on the organization's resources. As one director said: "In every other place, they tell you to talk to your colleagues or reward you when you do it. Here you don't have any other choice if you want to get the job done." Organization Bank responded to its uncertain environment by forcing bankers to dis-tribute the cognitive load across a high-capacity organizational system.

PART 2

PSYCHOLOGICAL TRANSFORMATION

As important as the divergent uncertainty-management practices were for Individual and Organization Bank, work practices should not be analyzed only by examining how they accomplish business activities. Work practices do influence how people accomplish tasks, but they also contribute to a business by changing participants in fundamental ways. As Martin Packer (2001; see also Packer and Goicoechea, 2000) has argued, we must attend not only to epistemology but also to ontology – not only to *what* people come to know but also to *who* they become. Different organizational practices require participants to use different sets of tools and engage in different activities. As a result, participants change as people. They develop a different sense of identity and exhibit distinct cognitive, motivational, and relational tendencies. Because Individual and Organization Bank used very different work practices, Individual Bankers and Organization Bankers developed into different kinds of people. This section describes how by following newcomers during their first two years with each bank.

We describe four time periods: recruiting, which took place a year before the bankers started their new jobs and lasted for about six months; five weeks of introductory training; the bankers' first six months on the job; and the period from six months to two years of service. The recruiting data were obtained during a one-year exploratory study. We classified the second, third, and fourth time periods into these three segments based on bankers' observations about important transitions. At both banks, for example, senior bankers told newcomers that "it will take about six months until you know the ropes around here." Our ongoing measures of the bankers' psychological processes, such as self-reported stress measures, also revealed changes after introductory training and after the first six months. In addition, other work on socialization in organizations has reported that an important phase of learning is usually completed after six months (Ashford and Black, 1996; Van Maanen, 1976; Van Maanen and Schein, 1979).

Individual Bank and Organization Bank recruited very similar people and their entering cohorts of junior bankers were indistinguishable. Both sets of newcomers experienced high anxiety at first, worrying about what they would be asked to do and whether they would measure up. Individual Bank mitigated this anxiety, providing clear guidelines for newcomers and helping them specialize in manageable areas. Organization Bank amplified this anxiety, denying junior bankers guidelines and throwing them into many new situations. New Individual Bankers thus experienced less stress over the first six months than new Organization Bankers. After six months, however, Organization Bankers began to change, becoming less focused on their own attributes and more open both to using resources – including other bankers – and to the features of specific situations. We argue that this represents an unusual but productive transformation in the Organization Bankers as people.

4

Recruiting

Before we describe the divergent developmental pathways that new Individual Bankers and Organization Bankers traveled, we first establish that most of the banks' recruiting practices were similar. This chapter provides evidence that the banks chose similar types of recruits. In describing their comparable recruiting practices our goal is to rule out an alternative explanation for our findings. One might argue that the divergent developmental processes we describe in Chapters 5 and 6, and the differential performance consequences that we observed at the two banks, were not caused by the banks' different uncertainty-management practices but instead by selection effects. According to this view, the bankers developed differently because they were different people to begin with. One bank might simply have recruited people who were smarter or differed along other important dimensions. This explanation might be valid if the banks used different selection processes and criteria or if applicants systematically chose a bank based on their preferences for the banks' different cultures. Candidates who were interested in a superstar culture, for instance, might have chosen Individual Bank but not Organization Bank. This chapter shows that neither the banks nor the applicants based their selections on such factors.

Even though the banks' recruiting processes and selection criteria were similar, however, recruitment served different functions at the two banks and thus launched new bankers' trajectories in distinct ways. Both banks recruited candidates who had a history of strong personal accomplishment and a "big ego." Individual Bank recruited high-achieving newcomers because they brought with them the tools and personalities that they would need to succeed as individual experts. This recruiting strategy supported the bank's individual-centric strategy. Organization Bank also valued high achievement and ego, but it then subverted its junior bankers' ability to succeed through their own talents. It created situations in which bankers who relied on their personal skills would fail. This caused bankers to consciously evaluate and discard the individual-centered approach to knowledge and to adopt a more organization-centered approach. Thus, even though Organization Bank initially focused on bankers' individual identities as it selected them, it then treated them in such a way that their own individual skills became less relevant.

This chapter has four sections that present the recruitment and selection processes from both the banks' and the recruits' perspectives. We describe the banks' overall approach to recruiting and the mechanisms by which they made the recruits' individual identities salient, the recruiting process, selection criteria, and recruits' decision making processes.

APPLICANT IDENTITIES AND THE BANKS' RECRUITING APPROACHES

The banks described their selection processes as "recruiting," a notion that they contrasted with the "hiring" processes of traditional companies. Both banks recruited bankers but hired back-office employees – distinguishing back-office functions and personnel from the revenue-producing positions into which bankers were recruited. Hiring typically refers to the engagement of a person in return for payment. This is a market transaction in which each party delivers a predetermined commodity. The employee supplies a set amount of effort and the employer provides a negotiated wage. In contrast, the term recruiting carries connotations from nonmarket settings, such as the military or athletics, and evokes images of elite institutions to which an elite group of participants unconditionally devote their effort. People who enter these settings often do not perceive their relationship to the organization in terms of a market transaction. Such organizations often extract extreme effort from their members, sometimes in return for uncertain and intangible rewards. Recruits become a part of the organization as "members," a term that evokes a quasi-organic unity between individual and collective. New recruits, as opposed to new hires, do not complete discrete tasks but "refresh" or "restore" the organization.

For example, aspiring Individual and Organization Bankers acted like recruits and not hires when they suppressed their interest in finding out about and negotiating compensation. By treating compensation as secondary, aspiring bankers signaled their willingness to exert themselves unconditionally for the banks and to subordinate their desire for high salaries to a focus on the goals of the organization. Many of the bankers we spoke with, both junior and senior, openly admitted that money mattered to them. The stereotypical image of an investment banker is someone who is motivated primarily by money. During the time of our study, for example, a business periodical featured a cover story about the extraordinarily high salaries in investment banking, with an image portraying a banker in the form of a money hog. The bankers did not appreciate this image, but they readily agreed that money mattered to them. An Individual Bank vice president said, for example: "Of course I work here for the money. That applies to all of us. Whoever tells you something different is bullshitting you." Similarly, a senior Organization Bank associate said: "Money is definitely part of why people work in investment banking." Many of the applicants for investment banking positions also expressed a fascination with high investment banker salaries. One MBA student who interviewed with both banks said:

> Whenever we have a guest speaker with some background experience in i-banking, students more or less delicately try to find out how much you'd earn at the different career stages. . . . I don't think that everyone is only in it for the money. I think part of this interest in what i-bankers earn comes just from hearing about a world that is so different from what you are used to. But I think it is safe to say that money is important to many of us.

Incoming associates often had a general sense of what they would be earning because of related prior work experience or personal contacts with other investment bankers. Undergraduates who entered the banks as analysts, however, typically found out about salary only when they received the official offer letter, after multiple rounds of interviewing that could extend over months. Many recruits did not even have a rough estimate. One Organization Bank analyst said: "I just figure it will be enough to live on. I probably won't have much time to spend it anyways." Nevertheless, most applicants realized that a career in investment banking would be very rewarding financially.

Despite everyone's interest in money, however, salary was a taboo topic in interviews. One Individual Bank director explained: "There are always alarm bells going off when people show too much interest in their salary during interviews. You want them to be excited about being part of the firm, not about the money." Similarly, in an interview debriefing session, one Organization Bank vice president announced her misgivings about a candidate: "In two separate interviews, she tried to find out what exactly she would be earning. She also said that she was offered $50,000 by [name of company] and that she was trying to compare this to what we'd be offering. So I am not sure how much she really wants to come here."

These quotations indicate how senior bankers expected recruits to value firm membership independently of its financial rewards – or at least to behave as if they did. Recruits who asked about salary received the same type of answer at both banks: "We take good care of our own." The tone in which this answer was delivered, and the lack of specific information, sent a clear message not to investigate further and discouraged attempts to negotiate. One Individual Bank associate who had asked about his salary made the following comment: "I felt embarrassed the second that question had left my mouth. You should have seen the look on [the interviewer's] face. I felt like I had dropped my pants in public, something that distasteful."

Thus, the banks' expectations about what it means to be a recruit were enforced subtly, through silences and facial expressions, rather than explained explicitly. Even though recruits could assume that the banks paid well, some of the recruits could choose from other, potentially more lucrative positions – such as Silicon Valley start-ups or private equity firms. Giving up one's right to negotiate salary could therefore have a high cost. Many applicants were happy to choose one of the banks, however, and they understood the benefits of being a "recruit" instead of a "hire."

The "we take care of our own" comment cited above was typical. Senior bankers often used family metaphors during recruiting, referring to the company as a "family" or a "mother" and talking about instances when the firm "helps people out who are in need," "makes sure you are comfortable," and "cares that you are safe." For some bankers, such metaphors gave the impression of belonging to a kinship-based community instead of working for a corporation. One Organization Bank analyst reportedly told a recruit:

> People here really care that you are safe and help you out even when the situation has nothing to do with work. One of my friends had trouble with the guy she was living with. He became violent toward her and she got scared. When she told that to [the banker who runs the analyst program], he immediately got her out of that situation and put her up in a really fancy corporate apartment until she could find a new living situation.

The analyst who related this story said: "This is what you'd expect your parents to do for you. You don't expect that from some employer." In a similar incident at Individual Bank, the son of a secretary had to undergo expensive surgery, and the firm's senior bankers paid for it out of their pockets as a gift to the employee.

By referring to the bank as a family, senior bankers encouraged recruits to identify strongly with the institution and to desire membership in the exclusive club of elite bankers. Their ways of speaking about the bank construed bankers as part of a closely knit group in which participants generously extend themselves on behalf of the community. Most recruits adopted this frame without objection. Some, however, took a more cynical view:

> I think they tell you all of this family stuff to change how you view your decision. In a family that takes such good care of you and worries about your well-being, you have the obligation to do the same for your family, to give of yourself what you can. You wouldn't really keep track of who gives what and of what you receive for what you put in. I think this is the kind of arrangement they try to get going with us, making us work around the clock without really asking ourselves whether it is worth it.

Despite such reservations on the part of an occasional recruit, most happily adopted the identity they were being offered as new members of an elite group focused on common goals and not on fee-for-service.

In contrast to the taboo on discussing salary with recruits for investment banking positions, there was no stigma attached to inquiries about money by candidates for back-office jobs. At Organization Bank, one back-office department also hired undergraduate students from prestigious universities. As one of these students was deciding between Organization Bank and another company, he listed salary as one of the considerations he was weighing. When Michel asked the hiring manager whether this was a legitimate question, she responded with surprise: "Of course it is. This is not a charity. Isn't that something that you would want to know about your job?" Both banks recognized that interest in salary was natural for a job applicant, but they deliberately tried to downplay the topic for their investment banking recruits. They did this not through persuasion or incentives but by fostering organizational identification – by encouraging recruits to view themselves as part of a group that provides a personal identity and to which one is personally obliged.

Associated with this identity as an elite banker were expectations about what counts as appropriate effort. As in the military and athletics, the banks made clear to recruits the extreme effort they demanded from their employees. The U.S. Marines recruit with the slogan "the few, the proud," and in one recruitment commercial they show a marine climbing an almost vertical rock to its top. The camera angle then sweeps over a vast landscape of mountains without another living being in sight. In a similar vein, the banks highlighted the grueling aspects of investment banking to candidates, echoing themes of rugged individualism and describing the very limited time for personal relationships. Senior bankers candidly spoke about the long hours they worked, the extreme physical and psychological exhaustion they experienced, and the negative health and family consequences they suffered. For instance, one Organization Bank director said at a university information session:

> When I entered [the bank], I thought that I'd put in a few difficult years as an analyst, that I'd pay my dues, and that life would become easier as I became more senior because I could delegate more. I actually counted on this because I had to promise this to my wife who often enough felt that she just couldn't take it anymore – never having meals together during the week, never being able to plan anything on weekends, canceled vacations. But I have been with the firm for fourteen years now and I still have all of these problems. I still work around one hundred hours most weeks. When I have time to chitchat in the office, we usually talk about who is more tired or who lost more hair. I promise you, these hours will take a severe toll on you. Even two years of work like that will really get to you.

While recruiting, then, both banks made clear to recruits how the commitment to an organizational identity could interfere with one's commitment to other identities, such as being a husband or wife.

Even before they entered the banks, most of the aspiring bankers said that fulfilling the bank's expectations was at least as important as, or even more important to them than, the expectations of their friends and families. One associate explained: "I am at a stage right now where I want to work hard and want to succeed here with the best and prove myself. . . . If that means I don't see or call my parents or my wife, they just have to accept this. . . . After all, this is [Individual Bank] – [Individual Bank], man." When asked whether they were prepared to endure the hardship associated with being a banker, recruits affirmed enthusiastically that they were. A new Individual Bank associate said: "I am definitely willing to push myself. I figure this is the only time in my life where I still have the energy and stamina to do this." Similarly, an Organization Bank associate said: "This is the time to work like this."

Associates were willing to sacrifice because it reinforced the identity that the banks had encouraged them to adopt as members of an exclusive club. The wife of a new Organization Bank associate described the pride that the newcomers experienced about their extreme work:

> When you ask him directly, he'll admit that these hours are insane, inhuman, and utterly unreasonable. But at the same time there is this

fascination with this kind of lifestyle that only few people would be willing to take on and actually only very few could endure for that long, even if they wanted to. It's always there in conversations at parties: who pulled how many all-nighters and under what crazy pressures.

Psychological studies predict this sort of response. Various cognitive psychologists have shown that role expectations are important sources of identity and self-esteem (Thoits, 1991; Tajfel and Turner, 1979). Individuals view organizational roles partly with respect to what they say about them as individuals, and they are willing to make sometimes-extreme sacrifices because their identity is at stake. The fact that this strong reaction occurred even before the candidates joined the banks is consistent with the minimal-group paradigm (Turner, 1975; Tajfel, 1981). According to this theory, the mere act of categorizing oneself as a group member is sufficient to evoke behaviors characteristic of group members. As the theory's name suggests, the extensive interactions that are typically part of group relations are not necessary. This research shows the profound influence that organizational identities can have on participants' behaviors, even when these identities are based on anticipatory self-categorization and not on prolonged personal experiences with the organization.

The gung-ho attitudes of the investment banking recruits differed from the reactions of those hired into back-office functions, who wanted and expected a more balanced life. Incoming hires usually wanted to know how many hours they would be working, and many considered a fifty- or sixty-hour work week as sufficiently unattractive that they declined positions. This contrasts with the 100 to 120 hours that incoming investment bankers knowingly signed up for. In some cases, undergraduates entered back-office positions hoping to move into investment banking. While some of them accepted the sixty-hour weeks for the back office only reluctantly, they said that they would not mind working twice as hard if they became investment bankers. One Organization Bank employee in human resources explained:

> I just don't see the need to stay here longer than six o'clock. Most of the work I am doing here is bullshit anyway. I am here until six o'clock in the first place because she [his boss] gets on my case when I leave earlier. In investment banking you work these hours not because you have to pull face time or because someone has these ideas about what it means to work hard. You work hard in investment banking because there is an objective need. There is a deal and it has to get done. It's not that people create work to make themselves look important, like here [in human resources].

This quotation suggests that the extreme motivation observed in invest-ment banking recruits is not necessarily an attribute of these individuals, but instead something that the investment banking job can extract from various people. This lends further support to our focus on organizational practices, not individual dispositions, as the most important explanatory factors in these settings.

Bankers at both banks explicitly used military and sports metaphors to communicate expectations to recruits. One Organization Bank vice pres-ident compared the banking experience with military training: "This is like a boot camp.... You can always ring the bell and quit." Other bankers used the term "athlete" to describe successful bankers: "We don't really have one particular background that we are looking for. It's more that we are looking for athletes. You need to be mentally quick and have a lot of stamina and always be willing to push yourself."

These metaphors frame the long work hours as a test of courage, char-acter, and endurance that people freely seek out to challenge themselves, not as an exploitative work arrangement that they are trapped in. It thus encouraged bankers to foreground their own identity attributes – they were attracted to investment banking because they were the kinds of people who had the requisite courage, character, and endurance.

Both banks thus made an organizational identity salient to recruits, encouraging recruits to view themselves in terms of their prospective membership as a banker at their particular firm. When organizational identities are salient, individuals are more likely to adopt the group's values, norms, and standards as their own, to exhibit intense effort on behalf of the group they identify with, and to accept high levels of stress as they strive to live up to the group's norms (Haslam, 2004). The banks' framing of employment selection as "recruiting" made salient particular types of norms and values – namely those typical of "total institutions" (Goffman, 1961) such as the military and distinct from more traditional jobs. A salient organizational identity, however, does not necessarily mean that participants forget their individual self. In fact, as the data above show, identification with the banks was partly motivated by individuals' concern with enhancing their sense of them-selves (cf., Hogg and Turner, 1985) – as exemplified by their personal desire to be viewed as part of an elite group. The important point is that the banks' recruiting approach made subjectively salient the candidates' identities, whether as group members or as independent individuals, in ways that fit well with traditional cognitive explanations of how motivation and identity work.

THE RECRUITING PROCESS

This section describes the specific processes through which the banks selected recruits. Three aspects of these processes are noteworthy. First, each bank tried to be first on a given campus because recruits often selected the bank that got to them first and built personal relationships with them. This supports our argument that recruits did not select the two banks based on their divergent cultures. Second, both banks structured the recruiting process to reinforce an organizational identity such that they became the kinds of dedicated recruits described in the last section. Third, the banks used comparable and highly systematic processes to ensure that they obtained the type of candidate they desired. Our account of these systematic selection processes shows that the two banks hired similar individuals from the same pool, without selecting ones that fit their particular culture.

We first describe how the deep investment of incumbent bankers in the recruiting process elicited organizational identification from recruits. Both banks expended significant resources on recruiting. By far the highest expense was the opportunity cost of senior bankers. Recruiting was orchestrated almost exclusively by bankers themselves. The banks' human resource managers were mainly concerned with logistics and formalities, such as sending out benefit information and helping with relocation. In contrast to the central role that human resource managers typically play in the hiring process, in recruitment they made no substantive decisions. Decisions about where to recruit, whom to select, and what to pay all were made by teams of bankers. One Individual Bank director described how he did it: "During recruiting season, I come in on weekends to interview. I also have dinners with recruits. Sometimes this means flying out to where they are. Just last week, I had dinner with someone in Boston. And I keep checking in with them on the phone, to see where they are in their decision process."

One Organization Bank associate said: "I sometimes see Bill [the department head] on the phone until late at night, trying to help a recruit make a decision." Another associate added: "And he logs these phone calls on a weekly basis, often over a period of months, until the candidate has made a decision."

This reliance on bankers was a costly choice. The time that a banker spent on recruiting could not be devoted to bringing in revenues, and these could be substantial. For example, when a banker brought in a "blockbuster" deal, a bank could earn $30 million in fees. At both banks senior bankers, including the heads of departments, nonetheless spent significant time in the recruiting process. Because senior bankers and department heads spent most of their time bringing in revenue from important clients, their time was particularly expensive. The banks were conscious of their bankers' opportunity cost and did not use their time lightly. For example, an Organization Bank human resource manager explained:

> Banker time is the highest cost of doing business. And it is crazy the kinds of things we do to protect this time. We have quite a few divisions that make money. But only the bankers get free meals delivered to their floor and coffee so that they do not have to waste time to go across the street. And when it is time to tighten the belt, we first remove the flowers from all the lobbies before we take the free meals away. And it's not that the bankers cannot pay for their own meals, even during bad times, believe me. And it's not a status thing, although that probably always plays a role, too. It's a business decision; one that people around here make very consciously.

This shows how carefully the banks allocated banker time, trying to save even the few minutes that it might take a banker to cross the street to go to a coffee shop.

Extensive banker time was nonetheless spent on recruiting. Bankers were willing to spend this time because people were crucial to the organization and because their involvement made it more likely that recruits would identify with the bank. An Individual Bank director said: "That's how you get people to identify with your organization, by putting a face on it and a person that you can relate to and who you want to become like." Involving bankers in the recruiting process let the recruits imagine themselves more vividly as members in the "club" of elite bankers. It gave the recruits a palpable image of the kind of identity they could embody if they became bankers. Candidates at both banks commented on the "power," "elegance," and "sophistication" that the bankers exuded in their "stylish suits, Hermès ties, and Alden shoes." They were also captivated with what they saw as the perks of a banker's work, including the "glamorous" lifestyle filled with "fancy dinners in the best restaurants worldwide," "personal relationships with senior executives of the Fortune 100 companies," and "all the travel in limousines, corporate jets, and in first class," "staying at the best hotels." The recruits' identification with the bank was not based merely on feelings of belonging. It was also motivated by an emotional attachment to an alluring vision of the self that the bankers embodied.

The banks were interested in fostering organizational identification because it allowed them to control and motivate their bankers more effectively. In addition, when recruits identified with a bank they were more likely to accept the bank's job offer. An Organization Banker who had rejected Individual Bank admitted:

> I felt terrible turning them down. I felt like I violated their personal trust or something. It was the bizarrest thing. I know that they matter-of-factly turn down thousands of candidates without feeling bad in the least. But they made me feel like we had this special relationship and that just because they wanted me to join and because they spent all that time with me, I was somehow personally obliged to them.

As one Organization Bank vice president said: "Every interaction is an opportunity to build a relationship and tighten the bonds between the candidate and the organization." The banks' internal research showed that a bank won over a contested recruit when it established contact first and could build loyalty. A recruiter at Individual Bank said: "I always try to be the first on campus with information sessions and interviews because the most desirable candidates have competing offers and usually go with the bank they met first." This claim was supported by the recruits themselves. For example, one associate who had offers from both banks said:

> Now that I am working for Organization Bank for a while, I can see that it is different from Individual Bank in many ways. But if you are not an insider – and I certainly was not – it is very difficult to decide between the banks. They are both highly prestigious, really the Rolls Royce of investment banking. They have the same kind of intelligent, hard-driven person working for them, which is important because you want to work with people like that. They offer the same benefits and perks. I think for many of us it was a matter of feeling a sense of commitment to the bankers with whom we had established a relationship, who had given you advice, and who had rooted for you throughout this process. It is not that I made such an important decision solely based on feelings of obligation toward someone I hardly know. Although I have to admit that there was some of that. It is also that you really come to like the people you get to know early on and have more contact with.

An Individual Banker who had decided against Organization Bank said:

> I had offers from Organization Bank, Individual Bank, and [top management consulting firm]. I had sleepless nights trying to decide between them. I kept talking to people, drawing up lists with the pros and cons but then one of my friends observed that I just tried to find good reasons for going with the firm for which I had decided early on, without really being aware of it. I think he was right. Individual Bank

was my first on-campus interview. They were about a week earlier than the other firms. And that was a week of fantasizing about working there, really warming up to the firm.

These excerpts indicate that, even though the banks had reputations for their different cultures, the recruits either did not know or did not care about these cultures when they made their employment decisions. They usually went with the bank that established a personal relationship with them first. This suggests that neither the banks' different cultures nor the recruits' personal dispositions caused recruits systematically to self-select into the banks.

We now describe the banks' systematic decision making processes, illustrating the considerable precautions they took to ensure successful decisions. Our account shows that both banks selected recruits based on similar objective hiring criteria, not based on the idiosyncratic preferences of powerful bankers or other bank-specific factors. Both banks involved a broad range of bankers with different perspectives and university connections, created competition among recruiters to motivate recruiting teams, and used a collective decision making process to separate accurate information from "noise."

For each university, the banks assembled a recruiting team that mostly consisted of banker alumni from that university. "This helps us to get an insight into what grades, prizes, and extracurricular activities really mean," explained one Organization Bank associate; "You know what the slacker courses are, who the professors with the tough grading are, and how much time it takes to have these leadership positions in the various clubs." The banks used competition to motivate the teams. For example, the Individual Bank team that recruited from Wharton was keen on bringing in more successful candidates than the Individual Bank team that recruited from MIT. Organization Bank used the same process. As one Organization Bank associate described it: "During recruiting season, you constantly see statistics about how each team is doing. And people here are competitive. If they see that their team is falling behind, they'll make a few more calls to candidates who sit on the fence, to professors, whatever. People can get quite creative when you get their juices flowing that way."

The banks kept track of success ratios describing the number of recruits brought in by a given team in relation to the eventual success of these candidates. By assessing this ratio – as opposed to rewarding teams based only on the number of candidates they brought in – teams had an incentive to select candidates carefully. They only brought in individuals whom they believed could succeed.

Before receiving an offer, a candidate typically interviewed with about thirty employees at all levels. In contrast, at many of the banks' clients, interviews were conducted by one human resource manager and two or three senior managers from the hiring department. Some of the banks' recruits compared this stressful experience with the "hazing" one has to undergo to join other tightly knit groups, such as fraternities or the military. As we described above, these techniques were partly designed to elicit commitment from the recruits. One Individual Banker said: "We do this because we are making an important investment here and we want to make the right decision. But many of us have been through something like this ourselves. The harder you have to work for something the more you convince yourself that you really want this." Because they were forced to spend an unusual amount of time and effort in the recruitment process, recruits developed strong identities as aspiring bankers and strong motivation to live up to these identities.

The first and second rounds of interviews took place on university campuses. The third and final round took place at the banks' headquarters, where all candidates from the various universities were interviewed on the same day. Initially, each candidate had about three interviews scheduled. If the initial feedback from these interviews was positive, additional interviews were added. Successful candidates often were kept interviewing until late at night. After interviews were completed, all bankers who had met the candidates assembled in a conference room to discuss each applicant. One Organization Bank associate described this event:

> These sessions are initially relatively unstructured. We want to hear whatever someone has to say about a candidate – anything, there is no censorship. Then when there are opposing opinions, we have people really hash it out. We are a meritocracy. When you have to give your opinion on something as important as recruiting in front of all of your peers, people take this pretty seriously and do their best to give good evidence.

An Organization Bank vice president described another way in which the bank motivated recruiters to make good choices: "We have batting records. We keep track of who advocated which candidate and then see how well their candidate works out down the road." This process motivated bankers to take recruiting seriously and encouraged input from various perspectives. When bankers differed in their assessment of a recruit, they had an incentive to collect the best possible evidence.

Each bank short-circuited its process if a desirable candidate had an offer from comparable organizations, including the other bank. For example, one candidate said:

> After my first round with Individual Bank, I had my first round with Organization Bank and really hit it off with them. They called me the same afternoon and told me to come out to [their headquarters] two days later. When I got an offer from them, Individual Bank also let me skip their second-round interviews and interviewed me [at their headquarters] before Super Saturday [the day for third-round interviews].

One Individual Bank director justified this process, saying that: "We all use the same raw material" – referring to the recruits. An Organization Bank vice president elaborated: "We use the decisions of some competitors, like Individual Bank, as input into our selection process and I know that they do the same. It just makes sense. We all have the same procedures, similar criteria, and always end up fighting for the same candidates."

Because the banks had similar selection processes, the judgment of one bank was an effective substitute for the judgment of the other bank. This is further evidence that new bankers at Individual Bank and Organization Bank did not differ systematically at entry.

RECRUITING CRITERIA

This section provides further evidence that the two banks selected comparable recruits. We describe how the banks used similar recruiting criteria – focusing on intellect, relational abilities, and ego. These criteria meant different things and served different purposes in the two banks' distinct cultures, however.

Both banks focused primarily on intellect in their recruitment decisions. As evidence for intellect, they attended to high grades in difficult courses, high SAT, GMAT, and GRE scores, and academic prizes. The two banks placed a higher emphasis on academic achievement than many other investment banks. One recruit said: "When I interviewed with [name of a Wall Street bank], they actually mocked me for my good grades. They said that I should try to find a job at Organization Bank, Individual Bank, or one of the 'high-flying' consulting firms."

At both banks, students who did not have a perfect grade point average were only considered when they had other redeeming features. In one such case, a student had a 3.6 grade point average but was a championship athlete and also played a musical instrument at a high level of proficiency.

The student was invited to the first round of interviews. Most bankers said that they looked at both grades and extracurricular achievements. For example, one Organization Bank vice president explained to his team what to look for in résumés: "We cannot consider people who only have these high grades because they don't do anything else besides studying. I want you to look for people who get these grades even though they also take on significant responsibilities in clubs or who excel at sports or art." Even though the banks valued hard work, they suspected that some candidates only got good grades because they put all of their effort into academic activities. Both banks thought that such one-dimensional candidates lacked the "pure intellect" or "raw intellectual horsepower" that the banks valued.

The banks differed, however, in how they defined intellect and why they valued it. Individual Bankers defined intellect mostly in terms of a person's mental ability. Definitions of intellect included "brilliance," "raw intellectual horsepower," "superior insight," and "genius." The bankers valued intellect in significant part because they believed that it was a necessary ingredient for cultivating a superstar. One director said: "Our superstars need to constantly come up with innovative and compelling solutions to some of the world's most complex deals. That requires a superior mind." In addition, the bank prided itself on attracting the "best and the brightest" from the world's top universities. In one client conversation a managing director said: "When you hire us, you have some of the most brilliant intellects at your disposal. . . .This year, our incoming MBA cohort had an almost perfect GPA." In client conversations, emphasizing the brilliance of the bank's superstars had the intended effect of differentiating Individual Bank from other banks that were less discriminating. As a director said, "In our business it is all about the quality of the minds you can attract. That's what determines the quality of your products." Another implicit comparison was with the client's own finance staff, which was typically recruited from less prestigious universities and earned considerably less than a banker. The higher quality of the bankers helped justify the substantially higher payment for the bankers' time.

In contrast, Organization Bankers defined intellect mostly in terms of context-dependent and relational processes, including the ability to mobilize a broader set of social resources. One vice president defined intellect as "an engine . . . that powers your search for the best tools, that makes you seek input." Other Organization Bankers defined intellect as the "ability to see connections," the "ability to understand what is going on in a situation," "acting effectively in a situation," and being "good with feedback."

A highly valued capability often mentioned in relation to intellect was "judgment." One Organization Bank vice president defined judgment as "knowing what the right thing is to do in a situation." None of the Organization Bankers used the related term "talent," which is often used by other highly successful professional service firms. An Organization Banker explained:

> When I think of talent, I think of something like juggling, playing chess, or singing. People who have talent practice one particular set of skills in a setting that is relatively well defined, like a chess board, or where the setting doesn't matter that much, like in singing. This is vastly different from what makes someone effective in investment banking or trading. The same types of strategies that work well in one kind of environment can be disastrous in another type of environment. What matters is not how well you have practiced a certain set of responses but how well you can act in concert with whatever environment you are in.

Organization Bankers viewed intellect more as an ability to connect and perceive in specific situations, not as a decontextualized skill or a purely mental gift.

Organization Bankers valued intellect because it helped bankers contribute effectively to its sociocentric, uncertainty-amplifying work practices. One vice president explained: "It requires someone with a keen mind to not make assumptions and to ask the kinds of probing questions that help you figure out what kinds of resources the client needs." A director said: "We need someone with a very flexible mind, who has the ability to recognize what kind of behavior is appropriate and to just behave in this way without a lot of training." Like some Individual Bankers, Organization Bankers spoke about the "collective intellect of our organization" in an attempt to solicit client business and to justify fees, but they used this term to refer more to the organization than to individual bankers' minds.

For both banks, demonstrated intellect was the criterion that got a recruit invited to the first interview. Subsequently, a different set of criteria was used, including the recruits' abilities to relate to clients and colleagues. One Individual Bank vice president said:

> Whoever comes through the door here with a 4.0 GPA from the kinds of schools that we are recruiting from can do the job. The three things that we want to know about the person are: First, how would I feel about this person sitting in front of our clients? Second, do I want to sit next to that person at three in the morning? Or, more generally, how will this person interact with internal clients – colleagues. And third, can I imagine this person as a managing director down the road?

The first two criteria refer to relational processes, which were also important at Organization Bank. The third criterion goes beyond the first two by adding a developmental perspective. Bankers at both banks not only were interested in what a person would be able to produce, but also tried to envision how that person might develop.

When asked what qualities were used as a predictor of successful development, one Individual Bank vice president explained:

> I think the best predictor for who will eventually be a good managing director is . . . if I had to tell you what to look for in a few words, I'd say: We are looking to hire insecure overachievers. We are looking at high grades and outstanding extracurricular activities partly as an indication of the person's ability to figure out what it takes to succeed in a given setting and to make himself into that kind of person.

To define the term "insecure overachiever," bankers sometimes used the term "ego." One Individual Banker said: "An insecure overachiever is someone with a big ego. Someone who always needs to be the best in whatever they are doing and who constantly needs the validation of others, even though they might not admit this."

Another Individual Banker offered her explanation with a laugh: "Insecure overachiever – to me that is the politically correct term for egomaniac, which around here is a compliment. It means you fit in." Other Individual Bankers also used the term "ego" with appreciation. For example, a managing director said: "Ego produces the superstar personalities we have around here. That's what our clients are buying." An Individual Bank director said: "You need a healthy dose of ego to wake up every morning and be pumped about swimming with the sharks." At Individual Bank, then, a banker's ego was important because it signaled the person's fit with the bank's superstar culture. An Individual Bank associate said:

> We all come here because of our egos, because we want to work for the most prestigious firm, the one who makes the fewest offers, the elite club. And once we land the job, we keep fighting for all the other things that feed our ego. We fight to get into the department that is the most respected inside the firm, to work with the most admired senior people, to be on the biggest client teams. Ego is good, ego works.

Affiliation with a prestigious bank and department feeds an insecure overachiever's ego. Hiring new bankers who derive an ego boost from the bank's prestige is likely to facilitate the bank's goal of fostering social identification with the bank.

Organization Bank also used the terms "ego" and "insecure overachiever" to refer to their preferred candidates, and they generally used these terms with a similar meaning as the Individual Bankers. When asked to define "ego," one Organization Bank director said: "It is when everything you do is all about how people perceive you and how you perceive yourself in relation to other people. It is a constant social comparison process and you just cannot stand to be on the bad end of that comparison." An Organization Bank vice president defined ego in the following way: "It doesn't mean that you are a jerk or that you don't care about what others say. Quite the opposite. If anything, you care way too much about what others think or say – but for the wrong reasons. It's not about them but about you, about how you are viewed or perceived." Note that this Organization Banker devalues more individual-centered ego and starts to articulate a sense in which the more relationship-oriented culture of Organization Bank might work for insecure overachievers.

Like the Individual Bankers, Organization Bankers valued "ego" for the kinds of development it made possible in junior bankers who had this characteristic. But they envisioned a different kind of developmental process. One Organization Bank managing director explained:

> When people come in here, they have egos large enough to cover the sun. Initially you need the big ego as a driving force. There is really nothing else that makes people take the kinds of beatings you have to endure here day after day over a period of years. It takes time until you can get your charge from other things.

This managing director depicts the ego as an auxiliary device that energizes bankers until they can begin to derive energy and direction from the task itself. While the Individual Bankers expected the ego to stay in place, then, the Organization Bankers expected it to go away over time as it was exorcised by the banks' practices. One Organization Bank director said:

> We are looking for people who are constantly looking outside for what to do. In the beginning, when people are still young they do this because of ego and insecurity. They'll do anything to be seen as smart and successful. That's why they pay attention to others, to figure out whether they have their approval. But this job matures people fast. It's not that the drive to succeed goes away but, believe it or not, the ego goes away, despite what you always hear about Wall Street types. Well, it doesn't go by itself. It is kind of bludgeoned into submission.

At Individual Bank, ego was valued because it encouraged bankers to develop and exhibit independent and flamboyant superstar personalities. In contrast, at Organization Bank ego was viewed as an attribute that made bankers susceptible to social control. According to one Organization Bank director:

> Contrary to what you might think, it is relatively easy to control a person with a big ego because they are so dependent on external validation. It doesn't matter how loud or rebellious they seem. I think that's why so many firms cultivate that kind of personality. It is infinitely more difficult to control someone who acts not from a perspective of insecurity and all wrapped up in emotions but from a cool inner strength. But the trouble with an ego is that you don't only make bad decisions for yourself but also for the firm, when you are with a client.

In contrast to Individual Bank, which valued the display of independence that comes with a big ego, Organization Bank recognized the potential for social influence. Organization Bankers believed that over time they could orient young bankers' strong drive away from ego-based concerns. As described in Chapter 6, many Organization Bankers could recall points in their development at which they made the switch from a preoccupation with their ego toward a concern for concrete tasks.

THE RECRUITS' DECISION-MAKING PROCESS

This section describes the newcomers whom we followed for a two-year period at the two banks. It reports on the first interactions between these recruits and the banks, including interviews and follow-up conversations. These recruitment interactions began one year before the recruits joined the banks and lasted for up to six months. In this section, we also describe what attracted the recruits to a career in investment banking. By describing the similar processes and criteria through which aspiring Individual Bankers and Organization Bankers selected one bank or the other, we further support our argument that the banks hired similar kinds of people. By describing the recruits before they formally joined, this chapter also provides a baseline description of what the recruits were like before the two banks' work practices transformed them.

Many recruits did not have a clear vision of what kind of career they wanted and chose investment banking partly because it was popular among peers. This shows the susceptibility of many recruits to social comparison – an attribute that was convenient for the banks, which relied on social influence to enforce their values, norms, and standards. The recruits appreciated the future career options that investment banking made possible and the prestige that came with the job, but they generally did not reflect on the profound changes that this work would produce in them as people, even though the banks talked explicitly with them about this.

Recruits were attracted to a career in investment banking for three primary reasons: identity-related concerns, learning opportunities, and future career options. An Individual Bank associate explained his decision this way: "The place you are working for says something about you. When you tell people that you work for Individual Bank, they are usually impressed because they think that you must be really smart because you made it through a highly selective process.... It also means that you'll work with other people like you, which is important to me."

Another associate also talked about his attraction to the kinds of employees that Individual Bank hired:

> I became interested in Individual Bank during the information session on campus. At the time, I was not really that much into investment banking or consulting. I just showed up for the heck of it. But then I was really impressed with the bankers they sent and with how they comported themselves. I still remember one of the senior bankers saying: "We are looking for people who have strong intellectual horsepower." And you could clearly see that the people they brought along had that kind of intellect by how they spoke and answered questions. That made an impression on me. I wanted to be part of a firm that hires people like that.

An Organization Bank associate said: "I have to admit that I was always fascinated by Organization Bankers, their reputation for being the best and most intelligent in their field, their drive to succeed. That's the kind of person that I want to be."

Prospective bankers were attracted also to the occupation's "prestige" and "glamour." As one Organization Bank associate said, "It is partly about the prestige. Investment banking currently attracts the best and brightest." An Individual Bank associate said: "It might sound shallow but I really want to experience all that glamour that you always hear about, the high-powered clients, the mega-deals that you read about the next day in the *Wall Street Journal*." An Organization Bank newcomer said:

> It is just incredible the amount of money that these firms spend to find good people.... They flew me to New York twice, first by myself and then with my fiancée, to get her on board, too. We both stayed in this

incredible hotel in the Wall Street area – the best hotel I've stayed in, that's for sure. And everyone I met kept telling me that this was all a reflection of how important it is for these banks to find the best and the brightest. That is part of the attraction for me. It's not just the glitz, even though I can definitely use some more glitz than I have currently, but also the chance to work with those kinds of people.

As noted above, the banks were well aware of recruits' interest in these markers of an elite and exclusive identity, and they made these attributes salient during the review process.

Fit with the specific culture of the bank not an important criterion for the recruits, although they often said what they thought the banks wanted to hear. One Individual Bank newcomer said: "You know what they want to hear from their website and that's what I am telling them. It's all about how you admire and fit into their great culture." An Organization Bank associate agreed: "I think they like to hear how much you like their culture and how much you can identify with them. This is what I emphasized in interviews." When asked what this culture consisted of for a given bank, most candidates answered that they could not discern differences between banks. Nor could they differentiate the top banks from other top professional service firms. One incoming Organization Banker said with some exasperation: "It is not that I don't care about the culture but they all sound the same to me. It is all about excellence, valuing the client and the individual, teamwork. . . . I have the same speech for all of my final interviews and so far it seems to work." A new Individual Banker said: "I think these websites are pretty generic. I also did not get any more individuating information from the people that I spoke with. They all tell me things about how you learn a lot, work really hard, but also have a lot of fun."

A few candidates believed that Organization Bank "works its people even harder than other banks" and that it "works its people to the bone." One candidate, who eventually joined Organization Bank, said: "I heard this place is a sweatshop." In general, however, our conversations with recruits and junior bankers indicate that there was not a systematic banker self-selection effect based on the banks' different cultures.

The excerpts above also show that recruits were flexible in how they presented their interests to the bank. They wanted the job, but they were not very interested in the details of what the banks were like. One might imagine that these highly accomplished candidates, who typically had a variety of job options, would use the recruiting process to learn more about how they fit into the organization and what the organization could offer to them. Surprisingly, however, many candidates knew very little about the kind of work they would be doing – even after they signed the contract. Like the following incoming Organization Banker, bankers at both banks had only very general notions about what they would be learning:

BANKER: I am interested in this job because I want to learn.
RESEARCHER: What, in particular, are you interested in learning?
BANKER: I guess you'll learn about finance and also about dealing with people.
RESEARCHER: Are you interested in finance?
BANKER: I am not sure. I haven't taken any finance courses or anything.
RESEARCHER: Could you envision a career in finance?
BANKER: Probably not. I don't know what I want to do with my life.
RESEARCHER: Do you know what you will be doing on a daily basis on your job?
BANKER: No, not really.
RESEARCHER: You probably have some ideas.
BANKER: No, actually I really don't.
RESEARCHER: How come? Did you ask anyone about what the job would entail?
BANKER: Only in general terms. I know that there is a lot of travel and long hours. I also know that every day is different, that people come and go at all hours, that most of what you do is in teams.
RESEARCHER: What about the tasks that you do?
BANKER: I told you, I just don't know.
RESEARCHER: You said that you are interested in what you learn about dealing with people. Can you elaborate on that a bit?
BANKER: I think you'd be dealing with some pretty intense characters. And I heard that you'll also have access to pretty senior people in the top organizations worldwide. I think that will be interesting. I think those are also good contacts to have.

Like this recruit, many new bankers did not have specific interests. They were just interested in general learning opportunities. Because they did not know what they wanted to do long term, and because they believed that work in a prestigious investment bank would give them attractive career options, these jobs at Individual Bank and Organization Bank were desirable to them. As one incoming Organization Banker said, "I heard that there are many paths open to you from here. You can go into private equity, have a leading position in government or in another division of the firm or another country, or build your own business." Another banker said: "It's just a great résumé builder. A few years at Individual Bank and you can do almost anything." The recruits often did not view investment banking as intrinsically attractive, but instead saw it as an instrument for building their future careers and as a place to learn more about what they wanted to do. One new Organization Banker said: "For me, going into investment banking is a way to postpone making a commitment about my life and my career." An incoming Individual Banker said: "It is a way to take a few gap years on your résumé while continuing to look like an overachiever." The notion of "gap years" suggests that this banker did not expect his eventual career to be related to the investment banking position. New bankers typically only mentioned their lack of certainty about the job after they had signed their contract and after reminding the researcher of her obligation to keep this information anonymous. They did not want the information to be shared, fearing that their future colleagues would see them as "undecided," "clueless," or "like I don't have a plan for what I want to do with my life."

In the absence of strong personal feelings about a career, many recruits relied on their peers at school for judgments about the desirability of different jobs. A recruiting officer at one of the universities from which the banks recruited said: "For many, there is a herd effect. They do what is most admired and respected among their peers." This herd effect appeared to be most prominent in the most intelligent students. An officer from another top business school said: "Actually, precisely our best and brightest are the ones who are the least committed to any one career. They have so many options and are wooed so intensively by so many different types of employers."

One exception was the approximately 40 percent of recruits who said that they had an interest in finance. Of these, about 80 percent could envision a long-term career in finance or a finance-related field. These bankers were interested in learning "about the deal process," "finance skills," "how an investment bank works," and "about the clients that you work with and how they produce their products and services." The bankers with an interest in finance were attracted to the two banks because of the banks' clientele, their reputations in the field, and the quality and quantity of the banks' deals. As one Individual Bank associate said, "Whatever you learn you learn from the kinds of deals you work on. The last thing you want to do is spend all your time doing research or doing pitches just because the bank doesn't have a deal flow." Another Individual Bank associate with an interest in finance added: "I think that I'd be able to acquire a very marketable set of skills that could open doors for a variety of jobs in finance like private equity."

Recruits to both banks, then, made their employment decisions based on notions about a way of living and being that they understood only incompletely. They did not understand the tasks they would perform or the profound impact of the long working hours. After reading a version of this manuscript, an Organization Bank managing director said: "You're just not taught to think about how a job changes you as a person, except for what you earn, the skills you learn, and what it does to your health and sanity." The institutions that trained aspiring bankers, such as business schools, inculcated a perspective on work that focuses on the social transfer of concepts and on motivators. These schools fail to sensitize students to the more comprehensive changes in persons that take place through work.

This chapter has described how Individual Bank and Organization Bank used similar recruiting processes and criteria and how recruits to both banks used similar criteria for selecting employers. The two banks thus attracted similar junior bankers. Both banks' recruiting processes also encouraged the recruits to identify with the banks and to accept the banks' norms, values, and standards as their own. Recruitment – at Organization Bank as well as Individual Bank – thus sensitized new bankers to their own identities, making them feel like members of the elite club of high-end investment bankers. The next two chapters describe how both Individual Bankers and Organization Bankers initially interpreted information with respect to its identity-relevant implications, often ignoring more task-relevant information. At Organization Bank, however, junior bankers' egocentric focus was transformed by the bank's uncertainty-amplification practices. Even though the two banks used similar hiring criteria, including "ego," Individual Bankers and Organization Bankers understood these criteria in different ways, and the banks' very different organizational cultures catalyzed different developmental trajectories. The next two chapters describe these different trajectories, following young bankers as they entered the two banks and as their work practices transformed many of them into different kinds of people.

5

Individual-Centered Transformation

The world of our informants was oriented toward action, toward bringing in and executing deals. In order to accomplish these actions, resources were central. Bankers at both banks recognized and used people, objects, and psychological processes as potential resources for accomplishing deal-related actions. Individual and Organization Bankers differed, however, in the types of resources they found important and in how they combined resources. Chapters 2 and 3 described the core differences, showing how Individual Bankers oriented more toward abstract conceptions of themselves and toward decontextualized guidelines for action, while Organization Bankers oriented relatively more toward human and nonhuman resources in the organization and toward properties of specific situations. This chapter and the next describe how the two banks socialized junior bankers into these different orientations. We show how Individual Bankers and Organization Bankers became different kinds of people over their first two years as they worked in these very different environments.

This chapter describes how Individual Bank's work practices socialized bankers into what we called in Chapter 1 a distinct type of involvement. Individual Bank's *identity-induced involvement* encouraged bankers to use their own identities and abstract concepts that they had accumulated as resources for action. Individual Bankers' actions were mediated by these abstract concepts and scripts. Organization Bank, in contrast, forced bankers to abandon such abstract concepts and to attend to specific situations. This created *direct involvement* in which bankers brought together resources tailored to a specific situation without letting abstract categories intervene.

Table 5.1 contrasts these types of involvement and uses two key ideas to describe how new bankers were socialized into them. The first concept, *self-interpretation*, describes the bankers' implicit view of what it means to

TABLE 5.1 *Psychological transformation*

	Individual Bank	Organization Bank
Introductory training (five weeks)	Bankers: Uncertainty about tasks and identity. Bank: Reduced uncertainty through abstract and clear identity categories and guidelines. Focus on banker role (individual self as the primary resource). Offered supportive resources, e.g., mentors.	Bankers: Uncertainty about tasks and identity. Bank: Amplified uncertainty by withholding identity categories and guidelines. Provided fuzzy and often contradictory information. Focus on bank's resources. Bankers needed to find resources.
Months two to six	Gradual, systematic learning reinforced an **individual-centered self-interpretation**. New bankers saw the person as the cause of behavior (trait-based identity) and expertise as a personal resource. Learning meant building role-related expertise. Interactions with others based on exchange of favors. **Individual-centered cognition, emotion, and motivation.** Deductive cognitive style: Learned but did not apply trait-based self. Cognition, emotion, and motivation oriented toward abstract traits. Mostly adaptive resource usage.	"Trial –by fire" challenged an **individual-centered self-interpretation**. New bankers saw the person as the cause of behavior (trait-based identity) and expertise as a personal resource. Learning meant building role-related expertise. Interactions with others based on exchange of favors. **Individual-centered cognition, emotion, and motivation**. Deductive cognitive style: Trait-based identity. Cognition, emotion, and motivation oriented toward traits. Maladaptive resource usage.
After six months	**Individual-centered self-interpretation** Preference for using personal resources. Habitual resource usage, determined by abstract internalized concepts. Objects passively represent banker knowledge.	**Sociocentric self-interpretation** No preference for a particular type of resource. Dynamic resource usage, determined by specific, concrete situations. Objects actively help generate knowledge.

TABLE 5.1. (*Continued*)

Individual Bank	Organization Bank
Individual-centered cognition, emotion, and motivation	**Sociocentric cognition, emotion, and motivation**
Deductive cognitive style: Applied trait-based abstract identity. Strong emotions of anger and anxiety disconnected bankers from situations and caused maladaptive resource usage.	Abductive cognitive style. Contextualized identity. Cognition, emotion, and motivation oriented toward concrete situation. Mostly adaptive resource usage.

be a person and how the person relates to the social context. The person does not necessarily mentally represent a self-interpretation, but can display it in conspicuous action (Dreyfus, 1999) – most notably in how he or she uses resources to solve problems. Individual Bankers believed that they possessed traits. A trait is a relatively stable attribute of a person, such as expertise, which the person views as a primary cause of behavior. Because the Individual Bankers viewed the self as the primary cause of action, they developed a preference for relying on their own personal resources. The Organization Bankers also initially focused on their individual traits and preferred to work independently. After about six months, however, their focus on traits diminished and they used personal resources more interchangeably with those of the organization. The second set of concepts, *cognition, emotion, and motivation*, describes how these psychological processes functioned. At Individual Bank, these processes oriented toward the bankers' trait-based identities. Individuals' cognition, emotion, and motivation were mediated by abstract understandings of who they were as individuals. When the Organization Bankers' trait-based identities became less salient after about six months at the bank, their cognition, emotion, and motivation oriented toward the context, such that they attended to the situation and not to aspects of themselves.

This chapter and the next describe how new Individual Bankers and then new Organization Bankers were transformed over their first two years on the job. Both sets of bankers started out with a concern about their identities, as described Chapter 4, but the different work practices at the two banks propelled them along different developmental trajectories.

We organize Chapters 5 and 6 chronologically, starting with the first five weeks of introductory training, then the official learning period (months two to six), then the next year and a half (months seven to twenty-four). Chapter 7 builds on the developmental data presented in Chapters 5 and 6, returning to the concepts of identity-induced involvement and direct involvement and giving a fuller theoretical account of how these processes work.

When they entered the bank, new associates were uncertain about the tasks that they would be doing and the kinds of identity they would adopt. During introductory training, Individual Bank reduced both types of uncertainty in its characteristic way, offering abstract categories, expectations, and behavioral guidelines. When they moved from introductory training into their jobs, Individual Bankers were assigned a mentor who systematically reinforced these abstract categories, expectations, and guidelines as he or she shaped the newcomer's behavior, thus moving the junior banker toward the Individual Bank ideal.

During months two to six, the bankers further developed the individual-centered self-interpretation that they already had exhibited when they entered the bank. That is, they treated their own self as the primary resource for action. One important aspect of being an Individual Banker was possessing expertise that consisted of abstract personal resources – such as role-related concepts, skills, and guidelines for action – that one builds and then applies to different settings. Other important personal resources included the alliances that Individual Bankers fostered and the loyalties and favors they received through these alliances. This system of building alliances and exchanging favors reinforced the individual-centered view that a person has unique traits, including knowledge and personal relations, that contribute to successful action. Using this trait-based, individual-centered account, Individual Bankers located the cause of action in the context-free, inner attributes of a person. In this they followed a traditional cognitive account of how thought, action, and identity work.

Individual Bankers' trait-based identities shaped how their cognition, emotion, and motivation functioned. The bankers exhibited a deductive cognitive style with which they encoded situations and people, including their own identities, using abstract concepts. When people engage in such deductive cognition, they use familiar concepts and ideas to understand and react to situations. As a result, they experience their own self and their ideas as the cause of action, which reinforces an individual-centered self-interpretation. Individual Bankers clearly exhibited an individual-centered self-interpretation in which their own identity traits were the primary anchor and explanation for psychological processes. For example, bankers interpreted situations with respect to the consequences for their own identities. When their action in a situation allowed them to exceed their internalized expectations and identity standards, they experienced pride. When they failed to reach these expectations, they experienced anxiety, stress, embarrassment, and guilt. Failure to live up to their image of themselves motivated them to act.

When people mediate cognition, emotion, and motivation through an abstract, trait-based identity in this way, they attend more to abstract concepts than to the concrete situation. Individual Bankers thus were often disengaged from the immediate social context. As we describe below, this had negative consequences for Individual Bankers' performance when compared to the Organization Bankers. We emphasize that this disengagement does not mean Individual Bankers did not care about the bank or their work. To the contrary, the bankers cared so deeply for abstract notions of the bank and their work that they incorporated them into their identities. Because these abstract identities became so salient, they failed to notice concrete cues for acting on behalf of the bank and their work, despite their intense efforts to promote the bank's goals.

During the Individual Bankers' first six months there were only glimpses of this disengagement because the bankers did not always use abstract identity traits to interpret their experiences. Even though the bankers already had developed a sense of their abstract identities, and even though they strived to live up to this conception, they believed they were still learning and thus they often did not attribute their successes and failures to their own identities and capacities. This prevented such disruptive emotions as anxiety from interfering with new bankers' performance. This evidence shows that disengagement from specific situations, which we observed in more senior Individual Bankers, requires both an abstract self-concept and the belief that one's own traits are the primary causes of one's behavior.

After about six months, when the official socialization period was over, the Individual Bankers began to rely more heavily on their personal resources, and thus they curtailed their use of social resources. While they did not intend to stop using as many resources from outside their own expertise, Individual Bank's work practices encouraged this change. They followed other bankers' examples and imposed abstract categories on task situations. As a result, they often followed habitual courses of action even when the usual categories were not relevant to a particular situation. After six months, then, self-reliance and a reliance on habitual resources accelerated among junior Individual Bankers.

As these Individual Bankers increasingly relied on abstract concepts and guidelines, their cognition, emotion, and motivation began to focus more intensely on their own identities. Powerful emotions, often anxiety or anger, sometimes disconnected bankers from concrete situations and interfered with effective resource usage. These emotions further impeded functioning when they spread contagiously among participants in meetings and diverted collective attention from the task. Emotions are triggered by external situations and internal cues, and they generally engage script-like responses (Kitayama and Markus, 1994). These responses are rarely tuned to the tasks and affordances of a specific situation, and thus Individual Bankers sometimes reacted to face-threatening situations in unproductive ways.

Before describing the development of the Individual Bankers in more detail, we describe a striking contrast between junior Individual Bankers and Organization Bankers. Table 5.2 presents data on self-reported stress levels across the two-year period. In contrast to the emotions described in the last paragraph, which were triggered by specific situations, the stress that bankers experienced was a more "existential" type of emotion (Kitayama et al., 1995) and was present across situations.

Note first that Organization Bankers started out with much higher stress levels. As we describe in Chapter 6, new Organization Bankers found it extremely upsetting when the bank denied them abstract goals, concepts, and guidelines. New Individual Bankers, in contrast, were given clear goals and guidelines, so they at least knew what to aim toward. By the end of the two-year period, however, Organization Bankers experienced somewhat less stress. Their jobs were still very hard, but Organization Bank's uncertainty-amplifying practices forced them to change their approach and they became comfortable with an alternative way of working. Individual

TABLE 5.2 *Self-reported banker stress levels*

Months w/bank	Individual Bank			Organization Bank		
	Medium %	High %	Extremely high %	Medium %	High %	Extremely high %
1	28	65	7	0	4	96
5	12	74	14	0	0	100
7	0	22	78	0	40	60
12	0	15	85	0	80	20

Note: The cell values indicate, for each site, the percentage of respondents who rated their stress to be at a particular level during the indicated time period.

Bankers, in contrast, experienced more stress toward the end of their first two years. We argue that this generalized anxiety came from constant concerns about whether they were living up to their own and others' conceptions of who they were. We will return to and further explain these striking changes in stress levels across the two banks as we present the developmental data in this chapter and the next.

INTRODUCTORY TRAINING

The first five weeks at Individual Bank consisted of introductory training. New Individual Bankers were initially uncertain about the kinds of tasks that they would be conducting and the kinds of identities they would have in the new context. The bank reduced this uncertainty by conveying comprehensive information about both task and identity concerns. This information was abstract. The bank told newcomers about generic types of situations they would encounter, the types of norms they should follow, and desirable types of identities for bankers like themselves.

New associates were eager to find out what kinds of tasks they would be doing, how they would learn to do these tasks, and what the quality standards were. In response to an open-ended question about what his concerns were as he was starting his job, one associate replied:

> I think I have some ideas about what I will be doing here. I actually worked in an investment bank before, during summers and as an analyst. But every bank is a little different. Some banks are highly systematic and teach you in advance everything you need to learn with extensive training. Others have strong mentorship programs where you learn by working with senior bankers. And some just throw you into the fray and it is swim or sink. . . . So I kind of know what it is that I will be learning but I don't really know how this learning will take place. That's something that I want to find out.

An associate who overheard this comment added: "You see, I have no background at all in investment banking. So I hope this is not the sink or swim type of situation. . . . And I want to know some really basic stuff like what kinds of tasks will I be doing? What will my day look like?" Other new bankers said that they wanted to learn about the social standards that governed task completion: "I want to get to know the rules and norms around here: how things are done, what the working hours are, what counts as good work, whether people work in teams, how clients are being served, and so on."

The new bankers' second type of concern had to do with establishing who they were in the new context. As one newcomer explained:

> Whenever you are in a new group of people, things sort themselves out. In high school there were the jocks and the geeks kind of thing. In college, people looked at each other and thought who was most likely to succeed. . . . I am curious what the groups are here, like you want to know what kind of person you are going to be.

This banker suggests that, in a new social context, people generally adopt or are assigned an identity. Another associate argued that a banker's identity can influence how colleagues evaluate that person's potential: "The people you work with are looking for indications about who you are and whether you can do the job. . . . I am looking for the kinds of signals that people are expected to send, the codes for saying: 'I am someone who will succeed here.' " To the new associates, then, knowledge about tasks and about one's identity were two crucial factors that would allow them to be successful. They urgently wanted to learn about these things.

Individual Bank was responsive to both types of concerns. Most of introductory training was devoted to helping the bankers understand their role in the organization, including the rules and norms that pertained to associates. Panels of incumbent associates talked to them about "lessons learned." One important theme was norms concerning appropriate working hours. For example, one associate told his new peers: "During the week, you should expect to work until about midnight. You won't always have enough work to keep you there that long. But remember you are building a reputation. It just looks bad if you leave at ten or eleven at night while everyone else is still there." Another associate advised:

> Everyone will tell you that people here are so busy that face time is not important. But I tell you that it is. You'll find that out the hard way, if you leave a few times before the senior bankers sitting around you leave. I assure you that they'll take note, whether they work with you or not. So do yourself a favor and hang out at least until the directors around you leave.

The new bankers also heard from administrators who gave them detailed guidelines. As one new associate described:

> And then we had people from HR come in, wagging the finger at us and telling us what we can and cannot spend money on. There are rules for everything, the hotels you stay in, the restaurants you can eat in. I mean,

frankly, it got to be a bit ridiculous at times with rules about how much you could spend on wine for your client.

Although they found the detail of some rules ridiculous at times, incoming Individual Bankers generally appreciated the information they received in training.

Administrators and bankers also told newcomers about situations in which bankers had conducted themselves poorly in the past, and they gave advice about how to behave more appropriately. In one scenario, a vice president said:

> You might have read about some of the situations that we are going to talk about. And that in and of itself should be a lesson to you, that you might be able to read about what you do at night when you think no one is watching, on the cover of the *Wall Street Journal* a week later. In one such highly publicized situation, a banker took out clients to nightclubs, on the firm's expense. How do you feel about that? Should that be an issue? ... What if the client insisted on being entertained in that way?

For this scenario, the right answer was that nightclubs and gambling were inappropriate ways to entertain, even when clients insisted. Associates were given a list of more appropriate choices, including golf outings and sports events in the bank's private box and instructions for how to respond to clients. For example, one director told them:

> Whenever you have situations like that, you should off-load them onto a senior banker. Just tell the client that you need to check with the senior banker on the team. And try to leave it at that. When the client probes further, you can say that these kinds of events commit the firm's resources and that you, as a junior banker, need approval for these kinds of decisions.

Some bankers in the past had also been caught using company meeting rooms for sex. The senior bankers downplayed these prior incidents by noting that these were "isolated events – hardly on the scale of the 'boom-boom rooms' you undoubtedly read about at other banks." The new associates were informed that this kind of behavior would not be tolerated, and they received guidelines about dating colleagues.

Thus, Individual Bank fulfilled the new bankers' desire to learn task-relevant information. This training reduced new bankers' uncertainty by providing general rules, concepts, and guidelines – following the bank's uncertainty-reduction strategy as we described it in Chapter 2. The rules, concepts, and guidelines oriented bankers toward abstractions, describing general types of situations (e.g., "before 11 PM," "until the directors around you leave") in which clearly specified types of behaviors were appropriate (e.g., "stay at least another hour") regardless of a situation's unique attributes (e.g., whether you have work or not).

In about 60 percent of the training sessions, speakers also gave the new associates information about how they were informally judged as people by their colleagues. The other 40 percent of the sessions were conducted by either administrators or outside vendors, including finance professors or consultants who were in no position to offer such information. This information about identity-relevant behavior addressed the associates' concerns with their own and others' identities. Like the task-related information, this identity-related information was presented in a way that encouraged bankers to think in relatively abstract terms – this time about the self as a socially recognizable type of person. One vice president, for example, talked about how associates come to be viewed as successful:

> One of the most important tasks during your first few months is to communicate symbols effectively. You want people to think of you as someone who has a great attitude. So you want to do and say the kinds of things that show that you are enthusiastic about working here. ... You also want people to classify you as someone who has intellectual horsepower. This is just as important. You want people to look at your work and say: Wow, John was really careful with his analyses. ... For example, each of our pages in a pitch book has a little blurb that summarizes the main message of this page. I know that I am working with a smart associate when he or she goes through the trouble to put something into this box instead of waiting for me to do it and if that something is compelling.

This vice president explains how Individual Bankers used an associate's observable behaviors to infer underlying abstract traits such as "intellectual horsepower." Such a trait supposedly causes different types of behavior, and knowledge of the trait helps one predict future behavior. As we have described, Individual Bankers tended to interpret a person's identity as consisting of traits. In this training session and elsewhere, senior bankers socialized newcomers into this view. Thus the vice president's advice made sense for Individual Bankers: the management of symbols that communicate about identity was "one of the most important tasks" that associates should be attending to. Such recommendations increased the associates' existing preoccupation with how they were perceived.

As training progressed, other speakers fed the new associates' intense interest in how behaviors could signal underlying traits:

> People here look very closely at what you do and say because they want to know whether you have what it takes to succeed here. One thing that is important is that you show that you know the norms around here and behave appropriately....For example, some people want to show that they are really smart and start offering advice in client meetings. That is not how you show that you are smart. That is how you show that you are too dumb to understand that associates, at least at your level, sit in the meeting and listen so that they can support the senior bankers.

Many panelists offered further advice on how to avoid communicating undesirable identities, as did this one:

> When people come in, they sometimes try to take their cues from more senior bankers. And let's face it, some of the senior bankers around here can be quite vocal and opinionated. . . . But that is their job. They need to convince the client that they have the confidence to give strategic advice. But that is not your place. When you talk a lot, especially spouting your opinions, people will think that you are cocky or a bull shitter. Not a good impression to make. So in meetings it is better to be quiet and to only say something when you are asked, at least initially.

The new associates were pleased with how the bank's training addressed their concerns about tasks and identity. They were "impressed by how detailed and systematic the training here is" and found the information "practical" and "useful." One newcomer said: "I feel that I got a great overview of what will be expected from me and lots of specific instructions and tactics to use for making a good impression." Another added: "That's the benefit of working for an established firm. They have things thought out and codified so that not everyone who comes through the door has to recreate the wheel." The associates were not daunted at all to hear that their behaviors would be interpreted as evidence of stable, underlying dispositions. As one associate said: "I think this is how all places work. People don't have the time to get to know you closely. So these cues are all that they have to go by. I am glad that they spell these things out for us so that you have some control over how you come across." Another associate agreed: "I think this information is very valuable. This is exactly what I hoped to learn."

Individual Bank also provided extensive, ongoing training, and support. During introductory training, the bankers received basic training in corporate finance and accounting. The training department also told them about other resources that would be available to them on demand once they started their job, such as access to professors and accountants on retainer, ongoing training sessions, and interactive CDs. At the end of introductory training, junior bankers were matched with a senior banker in their department who functioned as a "big buddy." The newcomers were assured that their learning was planned out systematically and that no prior knowledge was expected of them. In the concluding speech of the introductory training, the coordinator of the program said:

> Introductory training is over and you will start in your departments next week. . . . You might be nervous to start on your job with only a few days of introductory corporate finance and accounting training. But don't worry. The purpose of the last few weeks was mostly to help you get to know the firm and what will be expected of you. The people in your department will not assume any prior knowledge and your big buddy is there to systematically teach you everything you need to know to be effective at your job.

The bankers' informal conversations with the prior year's associates confirmed this information. One widely circulating story had to do with several European associates who lost all of their training material during the first week of last year's training program and yet appeared to fare no differently at work than their more diligent peers. The new associates found such stories comforting.

We assessed the associates' stress levels throughout their first two years because stress was one important theme that we observed early on in both banks. Everyone said that investment banking was high-stress work that tended to burn people out. In fact, the average banker in both banks was only thirty-five years old. One Individual Bank director explained why bankers typically leave at a relatively young age: "The stress you have to endure here is so extreme that many people simply cannot take it any longer, health-wise and in terms of their mental sanity. We had people here with heart attacks in their early thirties. I mean, just look around, how many men do you see with full hair, even in their twenties?"

At the end of their introductory training, 93 percent of the Individual Bank associates judged their stress level as either medium or high (see Table 5.2). They agreed that their stress level was "definitely bearable," mostly because they had faith in Individual Bank's well-designed system.

One junior banker, who was undecided about whether to rate his stress level as "medium" or "high," explained:

> Yeah, I guess I am pretty stressed. At this point I just don't know yet what is expected of me and whether I can hack it here. . . . But then also I heard that they are pretty good here at spelling things out for you, you know what's expected of you, . . . and taking care of you. They have pretty good on-the-job training, little buddy systems, so that does make me feel better.

Even though new Individual Bankers experienced uncomfortable uncertainty about their responsibilities and their abilities to do the job, they expected this uncertainty to be transient and expected that Individual Bank's practices would provide the necessary support.

The new Individual Bankers approved of Individual Bank's training practices because they shared the assumptions underlying these practices. They believed that they would be able do their job better if they learned about the types of situations that they would encounter and about general procedures for dealing with these situations. Like traditional cognitive psychologists, they believed that abstract knowledge is separate from and can be deductively applied to circumstances. Incoming bankers also shared Individual Bank's trait-based construal of identity. They wanted to know what kinds of behaviors indicated desirable types of identities and they agreed that one could characterize people in relatively context-free ways. The newcomers already exhibited an individual-centered interpretation of self at entry. Individual Bank reinforced this through its uncertainty-reduction practices. The fact that new bankers fit with Individual Bank's approach is not surprising because, as we argued in Chapter 1, uncertainty reduction and individual-centered orientations are common in Western institutions. Individual Bank simply built on practices that were already familiar from bankers' experiences with school, government, and other institutions.

THE FIRST SIX MONTHS AT INDIVIDUAL BANK

This section first describes how junior Individual Bankers elaborated the individual-centered self-interpretations they already had at entry. We show how Individual Bankers interpreted their personal resources, including their expertise and relationships, as the primary causes of their behavior. Consistent with traditional cognitive theories, they construed learning and expertise as the development and possession of abstract concepts that applied across different situations. This contrasted with more senior Organization Bankers, who viewed social resources as the primary cause of outcomes and considered expertise to involve context-specific action in concrete situations. The second part of this section illustrates junior Individual Bankers' individual-centered psychological processes, in which their cognition, emotion, and motivation all oriented toward the bankers' identity traits. This focus often disengaged bankers from the concrete aspects of situations.

Self-Interpretation

The junior Individual Bankers' on-the-job training was gradual and systematic. New bankers worked on deals as soon as they finished introductory training. At first they were not formally staffed on projects, but just helped out on their big buddies' projects. These deals usually were fully staffed and the newcomers rarely had significant responsibilities. They shadowed their big buddies, who let them work on small parts of tasks – often using a scaffolding technique in which the big buddy first showed a junior banker what to do, then watched, and, if necessary, assisted as the junior banker completed increasingly larger chunks of the task. One junior banker described how he learned to complete a common stock comparison through such scaffolding:

> George first explained the big picture to me, how this is being used in the presentation and how this analysis flows into the evaluation of the company. The first time around, I watched him do it and just looked over his shoulder when he entered the data and talked me through it. The second time around, he watched me enter the data. He actually might have watched a few more times but not all the time, just checking in with me. I can now do all of this by myself and he just checks the numbers [the results of the analysis, not data entry] to see whether they make sense. I guess the next thing is that I'll figure out which companies to use. Right now he still tells me which companies to use.

This scaffolding process ensured that bankers only stretched their abilities in manageable ways. Associates thus felt that they had some control over how quickly they developed, and this reduced the stress and uncertainty they experienced: "This job is objectively stressful. It is stressful for everyone, period. But they ease you into it. To some extent you feel that you have some control over how fast you go and that helps." This feeling of control indicates an individual-centered self-interpretation because the new bankers experienced themselves as having an influence on outcomes. This scaffolding and apprenticeship process that new Individual Bankers experienced is typical in the professional service industry. It differed dramatically, however, from the "trial-by-fire" method used at Organization Bank – where, as described in the next chapter, junior bankers were fully functioning members of deal teams from the first day and were expected to deliver flawless products on a timely basis.

The learning process at Individual Bank was highly systematic. Bankers had predetermined responsibilities on each deal that carried a known set of tasks. Associates were responsible for supervising analysts, completing financial models that were too complicated for analysts, and managing daily client interactions. Many junior bankers had lists of all the tasks that fell into each of these categories. For example, the category "financial models" contained such tasks as "common stock comparison," "leveraged buy-out analysis," and "deal comparison." The junior bankers used these as checklists on which they ticked off the tasks that they had learned. As one associate said:

> Jeff is my big buddy. On the first day, we sat down and put together a list of all the things I should be learning during the next six months. When I feel that I know how to do something by myself, I cross it off the list. If I am not staffed on deals where I can learn these tasks, Jeff will sit down with me and teach me.

This approach to training reduced the junior bankers' cognitive uncertainty because they knew what they should be learning, they could check their progress against clearly articulated learning goals, and they had a reliable process for acquiring this knowledge. Having clear learning goals and being able to monitor and regulate one's progress against these goals further reinforced the feeling of personal control that the associates valued. The gradual, systematic learning process and the feeling of personal control explains why new Individual Bankers experienced their initial months on the job as "challenging" but not as confusing or overwhelming. One banker explained: "We have a great system here for getting people up to speed. I have never spun my wheels for long."

The bank's learning process shaped bankers' sense of what it meant to have expertise at Individual Bank. The goal of training and apprenticeship was to enable bankers to work independently. Having expertise at Individual Bank meant having a set of personal resources, such as concepts and guidelines, which allow one to complete tasks successfully. One associate admiringly characterized a senior banker whom he tried to emulate:

> That guy is just a walking encyclopedia. You can ask him anything and he'll just rattle it off for you. . . . He told me that, as an analyst, he would come home at twelve at night and then learn tearsheets [summary information about companies] by heart for half an hour, every single day. That guy is intense. And he just doesn't stop. I mean even when you see him walking to the bathroom he has a stack of 10Ks [a public filing that companies are required to do] under his arm.

The associate here describes his view of effective learning as a process of creating a store of relatively context-free information that people can retrieve in appropriate situations.

Junior Individual Bankers already exhibited this view of learning and expertise when they entered the organization because it is the dominant theory in the West and they had been exposed to it in institutions such as graduate school. In response to an open-ended question about what he learned at Individual Bank and how, one banker elaborated:

> One of the things you learn is concepts, mostly financial and analytical tools, to hone a set of skills that you can use. . . . That's what all learning is about. You get to know fairly general concepts that you can then apply to a variety of situations. Think about the typical case study. You'll often get a set of readings that introduce you to a conceptual framework or a model and you then work that model in case study after case study. It's the same here. You learn certain analytical and inference skills and then apply them to different kinds of projects.

This individual-centered view was also shaped by socially shared conceptions of investment bankers as professionals who possess a set of general skills that they bring to diverse situations (e.g., Abbott, 1988; Nanda, 2005). As one associate said:

> Learning in investment banking is different from learning in an industrial company. I am sure you heard people say that the assets ride the elevator. What they mean with that is that banks have experts who carry the knowledge that the bank needs to do its business in their head. That's what I am doing here. I am learning to become an expert.

In all of these excerpts, the junior bankers expressed a belief that their minds, filled with corporate finance concepts, were the primary resources for them to draw on in doing their work. Learning, on this view, meant accumulating such concepts. This differed from the more organization-centered resource orientation that the Organization Bankers developed, in which the bankers' minds were subordinate to organizationally available resources. Even though the Organization Bankers started out like the Individual Bankers, conceiving of learning as the accumulation of concepts, Organization Bank changed their focus by forcing them to notice opportunities to bring more effective external resources to a task.

The Individual Bankers' individual-centric self-interpretation was reinforced by the bank's internal politics. Junior bankers learned early on that an effective banker not only possesses a store of specialized concepts but also has valuable personal connections that he or she mobilizes to achieve goals. For example, during one of their big-buddy-to-little-buddy conversations a vice president told an associate how to act toward analysts:

> It is absolutely critical that you develop a reputation for being an advocate for analysts. If you want to be successful here, you have got to be on the good side of the analysts. If you develop a bad reputation among the analysts, the best ones will find ways not to work for you and then you are stuck with the duds. . . . Analysts are the engines around here. They do all the work. Working with an incompetent analyst is worse than working by yourself because you first have to spend time teaching them and instructing them and correcting their work and then you end up doing the work again by yourself. . . . There is a lot of "black market" staffing that is going on around here. Some of the best analysts and also associates are simply never available to be staffed by [the department's work coordinator]. That's because they have developed friendships with senior bankers who just staff them informally.

This vice president describes how analysts, too, could be seen as personal resources. Astute senior bankers "possessed" the loyalties of the best analysts just as they possessed abstract concepts and guidelines.

The last excerpt also highlights the favor-based mechanism of exchange that lubricated work-related interactions at Individual Bank. Another example of this involved banker-to-banker alliances. Individual Bankers could advance their own interests by supporting colleagues in situations that mattered to their careers. Individual Bank usually promoted analysts and associates in cohorts. To become an associate, an analyst had to stay for two years and then return after completing an advanced degree, usually an MBA. Highly competent analysts could sometimes opt to stay a third year and get promoted directly to associates after that time. Associates were normally promoted to vice presidents after four years. This system was the same at Organization Bank, and was also common in other professional service firms. At Individual Bank, however, exceptions were relatively more frequent than at Organization Bank. Some analysts were promoted directly only after two years and some associates skipped one or more years on their way to becoming vice presidents. Officially, these bankers on the fast track were given credit for previous work experience or schooling. Informally, bankers gossiped about the personal exchange of favors that made such acceleration possible. For example, one senior associate vented about the unexpected promotion to vice president of another colleague, Chad, because of his relationship with the group head, Frank:

> I guess that happened because he was Frank's butt-boy for the last two years. I heard that he did whatever Frank wanted from him. For two years that guy (i.e., Chad) was permanently stuck behind the computer – no weekends off, not even a day of vacation. I heard that when he finally got out and walked his daughter to the kindergarden, he got this huge rash on his skin because he couldn't tolerate sunlight any more. And that was in December!

Incoming Individual Bankers concluded from such stories that doing one's work competently was not enough. To advance quickly one also had to do favors for important people. This exchange of favors reinforced an individual-centric self-interpretation. It focused bankers' attention on the power of specific individuals (e.g., powerful advocates) to advance other individuals. In contrast, Organization Bank's routinized promotion process, in which bankers were promoted more uniformly in cohorts, was more organization centered. It directed attention away from both the specific abilities of individual associates and the power of potential senior advocates.

At Organization Bank, bankers helped out on a task when they possessed the relevant knowledge. In contrast, junior Individual Bankers noticed that incumbents were more discriminating with their help. One junior Individual Banker explained:

> For now, I have never had any issues. Whenever I need something, I can go up to whoever has that information and people are usually more than happy to help. But that might just be how they treat you in the beginning. You know, you hear and see things. I have seen some associates run after vice presidents who basically let them speak to their ass. They just couldn't get more than a few syllables out of them. And for other associates, the same vice presidents make time in their office and close the doors. I guess that means that you have to be really careful about building your network around here.

Cooperation was not something that colleagues at Individual Bank provided freely upon request. The quality of the advice one could expect depended on the personal attributes of the person who needed help and the relational history of the two bankers. One associate complained about this:

> I have seen how Tim (a vice president) helped Mark (an associate) build a whole pitch book from scratch. There was not a word in the revised book that was Mark's. And Tim wasn't even on the deal! When I saw that, I thought: "Looks like Tim is really into mentoring junior bankers." And when I didn't know what to do with a pitch I just went to him, thinking that he would give me the same help. And he was all like: "Sure, anytime. Would love to help." But then the comments I got were maybe two or three minor points that were missing. It was just very clear that he had not spent any time or thought on this. I knew of course that Tim and Mark are also friends. I have seen them go to lunch and to the gym together. But I just think that people here should help when they can and they should help everyone, not only their buddies.

Senior Individual Bankers disagreed, however: "You only have so much time to worry about the junior people around here. So you have to pick and choose and most people like to place their bets on a winner." Another senior banker said: "Time around here is probably the scarcest resource. If you spend all that time mentoring someone, of course you'll expect them to show some gratitude and help you out when you need them to." In contrast to what the associate had hoped for, these senior bankers made it clear that their help was contingent on the personal benefits they reaped, such as being associated with a winner.

This section has illustrated two ways in which new Individual Bankers were socialized into the bank's individual-centric self-interpretation. First, bankers were encouraged to construe expertise as something that resided in the mind of an individual. According to this view, people learn by building up abstract concepts that they can then apply to diverse, specific situations. Second, individuals also built idiosyncratic stores of loyalties and favors that they could draw on when needed. Individual Bankers did not help one another based on the needs of the situation, but instead based on a banker's specific attributes – such as being seen as a winner or having done favors for someone in the past. Incoming Individual Bankers thus discovered that they would have vastly different career opportunities depending on how they were perceived as individuals. The bank's practices made the bankers' own traits highly salient. The next section illustrates how new bankers responded to this situation: quite rationally, they focused on understanding and managing their identities.

Cognition, Emotion, and Motivation

During the first six months, Individual Bankers' self-reported stress levels mostly stayed at "high" (see Table 5.2). The source of stress changed, however. One initial source of stress had been uncertainty about whether task demands would exceed the bankers' ability. This task-related uncertainty was transient because task demands at Individual Bank were clearly articulated and manageable. Junior bankers thus began to attend relatively more to identity-related concerns, and uncertainty about their identities now became the primary source of stress. Bankers wanted to ensure that they managed impressions effectively, and they recognized that they still lacked information about how their behaviors would be interpreted. One associate explained his "high" stress rating as follows: "This is a critical time. You are building the basis for how people are going to see you and treat you." Another associate said: "There is a lot of gossip here. I feel like we all trying to size each other up to see who will make it." Incoming bankers said that these identity-related concerns caused them stress partly because colleagues' perceptions of them would have such a large impact on their career chances.

This section first describes central aspects of the bankers' identities. We describe how the bank made identity salient to the bankers so that they were more likely to use aspects of their own and others' identities to interpret behaviors. More organizationally relevant aspects of identity developed as bankers inferred who they were by observing their behaviors in light of the bank's expectations and interpretations. What matters most for understanding the bankers' development, however, is not the type of identity components but the fact that the bankers experienced their identity attributes as traits – as relatively stable causes that underlie and explain behavior. We explain how the bank's practices reinforced the bankers' preexisting conception of identities as being composed of traits. Because identity traits were highly salient and meaningful to a banker, they dominated how the banker thought, felt, and acted, sometimes disengaging bankers from more immediate cues in particular situations.

Junior Individual Bankers attended to various aspects of their identities. One aspect involved identities that bankers brought to the job, including their nationalities and educational backgrounds. Bankers paid attention to national identities, and social groups organized around such identities. After a few weeks, junior banker cliques developed. The groups went to lunch and gossiped about other cliques. One such clique contained bankers of European origin. One American banker said of the Europeans: "You can immediately tell where they are from by how they dress. I guess you could call it edgy: ties with huge knots, massive shirt collars, and shirts with patterns." The Europeans, in turn, teased the Americans for their obsession with physical fitness, health-conscious eating, and "lavish attention to each and every body part ... with facials, manicures, pedicures, waxing, plucking, hair dying, botox injections, and God-knows what kinds of enhancements. ... I wish they'd pay that much attention to what is going on politically." The Europeans also commented on Americans' "fraternity-like" dating habits that seemed to conflict with an otherwise "puritanical" outlook, as well as on their "pedestrian" leisure choices ("dinner and a movie"). As these characterizations illustrate, the cliques led Individual Bankers to view themselves and others in terms of abstract attributes and stereotypes.

National identities became important to the bankers not just because they were made salient in social interactions but also because people believed that they predicted work-related behaviors. For example, European bankers were viewed as poorly attuned to the etiquette of their American clients: "I guess in the Netherlands you can tell people what you think. But here you have to be more indirect and subtle." Senior European bankers, in turn, hesitated to staff American bankers on European deals, fueled by stories such as the one about the American associate who supposedly addressed a European CEO not only using his first name (which was Herbert) – God forbid – but also by abbreviating it to Herb.

The same was true for identities derived from educational background. Harvard graduates believed that they were unusually suited for presenting themselves in sophisticated ways to clients ("the school puts a lot of emphasis on effective communication and presentation of the self"), while Wharton students derided this ostensive sophistication as "bullshitting." The Wharton students self-stereotyped as "quant jocks" and felt as if they were the ones to complete challenging analytic tasks ("they [the Harvard grads] are the talkers, we are the doers"). All of these examples show the junior Individual Bankers' theory that personal attributes, including skills, heritage, and educational backgrounds, explain why individuals behave in particular ways. This is consistent with the Individual Bankers' more general sense that a person's identity consists of traits, which are relatively enduring attributes that persist across different situations and explain performance.

Other aspects of banker identities emerged more slowly because they had to be inferred from ongoing behavior. It was particularly important for bankers to develop an image of being both helpful ("a good guy," "reliable," "willing to help out," "takes time for others") and competent ("knows what she is doing," "smart," "can figure things out"). These two attributes were a frequent topic of gossip during the first few months. Bankers spoke about how they helped others, how others helped them, when someone was not as forthcoming with information as they should have been, when someone gave particularly brilliant or dumb advice, and when someone acted in an arrogant or superior way when giving advice.

Other emerging aspects of identity involved bankers learning to portray themselves as professionals. Informal social interactions, such as teasing, were important. One associate recalled how his colleagues mocked him because he showed up in an olive green suit: "Hey, look at Jim, Jim got a job in advertising," and "I'd say he is making a bid for the Frankfurt office." Looking back, Jim commented on this incident:

> Before that, I never really thought that much about what to wear, as long as it is a suit, shirt, and tie and as long as it is clean. I have definitely become more thoughtful since then about how to present myself. In this job you have to think about what your clothes say about you because that is the reality of how people look at you.

Here the colleagues' mocking comments introduced uncertainty by challenging the associate's more functional view of attire. But they also resolved uncertainty, replacing his view with a conception in which attire identifies one as a particular type of person. Individual Bank had both implicit and explicit norms about attire and in many other areas that were reinforced through casual interactions. Another associate echoed this theme: "I'd say there is definitely a strong culture [in this department]. You can tell who works here just by looking at when they come to work, when they leave, what buckle belt they have, where the cuff of the pant ends. Dude, you don't want to be caught dead with a cheap watch – that's for [Organization Bankers]."

Because of all the attention paid to personal identities, and the important consequences of being classified in a particular way, Individual Bankers were highly sensitive to identity-related issues. After about a month on the job, bankers started to talk informally about how a wide range of choices reflected organizationally relevant traits. These choices included how bankers should dress ("Rolex is for traders," "Bankers wear Hermès ties") and walk ("I heard people comment on how quickly Maggie always walks and how that means that she is constantly busy. So I am picking up my feet when people see me"), how their office should look ("You do want it messy so that people see you are busy. But if it is too cluttered, they'll think you can't handle the work"), and where they ate ("If you don't eat at your desk, you clearly don't have enough to do"). Junior Individual Bankers said that it was important to learn what these cues indicated to their colleagues and that they consciously tried to manage the impressions they made through their choices. One junior banker described himself as "classy:" "I have always been hard driving, you know the go-getter type. . . . And people always tell me that I am kind of classy, you know." In order to project these traits, he bought a Patek Philip watch: "You see lots of Rolexs and Breitlings around here. But this one [i.e., the Patek] you just don't see that often. I also think that it looks kind of classy, you know. It has a certain sophistication. I like that style." Because they considered identities an important predictor of behavior, it makes sense that Individual Bankers devoted considerable effort to learning about their colleagues' traits and managing others' perceptions of their own traits.

The situation was very different at Organization Bank. Senior Organization Bankers showed less interest in a person's traits, and prior identities were rarely brought up. One senior Individual Banker who had previously worked at Organization Bank said:

> At Organization Bank people did not give a hoot whether you were Jewish, Catholic, athletic, rich, or God knows what. Most people didn't even know these things about others and they most certainly did not use them to pigeonhole people. It wouldn't have occurred to anyone to staff bankers on projects because of what they supposedly did or did not learn at graduate school. All of this stuff was just completely irrelevant. . . . Of course, when you screwed up you heard about it. But no one cared whether that is because of your nationality or because you did not study at Harvard. Just fix it.

Most Individual Bankers knew that Organization Bankers were not interested in bankers' individuating attributes. They said that the Organization Bankers were "clones." One Individual Bank vice president sneered: "We are proud of hiring interesting people. We actually like individuals and we are not going to try to take this individuality away to make you into some kind of Borg."

Although Individual Bankers were often self-conscious and stressed because of their preoccupation with what others might think about them, they experienced Individual Bank's gossip mill as "natural." "This is not different from any other place I worked at, or from university for that matter. . . . That's how you know what to expect from one another." This excerpt also supports a claim that we have made before: Individual Bank simply reinforced tendencies that bankers already possessed when they entered the bank, including the tendency to categorize people in terms of stable traits that explain and predict behavior.

One important practice that reinforced the bankers' trait-based conception of people was the bank's focus on superstars. Because superstars possessed highly idiosyncratic expertise, clients and colleagues often identified the bank's expertise with that individual and followed departing superstars to another bank. When new Individual Bankers observed such departures and heard about how others interpreted them, they inferred that bankers had traits such as expertise ("You just can't replicate Paul's experience in high yield") or charisma ("He gets the deal because people are just awed by his personality") and that these traits reliably caused outcomes. From observing such individual-centered ways of thinking and behaving, Individual Bankers developed their own trait-based accounts of themselves and others.

Another practice that caused bankers to experience identities in terms of traits was the bank's review process. As one junior banker said:

> When I heard about this review and saw the form, I thought "*O-h m-y g-o-d.*" Just the fact that *everyone* you are dealing with gets a chance to say something about you *to your boss*. I think it is only natural for us to obsess about this when we talk to people. I know I do. And they probably want us to. I keep thinking whether this person will now think that I have a "good attitude," "strong interpersonal skills," and whether I have "personal presence."

In this context, "good attitude" and "strong interpersonal skills" – categories on the official evaluation form – were traits that presumably characterized the person across diverse situations. Another associate explained why the review process was so important to the bankers:

> I think for most of us the review process is a pretty strong incentive to constantly think about how you are appearing to others. What people say about you in this review does not only determine the bonus you are getting but also your career chances, what kinds of projects you are working on and whether you'll get a chance to work with some of the legendary bankers around here.

"In most situations, I tick off a mental checklist," said another associate: "Did what I just said sound eloquent? Do I sound smart? Did I come across as someone with a good attitude?" All these comments suggest that the review process directed Individual Bankers to experience themselves in terms of socially valued traits.

The fact that Individual Bank reinforced new bankers' preexisting tendency to understand people in terms of abstract, trait-based identities that predict how a person behaves and what a person can accomplish had significant implications for new bankers' cognition, emotion, and motivation. When people repeatedly use a concept, and when this concept has important social consequences, it becomes more readily accessible to guide action even when it is not directly relevant (Bargh, 1989). New Individual Bankers soon began to focus on their traits even in situations that did not necessarily pertain to their identities. For example, a junior Individual Banker said he hesitated to leave before midnight because "people say things like 'Half a day today?' or 'Thanks for stopping by,' making you feel like a slacker. ... And I just don't want to be that kind of person." Another banker related the following incident:

> I was in this meeting with Gwen (a vice president) and a client and when Gwen went through the deal comps that I had put together, she said some things that were just plain wrong. And I thought to myself: Should I correct her or somehow let the client know? Or should I tell her after the meeting so that she could tell the client? But then I thought, you know what, this is a lose-lose kind of situation. Either way she is going to get mad at me and will think that I am a smart ass. They told us in introductory training that people hate it when you are still new and speak up. So I just let it slip.

As would be predicted by cognitive self-regulatory theory (Carver and Scheier, 1990, 1981), this associate's focus on traits – wanting to be perceived as a certain kind of person (not a smart ass) – functioned as a high-priority goal. In this case and many others, task-related goals were secondary. The associate followed the bank's rule about developing a good internal reputation instead of considering the potentially serious consequences for the client or the bank.

This excerpt also illustrates the connection between the reduction of cognitive uncertainty and the chronic salience of identity. Such practices as cultivating superstars, who are familiar with most of the situations they encounter, or review processes that direct attention toward abstract traits, aim to simplify situations. These practices also encourage deductive cognition in which bankers judge behavior based on how it corresponds to the bank's norms and rules. From the perspective of Organization Bankers, such simplifications inappropriately draw attention away from the messy, unique attributes of a situation and can make bankers feel unduly confident in their judgments. At Individual Bank, however, people found traits and rules to be valuable and they paid substantial attention to their own and others' identities.

Individual Bank associates' emotions were also influenced by the trait-based identities cultivated at the bank. Associates most frequently reported self-conscious emotions, such as anxiety, worry, embarrassment, pride, and guilt. They said that they often felt "self-conscious," "worried," "insecure," "mild anxiety," and "a bit nervous" about how others would perceive them. One associate said: "I think most of us are on the edge and kind of self-conscious a lot because we want to make a good impression but often do not really know how to do that." Another associate said: "I often feel insecure and a bit nervous because I don't know yet how what I am doing will be perceived." Embarrassment about having done something inappropriate was another frequent emotion. Associates said that they felt embarrassed when they had "said something stupid," "didn't know the answer to something," "dressed inappropriately," or "made a mistake." Some associates also confessed to feeling Schadenfreude when they saw their colleagues doing something embarrassing, or suspected that their colleagues would feel Schadenfreude when they witnessed others' blunders. Associates also reported feeling pride when they "told someone that I am working at Individual Bank," "worked really hard," "solved an impossible problem," "received praise from someone who is really difficult to please," or "learned faster than they expected me to." At one point, the wife of one associate said: "I am so tired of hearing them gloat about how much they work. The thing that gives them the most pride and joy is when they have pulled a few all-nighters, preferably without even changing or showering." Associates did report feeling guilt about spending limited time with their family and friends, canceling plans the last minute, and being emotionally unavailable.

Some of these common emotions were unstable, eventually turning into anger. After the initial embarrassment of being teased about a blunder, for example, associates complained about the "silly gossip" or "jerks who are on a power trip." After initially worrying about their standing in the department when a senior banker spoke to them sharply, they might feel anger about being treated in unduly harsh ways. Associates also experienced "anger," "annoyance," or "frustration" when they felt that important goals were thwarted. For example, associates felt that their career advancement depended partly on the types of deals they worked on and the types of people they worked with. Associates frequently felt angry when they did not work on enough deals but "wasted time" on business solicitations that were unlikely to result in deals. And they were angry when they worked on deals in which many bankers were involved and they had to do the "grunt work" without participating in client interactions.

The prevalence of self-related emotions indicates that Individual Bankers' emotions were strongly influenced by the extent to which they exceeded or fell short of the traits they aspired to. Individual Bank had clear expectations about what it meant to be a good banker. New bankers aspired to these traits, and they experienced strong emotions when they reached or fell short of the desired traits. These "socially engaging" emotions (Kitayma et al., 1995) showed the bankers' sensitivity to the norms, values, and goals of the bank. Self-consciousness, embarrassment, and pride all signaled that a banker was keenly aware of the bank's norms and cared about living up to them. Even the anger that the bankers felt could be viewed as a socially engaging emotion because this anger occurred when associates could not attain the performances and traits to which they aspired.

Despite their deep connection to the social context of Individual Bank, we argue that these emotions also had socially *disengaging* aspects. They oriented bankers toward abstract concepts and thereby disconnected them from immediate situations. Associates sometimes remarked that their anxiety, worry, and stress hindered them from enjoying their work:

> The job really is the way I thought it would be and it isn't. I am doing all the things that I wanted to do. I am traveling all the time, talking to CEOs and CFOs about their companies. I work on exciting deals and with interesting people. And all of these things could really be great. Except that most of the time this doesn't register because you are so stressed out about something, whether you get the model done in time or whether you get the model right and what people think of you if you don't, that you can't really enjoy yourself as much.

Another associate agreed:

> This job doesn't do much for your mental sanity, as much as I love the job. But you are constantly thinking so far ahead of what you are currently doing. All you are thinking about is when and how you are going to get to the 101 items on your to-do list and what X might be thinking of you and whether Y is making a better impression than you and what you can do about it. Sometimes it is only when I tell other people what I have been doing that I think: "Wow, this was really cool."

> But at the time, I didn't really experience anything because I was too frantic about something else.

This associate was not just taxed by his many tasks, but also anxious about how others would perceive him. Similarly, another associate said:

> Even though I am usually so tired that I could fall asleep standing, I often wake up early in the morning, an hour or so before my alarm goes off, and then cannot fall back asleep because I keep planning my day, thinking about when I am doing what … and worrying what people will say if I don't get my work done and how I can respond to their concerns. . . . I get really worked up this way.

Most of the socially disengaging aspects of these emotions became salient only after six months on the job, however. During the first six months, the bankers officially had "newcomer" status. Even though they formed an image of themselves in terms of socially valued traits, and even though they worked hard to live up to this image, they did not use these traits to judge their behavior as often as they would after six months at the bank. In the first six months, they saw themselves as learners and more senior bankers had relatively low expectations of them. One associate explained how she tried to contain self-judgments and emotions: "I just discipline myself. Whenever I catch myself fretting about these things, I just go 'lockbox' and try to think about something else." Another associate said: "At this point, it is too early to tell whether you are a success or a failure. Even if you do everything right, that may just be a fluke." A third associate pointed out why becoming emotional did not make sense at this point in time: "When you make a mistake, this really doesn't say anything about *you*. It doesn't mean you are stupid. You are simply learning." The bankers learned this attitude from others. One associate observed that "people hold back on their judgments until the official learning time is over." Because colleagues mostly refrained from evaluating associates during the first six months, emotions appeared to be relatively less intense and more manageable as compared to later.

Because associates believed that even embarrassing mistakes were "recoverable," they felt that "no question is too stupid to be asked." One associate explained: "When I don't know something, I see that as a great opportunity to interact with an expert, a chance to get to know them." Senior Individual Bankers agreed that most junior bankers "drew vigorously and deftly on the organization's resources." While the bankers had predefined tasks for which they felt personally responsible, they recognized when their own knowledge was insufficient and solicited help. We consider this to be adaptive resource usage, when bankers gathered the resources required to complete a task. It differs from the maladaptive resource usage we describe below, when Individual Bankers' intense emotions kept them from engaging effectively with tasks.

New Individual Bankers, then, developed a deductive cognitive style in which they construed persons, including themselves, in terms of traits, and in which cognition, motivation, and emotion were all strongly oriented toward a banker's identity. Associates understood situations in terms of their implications for their own and others' identities, they were motivated to live up to valued identity traits, and their emotions often registered the alignment between behavior and an associate's aspirations for him or herself. We refer to this overall orientation as "individual-centered cognition, emotion, and motivation" because these psychological processes were all centered on the person's identity such that abstract identity concepts mediated bankers' perceptions of and reactions to concrete situations.

The concepts that Individual Bankers identified with (e.g., "hard-working" and "intelligent") were often promulgated by the bank. Once these concepts became part of a banker's identity, however, they acquired an additional dimension, a special significance that Dreyfus (1999), following Heidegger, calls "mineness." Bankers felt differently about work that was "*my* work." This "mineness" shifted the function that these concepts served from organizational to personal. The bankers viewed the bank's rules and norms no longer primarily from the perspective of their social functions – such as ensuring that work gets completed – but from the perspective of what they said about the person who exhibited these behaviors, even when this focus on themselves distracted them from more substantive concerns.

Social identity theorists (e.g., Haslam, 2004; Brewer and Gardner, 1996) would urge us to differentiate between organizational and other types of identities. According to their view, we should distinguish situations in which bankers appraised themselves on bank-external attributes such as national origin from situations in which bankers affirmed their organizational identities through attire and the like. External attributes like national origin might be expected to create unproductive in-group and out-group distinctions within the bank, whereas organizational identities would more likely unite the bankers and make them think, feel, and act on behalf of the bank. We do not claim that this theory is wrong. We argue, however, that the content of a person's identity (i.e., whether the person defines the self in terms of organizational, personal, or other attributes) is not the only thing that matters. The *abstractness* of a person's identity-relevant information – whatever the particular content – also has important consequences for how the person thinks, feels, and acts. The Individual Bankers certainly did exhibit effort on behalf of the bank. But because their abstract organizational identity was so important to them, their psychological processes were oriented toward this abstract identity and away from the concrete cues of a particular situation. Even though the bankers might have wanted to act on behalf of the bank, their identity focus sometimes unintentionally undermined this goal.

AFTER SIX MONTHS AT INDIVIDUAL BANK

Self-Interpretation

This section describes in detail how, after about six months, the Individual Bankers had developed a preference for using their personal resources. Moreover, they often applied concepts in a relatively habitual and inflexible manner that was not necessarily appropriate to a situation. Self-reliance and habit limited the active role that other organizational resources could play.

When the official learning period was over, junior Individual Bankers felt compelled to start developing what the associates called the "distinctive personality," "brand," or "signature style" of a budding superstar. This meant, for example, that the bankers infused the bank's routines with their own personal styles and preferences. One Individual Bank vice president explained this trend:

> There are not a lot of things you can control and make your own at that stage. There is only so much personality that you can show in client meetings without the senior bankers coming down hard on you. So the first thing that you see associates do around here to make a statement is to create their own way of doing analyses. I don't know that this is always a good thing but that's what happens.

This vice president describes how junior bankers did analyses in a distinctive way out of their own personal needs, not in ways demanded by the situation. He also makes clear that one important need was the desire to be the cause of one's behaviors, which is an aspect of a trait-based identity. One analyst provides more detail:

> They all have their signature format. John likes it if you include these ratios here [points to the columns of a pitch book]. Jeff uses everything

that John uses but then also uses three additional types of ratios. I guess he wants to look extra thorough. And then Edwin thinks that John and Jeff are full of it and that they approach this all the wrong way. He likes to present himself as some kind of minimalist, focusing the client on only "the bare bones."

John, Jeff, and Edwin were all Individual Bank associates. They used analysts to do the analyses because that was part of the bank's division of labor. The associates exhibited self-reliance because they preferred to use their own concepts to analyze client situations. Moreover, they made these decisions not based on the needs of the particular deal or on input from colleagues, but instead based on a habitual style and their need to project an identity.

Even though the associates' behavior was in line with the bank's superstar business model, it also came at a cost. Analysts experienced the associates' idiosyncratic style preferences as a great nuisance because data were difficult to find for ratios that went beyond the bank's standard template.

Whenever I have to respond to one of these special requests, I have to rummage through 10Ks, 10Qs, Annual Reports, special filings – all to find one single number. This also means that I have to order and wait for extra financials. And I have to repeat all of this multiple times to find this number for multiple years. And then I have to do the same thing not only for the client but for all of the companies [on the common stock comparison]. This takes at least an extra day of my time. And I doubt that someone really thinks through all of this cost in relation to whatever minor benefit they are getting from having this additional number. I sometimes ask and usually the answer is something like: Just do it. So if there was a good reason for doing all this, I suspect they would have come up with a better answer.

Other analysts also complained that the additional effort was not justified by the insight it yielded: "For some of these extravagant ratios no one even knows how to interpret them. . . . In most of the meetings that I went to, when the vice president talks about the comparisons, they just skip over everything that is not standard or that they did not order themselves."

Analysts also often complained that associates asked them to do unnecessary analyses "just so that they could cover all bases and sound smart to the client." One analyst said:

I hate working with first-year associates. They are incredibly insecure. I just had to do two days worth of work that no one ever looked at in the meeting. I told [the associate] that we won't need this stuff before the meeting and he even agreed that this was unlikely to come up but he just wanted to be prepared for all eventualities.

It is possible that the analysts' complaints had little merit. Analysts did usually have less financial acumen than associates. But in this case, the analysts' judgments were backed by senior bankers.

The bank's chief operating officer had statistics indicating that junior associates used resources, such as analyst time, indiscriminately. Her own analyses of pitch books suggested that bankers often included unnecessary ratios and materials "to avoid looking stupid in front of the client," and that this unnecessary work wasted banker time, which she viewed as the bank's most valuable resource. She criticized this tendency: "No one expects you to have *all* the answers. Your credibility with the client doesn't take a hit just because you have to say: 'Let me check on this for you.' " In addition, the chief operating officer explained that indiscriminate resource usage also failed to provide good client service, because the additional material was often not relevant to the client situation: "I get to hear these complaints all the time. They (the clients) suspect that you just pulled out stuff from the shelves, cookie-cutter style and then just tweaked it a little." By behaving this way, Individual Bank associates used habitual scripts that reflected their own needs and conceptions instead of meeting clients' needs most effectively.

These examples also indicate another, subtler way in which Individual Bankers overrelied on their own mental resources. When they used the same set of analyses for each deal, they failed to draw on the specific cues that the evolving understanding of a deal could provide and they limited the potential role of other social resources, including artifacts, colleagues, and clients themselves. Junior Organization Bankers, in contrast, often started analyses in very rudimentary ways. They sometimes worked with analysts on spreadsheets or on blackboards to understand the fundamentals of the client business. They then used visual representations of the particular client's financial situation to decide on the financial ratios to include, the presentation format to use, and the materials to include in the presentation. The junior Organization Bankers were forced to work in this way because, in contrast to the junior Individual Bankers, they often were not familiar with the kinds of projects they were working on and therefore could not transfer habitual ways of doing a presentation from one deal to the next. These contrasting ways of approaching analyses generated different roles that social resources could play. In the typical Individual Bank case, artifacts such as presentation books passively reflected the associates' personal style and ways of thinking. At Organization Bank, as described more extensively in Chapter 6, artifacts such as blackboards and spreadsheets had a more active role. The bankers used them so that they could prompt the bankers to take next steps, and thus the artifacts functioned somewhat like the advice of another person.

The Individual Bank associates' eagerness to prove themselves also often limited the active role that clients could play. Junior Individual Bankers were responsible for managing the day-to-day interactions with the client, including working meetings. In characteristic style, the junior Individual Bankers tended to overprepare for and overstructure these meetings. They often produced small presentation books that summarized where the deal team was in the process and where the team was going. In one such meeting, an associate walked the client team through the presentation book page by page. He spoke without interruption for almost half an hour. When client executives tried to ask questions, the associate said things like "I'll get to that later," "let's finish this page first," and "let's just get through with this presentation and then open up for questions." In this way, the associate limited the ability of the client to give input, ask for clarification, and jointly direct the meeting. Instead of making this the collaborative working meeting that it was supposed to be, the associate turned it into a monologue.

This approach had some beneficial aspects. Clients were flattered by the attention that the bank lavished on them. Even when the Individual Bankers cut them off, clients attributed this to the bankers' zeal for the deal. Many senior Individual Bankers also appreciated the associates' "initiative" and willingness to "go beyond the call of duty." Some experienced Individual Bankers also saw costs in this approach, however: "When you present information in this way, it is very clear that you are telling the client what to do. That can sometimes backfire because clients want to feel like they are making the decisions. If you use a more conversational style, you are more likely to create buy-in." Another Individual Bank director said: "Our junior bankers are our eyes and ears on the ground. They talk to the client all the time and can help us uncover new needs. But most of them are in 'telling' mode." This banker suggests that the associates were focused on a one-way transfer of information and therefore were less receptive to what the clients were telling them and less likely to discover what the clients needed. When we compared these typical Individual Bank client meetings with the more collaborative working sessions that junior Organization Bankers used, we found that in Organization Bank meetings clients talked more, more new ideas were generated, and new next steps were more likely to emerge. These new steps most often represented new opportunities, and Organization Bank clients felt that the bankers listened and were responsive to their needs.

Individual Bankers tended to rely on their personal resources, even when this did not produce favorable outcomes. They structured situations in relatively generic ways and thus prevented them within the comfort zone of the individual banker. This allowed the banker to act like an expert, in line with Individual Bank's culture, and to act in ways that conformed to client expectations. The costs of this approach included reduced creativity, reduced sensitivity to the uniqueness of situations, and reduced efficiency in cases in which the bankers' ego concerns caused them to overprepare.

Cognition, Emotion, and Motivation

This section describes how junior Individual Bankers used the trait-based identities that they cultivated during their first six months with the bank as grounds for inferences about their behavior. As their official status as newcomers drew to an end, they followed their senior colleagues in attributing banker behavior to underlying traits. This intensified the junior bankers' focus on the identity-relevant implications of their behaviors and also resulted in self-conscious emotions such as pride, embarrassment, guilt, and anxiety. When experienced intensively, these emotions often disengaged the bankers from potential resources and yielded less effective solutions to problems. These emotions could also spread contagiously during social interactions, from one Individual Banker to another, thus impeding the productive engagement of resources even further.

One indication that young Individual Bankers entered a different developmental phase after their first six months was their higher self-reported stress levels. Around seven months into their work at the bank, 78 percent of the new bankers rated their stress level as "extremely high" (Table 5.2). After about one year this increased to approximately 85 percent, where it remained for the last twelve months of our study. These increases in stress were surprising because the bankers' working hours remained relatively constant and the task demands continued to rise only gradually to match the bankers' growing experience.

One associate explained his rating: "Now when you screw up, you can't blame it on the fact that you are learning or on an unfamiliar situation.

Now your mistakes say something about *you*." Similarly, another junior banker said:

> When you come in, you want to do really, really well here. And the first months are all about soaking everything up. It's literally like learning a new language, like what being a banker is all about and how people think and what is important. But now it's showtime. I mean people still cut you slack because you are still learning and stuff but you know from now on you gotta produce and whatever you do you are developing a reputation.

The bankers were more stressed because they believed that, from this time onward, mistakes allowed others to draw conclusions about their identities. This last excerpt shows a young banker distinguishing between the "learning" goals to which he aspired during the first six months and the performance goals ("you gotta produce") that guided cognition afterward. When people see their identities in more trait-based terms, mistakes are more likely to put central aspects of themselves at risk. Consequently, people think more about how they perform and less about what they learn (Dweck, 1986; Dweck and Leggett, 1988). The junior Individual Bankers' extremely high stress levels after six months reflected the threat to their selves, as they worried about whether others would see them as competent and expert.

This trait-based, self-focused motivation had consequences for how bankers noticed and used resources. When the junior Individual Bankers felt confident that they could complete their work, they put forth extreme effort. In these situations, bankers were willing to cancel dinners and vacations and work all night. The wife of one associate said:

> When he has to complete a project, he really goes at it until he thinks it is perfect. If that means working all night, not seeing the kids, or even canceling our vacation, so be it. . . . We came back early from a vacation just so that he had an additional day to really prepare himself for an important meeting, even though the book and everything had been done long before the vacation – otherwise he wouldn't even have gone.

Throughout their tenure with the bank, bankers were also eager to educate themselves. One banker said: "It does not matter how late I go to bed. Even if I do not go to bed at all, I will read at least two tearsheets [summary information about a company] every day until I know all the major companies by heart. Clients expect you to know these things." Other bankers read finance books in their spare time. Within Individual

Bank's culture of stars and individual expertise, these were adaptive ways of cultivating expertise. Junior bankers worked very, very hard to live up to the bank's expectations.

When bankers did not feel confident in their abilities to complete work, however, they used resources more maladaptively. Strong negative emotions often disconnected the bankers from the concrete details of situations and from people who could help them. An associate gave the following example:

> I was working on this doozy of a deal, a firedrill that had to be done over the weekend, with all those bigwigs. Really complicated transaction, completely convoluted financial statements, analyses I hadn't even heard of before. Friday night we had a meeting and they were all there. The head of the department, the head of investment banking, the [client] CEO, CFO. And, you know, this would have been a really interesting meeting. But all I could think about is whether they are going to make me do stuff that I was clueless about and that I didn't want to look stupid to these guys. And in my mind I kept going through the list of people I could call to help me out, you know, who owes me one. And what I would do if I couldn't get a hold of someone. Should I say that I got sick? Better to lie than to do a shoddy job. And it wouldn't even have been a lie because by that time, I really felt like throwing up.

This associate's strong emotions, caused by his identity-centered ruminations, distracted him from information that was necessary for completing the task.

The last three excerpts show how Individual Bankers' emotions were tied to their identities, with their emotions registering how well the bankers succeeded or failed with respect to their identity goals. The orientation toward an abstract identity made these emotions part of a deductive style in which situation-independent models of the ideal self drove a banker's behavior. Identity-induced emotions, such as pride in one's work, did sometimes produce a positive charge that made looking successful important enough to sacrifice other identity goals – such as being a good father and husband. Because the Individual Bankers' identities were aligned with the bank's goals – both wanted individual experts and stars – such emotions could aid banker performance. But identity-induced emotions such as anxiety could also undermine performance when their intensity and lack of task-focus impaired the bankers' use of resources, as in the last excerpt above. In these instances, emotions separated the banker from the specific situation by focusing attention on the banker's identity.

Concerns with their identities dominated how junior Individual Bankers used other organizational resources, including colleagues. While the bankers had often asked colleagues for help during their first six months and had approached colleagues based on their relevant experience, they now hesitated to ask for help and only approached colleagues who were friends. The junior bankers believed that asking a question might indicate that they were stupid, and they wanted to limit their possible exposure: "The problem when you don't know something is that you don't know how stupid your questions are. So you got to be careful whom you ask questions." This was also a theme among senior Individual Bankers, who readily admitted that they only sought out advice from their "allies" to limit possible signs of incompetence.

The bankers admitted that it was inefficient to go to friends instead of experts because friends often did not know the answers. Such requests usually resulted in a joint problem-solving session in which allies would laboriously arrive at a solution that an expert could have provided immediately. The associate quoted above, who was staffed on the "doozy of a deal," went on to describe how he eventually completed his task with the help of his close friend Jim:

> ASSOCIATE: I couldn't really go to anyone on my team for help because I just didn't want to look weak. In the end, Jim and I locked ourselves into a conference room for twenty-four hours straight to figure this out between us.
> RESEARCHER: Why did you ask Jim? Has he done this kind of deal before?
> ASSOCIATE: No, that's one reason it took us so long. We also had incomplete information. There were some questions I just didn't ask during the meeting. I am the one who is responsible for these analyses. ... The senior guys don't think through these issues because they rely on me.

These examples illustrate another negative consequence of the bankers' individual-centered psychological processes: Individual Bankers used up enormous amounts of the bank's most expensive resource, banker time, in order to avoid looking weak.

Another Individual Banker explained how he tried to manage people's perceptions of his competence by getting staffed on as many diverse deal teams as possible: "You gotta spread your screw-ups. That's my philosophy. If you do something really dumb on one deal, you can always blame it on all the work you are doing on another deal. But if you are working with the same person all the time, he'll catch on to what you don't know."

Junior Individual Bankers exchanged similar tips, such as shortening the presentation books ("every page is a risk – that's how I see it") and faking computer problems ("I'll just say that I was almost done but then lost all the data"). In these instances, the bankers acted against the interests of the bank in order to maintain a positive public identity.

This hesitation to draw on relevant resources did not keep Individual Bankers from using specialists located in other departments, such as capital markets or equity research. These interactions were routinized at Individual Bank. As a vice president explained: "There is a routine you have to go through for each type of deal. When you work on a sell-side assignment, you first have to meet with the research analyst.... Then you have to talk to people in capital markets and on the syndicate desk."

The chief operating officer elaborated: "I am not worried about these types of interactions. There really is no ego here. People usually do not hesitate to talk to equity research because that is part of the protocol. ... It doesn't reflect on them." Because these cross-departmental requests for advice were formalized, they did not imply that the banker did not know something. Such requests simply meant that the banker was doing his or her job. This example also shows that Individual Bank did have some sociocentric elements. This was not the norm at Individual Bank, however, and the bank had to script and enforce collaboration explicitly.

Junior Individual Bankers' preoccupation with their traits and the resulting distractions from task-related considerations could also be observed in senior bankers. This suggests that, after six months, Individual Bankers had reached the developmental endpoint for this organization. We have given various examples of senior Individual Bankers' concern with their identities. We also found that senior Individual Bankers – but not Organization Bankers – were highly sensitive to criticisms of their employer because they felt personally criticized when the bank was criticized. During one business solicitation, the client asked the Individual Banker team: "If I am giving you this business, I need to know whether [Individual Bank] will be [in this line of business] to stay." The director answered with indignation in his voice: "With all due respect, we are the preeminent investment bank in [this kind of business] – not some kind of bucket shop. I, myself, have been a principal in [this group] for close to ten years." The director subsequently disengaged from the situation. He let the vice president continue, looked down on his note pad for the rest of the meeting, and sometimes tapped his pen in an irritated manner when the client asked other questions that could be construed as challenging.

This director's irritation spread to the client executives, who asked increasingly more challenging questions in an annoyed tone. One client executive replied to the director: "Your preeminent reputation is one thing. But I want to be convinced that you can deliver on it for us on this deal with this team." Without even waiting for the answer, the client CEO asked the director directly: "I assume you are still interested in our business. So why do you think we should hire you and not one of your preeminent competitors who were just here this morning?" These questions responded directly to the director's positioning of the bank as "preeminent." Instead of assuming that all bankers of this preeminent bank provided high-quality service, the client asked for evidence of their potential contributions to his company in particular. The CEO's question clearly challenged the director and responded to his aggrieved tone. By using the term "preeminent" to describe the bank's competitors, he claimed that many banks use such terms to describe themselves, he implied that Individual Bank was not as extraordinary as the director claimed, and he made clear that the client has the power to select one bank or another.

The director's angry response thus focused participants on asserting their own power and sniping at each other. This diverted the group from its intended purpose. One might argue that the clients' questions were task-focused because they simply asked the bankers to demonstrate their capabilities. A satisfying demonstration, however, would have required the bankers to go through their presentation materials. By asking their questions before the bankers could complete their presentation, the clients forced the bankers into sound bites about the bank's market position that the client claimed were unsatisfying. Their questions thus prevented the group from working with ideas that the bankers had brought with them. This interpretation of the client's response is confirmed by the fact that, after the bankers had covered about 50 percent of their presentation, the client CEO excused both himself and the CFO. The bankers completed their presentation to junior executives who did not have any decision making authority. The bankers interpreted this as "a power play," "putting us into place," "an act of defiance," and "making it clear who has power over whom."

After the meeting, the director justified his behavior when speaking with his team. He complained that the client's comment indicated a "lack of due deference" toward "the institution" and toward himself: "Who does he think he is talking to? What does that [insinuating that the Bank was a 'bucket shop'] make me?" With reference to his two-sentence reply, he simply said: "I was not going to go into it any more. I won't dignify this bullshit with an answer." Our informants at Individual Bank agreed that the director's curt reply was a "judgment error" because he had dismissed the client's legitimate concern and responded instead to the offense he perceived. But other Individual Bankers, both junior and senior, acted in similar ways. In another client meeting, for example, we observed a senior banker disengage from a client who asked "obnoxious" skeptical questions about Individual Bank's products and start working on his own meticulous to-do list.

These examples illustrate the disengaging effect of the Individual Bankers' anger-related emotions. Some have argued that anger can serve a socially engaging function when it removes obstacles to joint accomplishment (Kitayama et al., 1995). In our examples, however, the Individual Bankers' anger directed the participants away from potential joint accomplishments and toward an abstract realm of power and status. Emotional contagion is also sometimes portrayed as a unifying force (e.g., Le Bon, 1911) because it can focus people on the same psychological reality and motivate them to act as one system. In our examples, however, anger had a divisive effect. It caused participants to behave as independent actors vying for power, and it thereby blocked productive collaboration.

SUMMARY

Over the course of their first two years as Individual Bankers, newcomers acted very much as traditional cognitive research on social identification would predict. From the beginning they were highly motivated to succeed and to establish themselves as successful bankers. From the beginning they learned that the bank valued individual expertise and that the bank provided abstract scripts and categories to minimize uncertainty. In their first six months on the job, however, they were given leeway to admit ignorance and experiment with various approaches. After six months, the junior Individual Bankers acted very much like senior Individual Bankers, relying on their own expertise and focusing on the consequences that actions would have for their own identities. This chapter has shown the implications for Individual Bankers' psychological processes, including identity, cognition, emotion, and motivation. Much as cognitive research on social identification would predict (e.g., Brewer and Gardner, 1996; Haslam, 2004), the bankers expended extreme effort to live up to their image of a successful Individual Banker.

We have shown how this identity had an unintended effect, as it disengaged bankers from their immediate situations and caused them to overlook or avoid resources that might have helped them solve problems more effectively. Individual Bankers used a deductive cognitive style in which they construed both situations and people using general, abstract concepts. The bank's goal of uncertainty reduction encouraged the deductive application of abstract concepts. We have described two types of consequences. The first is an individual-centered "self-interpretation" in which the person sees his or her own abstract traits as the primary resource for and cause of behavior. This kept bankers from noticing and effectively using available social resources. This focus on individual expertise fit with the bank's expectations and with wider cultural beliefs about authoritative individuals, but it often resulted in decreased creativity and efficiency.

The second consequence was the individual-centered functioning of cognition, emotion, and motivation. These psychological processes all oriented toward identity traits and other preexisting schemas for understanding. The bankers attended to the ways in which given situations might have implications for their own identities. When they perceived risks to their identities as successful bankers, they responded with self-conscious emotions such as guilt, embarrassment, and pride. And they were highly motivated to overcome these risks and reestablish themselves as competent, regardless of the consequences. We have described how this individual-centered functioning of psychological processes can separate people from concrete situations and distract them from noticing and using situational resources.

Our account shows how Individual Bankers enacted the dualistic worldview of traditional cognitive psychology, which casts the individual as separate from the world. Individual Bankers solved problems by focusing on their own, inner resources, separating themselves from the social context and defending their own interests. The next chapter shows that this is not the only way in which individuals can function. In different organizational contexts, individuals can function as parts of larger systems, not as autonomous carriers of expertise. Organizations can also clear away individual identities such that people come to think, feel, and act based on situational cues.

6

Organization-Centered Transformation

As shown in Chapter 4, new Organization Bankers began with the same individual-centered psychological functioning as new Individual Bankers. This chapter describes how Organization Bank's work practices socialized new bankers into a different orientation toward themselves, others, and resources for problem solving. We refer to this approach as direct involvement. Direct involvement involves a sociocentric self-interpretation. Organization Bankers believed that their personal capacities were merely one among many potential resources that could contribute to their work. They did not focus on their own identity traits as central explanations for action. Junior Organization Bankers, as they learned this new approach, attended less and less to individual traits. Instead, they learned to think, feel, and act with respect to concrete situational cues. This chapter describes new Organization Bankers' transformations, using the same three time periods as in the last chapter: introductory training (first five weeks), official learning (months two to six), and the rest of the time we observed them (months seven to twenty-four). For each of the last two time periods, we first discuss self-interpretations and then the functioning of cognition, emotion, and motivation.

At the beginning of introductory training, new Organization Bankers had the same types of uncertainties as new Individual Bankers – they wanted to know what tasks they would do and what identities they would have in the new context. In contrast to Individual Bank's uncertainty-reduction approach, however, Organization Bank amplified the bankers' cognitive uncertainty. It withheld behavioral guidelines and identity categories. Instead of the clear guidance that the Individual Bankers received, Organization Bank offered imprecise and contradictory information. New bankers who expected to learn about their own roles were confused when they learned primarily about "other people's jobs" – that is, about the bank's various resources. Early in their tenure at Organization Bank, the new bankers did not understand why they were not being told about their own jobs. They felt confused, helpless and disoriented. These feelings continued as associates transitioned into their jobs without a designated mentor, equipped primarily with the vague instruction to "make good use of the organization's resources."

During months two to six, junior Organization Bankers exhibited the same type of individual-centered self-interpretation and psychological functioning that we saw in the Individual Bankers – only more so. The bankers vigorously resisted the sociocentric self-interpretation that Organization Bank tried to cultivate in them. Despite a lack of knowledge, bankers tried to complete work independently, struggling to demonstrate their own competence. As described in the last chapter, new Individual Bankers only focused on their trait-based identities after the official learning period was over. New Organization Bankers, however, focused on their own identities immediately, worrying about their competence and misunderstanding the bank's sociocentric culture. Because the bank did not give them guidance, they believed that they were expected already to know how to do their jobs. They explained their unavoidable mistakes by citing personal incompetence. Like the Individual Bankers during the last eighteen months of the observation period, new Organization Bankers monitored each situation with reference to its implications for their identities. Because they invariably fell short of their aspirations, the bankers experienced intense self-conscious emotions and extreme stress. Just as we have described for Individual Bankers, these emotions disengaged new Organization Bankers from the resources they needed to do their jobs well.

Strikingly, however, as shown in Table 5.2, the bankers' stress patterns shifted after about six months. Although the Individual Bankers initially had lower stress, the Organization Bankers' stress levels declined below the Individual Bankers' levels at about month six. At the seven-month mark, only 60 percent of the Organization Bankers judged their stress levels as "extremely high" compared to 78 percent of the Individual Bankers. From the twelfth month on, only 20 percent of the Organization Bankers said that they felt "extremely high" stress as compared to 85 percent of the Individual Bankers.

The third part of this chapter, which describes junior Organization Bankers during months seven to twenty-four, explains this reversal in detail. We argue that the Organization Bankers' stress levels declined because their self-interpretation had changed from individual-centered to sociocentric. Bankers came to understand that their job was not to showcase personal knowledge, but instead to bring together organizational resources to solve client problems. Their trait-based identities faded into the background and their personal competence became less relevant. When a banker did not know something, other organizational resources could fill the gap. After about six months, then, Organization Bankers gave up their preference for self-reliance. They learned to use their personal resources together with organizational resources, fungibly, as dictated by the situation. After six months, the Organization Bankers' perception of available resources increased. Stress – the subjective perception of an unfavorable ratio of demands to available resources – consequently decreased. The anxious, self-focused ruminations that previously had kept junior Organization Bankers from focusing on the situation became less frequent.

As junior Organization Bankers shifted to a more sociocentric self-interpretation at about six months, they explained their lower stress by citing decreased preoccupation with "ego problems." Because Organization Bankers did not perceive situations as being about *them* – that is, they did not feel that their identities were at stake – they were less likely to feel anxious. As the bankers' trait-based identities came to be less important to them, they more often attended to situational cues. Bankers monitored the details of situations so that they could find the relevant organizational resources to solve particular problems. Their emotions tended to register situational dynamics – such as the enthusiasm that bankers felt when they found the perfect resource, the boredom or disinterest they felt when deals got bogged down, and the anger they felt when political processes threatened to impede deals. These emotions were neither self-conscious nor other-directed, which is a distinction that Kitayama et al. (1995) use to classify the emotions typical of an "independent" as opposed to an "interdependent" self. Bankers experienced these emotions not as being about the person, but instead as signals for engagement. The emotions motivated the bankers to take next steps, such as searching for the right resource until a banker felt that "charge," probing into obstacles to a deal's progress, and exposing political processes for their harmful effects.

Organization Bankers learned to adopt an abductive cognitive style, encoding situations and people, including their own identities, in concrete, contextualized terms, and developing new solutions tailored to the context. Cognition, emotion, and motivation were oriented toward the concrete aspects of situations in order to bring resources together in relatively unique solutions. As their trait-based identities moved into the background, the bankers understood themselves as just one of many fungible resources. The Organization Bankers did not construe their own traits as causes that influenced external situations. They saw identity and situation as united in action, as a configuration of resources that did not involve a fundamental split between the individual and the situation. They talked about the person-acting-in-a-situation, using notions like "task-orientation," not about their own identities and expertise.

Organization Bank thus illustrates an alternative way of socializing newcomers and using human resources. In contrast to Individual Bank's more familiar pattern of encouraging participants to internalize organizational concepts and see themselves as the primary carriers of organizational expertise, Organization Bank encouraged bankers to clear away such abstract mediating concepts and focus directly on the concrete aspects of specific situations.

INTRODUCTORY TRAINING

Introductory training at Organization Bank lasted for five weeks, just as at Individual Bank. Like their peers at the other bank, incoming Organization Bankers described themselves in terms of traits. During his first week at the job, one junior banker explained: "What attracted me to this organization is that you get a chance to work with the best of the best. I can identify with that. I have always tried to be the best in whatever I am doing and I want to work with people like me." Another banker answered an open-ended self-descriptive question by saying, "I'd say I am a go-getter: Hard-working, hopefully intelligent, clearly determined, and also reliable."

Individual Bank's introductory training supported new bankers' desire to exhibit traits that were relevant to the bank. Speakers and panels explained in detail which traits were valued (e.g., hard work) and what kinds of behaviors were associated with these traits (e.g., being hard-working means that one does not leave work before 11 PM). In contrast, Organization Bank frustrated the bankers' desire to understand and display the traits of a successful banker. Like Individual Bank, Organization Bank highlighted the importance of possessing certain attributes, such as "excellence." Unlike Individual Bank, however, it did not cite behaviors that indicated these attributes. This amplified the new bankers' cognitive uncertainty because it alerted them to a critical goal without telling them how to reach it. For example, during introductory training one speaker said:

You are here because of your extraordinary achievement. When you look around you, you see people who graduated at the top of their class from this country's finest institutions. You have among you Fulbright Scholars, a published poet, a prize-winning concert pianist. . . . This is why we selected you. This is what we all have in common, a commitment to excellence. This commitment is reflected in the very fabric of this firm. . . . It is a meritocracy where you will never be judged by who you are but only by what you contribute.

Another speaker told the new associates: "We hire insecure overachievers – people who are deeply committed to excellence and constantly fear that whatever they are doing is not good enough." Another added: "People here expect excellence from one another, even on tasks that seem mundane and trivial. . . . There is zero tolerance for low quality."

Such speeches presented "excellence" as a significant trait, and the new bankers urgently tried to find out what kinds of behaviors would count as excellent at Organization Bank. One trainee asked a speaker: "During the last few days, we heard a lot about this firm's commitment to excellence and about your expectations for us to show excellence in our work. But I guess I am not really clear on what that looks like. Can you give us some examples? Or tell us how people can learn this?"

The senior Organization Banker replied: "The recipe for excellence is not to have one." This joke was not well-received by the frustrated audience. After this training session, one associate complained: "I still don't know what [excellence] actually means. It would help me if they were clearer on what the goals and criteria are." In this and in many other instances, training at Organization Bank amplified new bankers' cognitive uncertainty because it raised expectations (of excellence, for example) while withholding information that would help the bankers understand and fulfill these expectations. As a result, bankers became acutely aware that they did not know how to succeed at the bank. One associate said about the training: "This was like a cliffhanger without a sequence. They raised all this urgency and these expectations about how important it is to be committed to excellence and then they left you hanging."

Organization Bank thus failed to reduce new bankers' identity-related uncertainty. It also did not live up to the new bankers' expectations that they would learn about their tasks. New Individual Bankers learned about their roles during introductory training and were satisfied with the information they received. Most Individual Bank associates believed that the bank understood their concerns and addressed their questions effectively. In contrast, the junior Organization Bankers learned mostly about their bank's resources and were dissatisfied with how their concerns were addressed. Organization Bank's speakers talked less about the associates' roles and responsibilities, focusing on their own jobs instead. This was consistent with Organization Bank's emphasis on organizational resources. However, instead of telling the junior bankers how they could use the speaker as a resource, the speakers focused more on personal impressions of their jobs. They left the disgruntled junior bankers to infer how this was relevant to them. Dick, a senior capital market specialist, said:

> Imagine you are sitting on a floor with over three hundred people. All of us are watching multiple computer screens, talking on the phone, and listening to market updates, all at the same time. So you can imagine that the people on the trading floor have the attention span of gnats, which is something to think about when you need our advice.

In a conversation with his peer, one associate wondered afterward: "I now know that capital markets people are apparently prickly. But I still don't know how to deal with that." The peer agreed: "I don't even know why this guy is talking to us. What is he trying to teach us? Sorry, I just don't see the relevance."

Another capital market specialist, Gina, explained Dick's behavior in a subsequent conversation with the researcher:

GINA: These young people often come here and they have a vice president riding their tail to get them market information quickly and so they bust right in while you are juggling three phones and expect you to talk to them right away. . . .And often they are not very concise. They uhm and ahm or have incomplete information and need to go back to their team to give me all the information I need to give them an answer. So I guess he just wanted them to see these kinds of situations from our perspective and keep that in mind when they come to see us.

RESEARCHER: Wouldn't it be easier to just give them a set of rules, telling them things like: "Come prepared with the following types of information before you talk to us," "Prepare what you are going to say so that you can say it quickly," "Be patient with us during market hours?"

GINA: That might be easier in the short run but probably counterproductive in the long-run. Dick said these things during introductory training, right? So he wanted people to actually learn something, not just mindlessly following rules but actually paying attention and stopping to think before they are doing something. In our world, that [paying attention] is a survival skill.

In other words, Organization Bank tried to achieve a different kind of learning during introductory training. Instead of encouraging associates to internalize organizational concepts, it created unfamiliar, uncertain, or confusing situations so that bankers learned to pay attention and to engage with situations as they searched for the right answer.

The associates, however, were not pleased with this training and persistently asked questions about their own role. One frustrated associate, Ben, asked another speaker: "We received a lot of information about what senior people in different departments do. But I am curious: What does the typical day of an associate look like? What can I expect of my work?" The senior banker at first gave an indirect answer, describing his own workday:

> I usually plan on getting up around 6 AM, but I am often awake earlier, my head reeling with all the things I have to get done that day. A typical day in my life is that I start the day with a to-do list that is about one or two pages long. And once I am in the office, what I thought was an urgent priority is usually eclipsed by even more urgent things and so I add another page in front of that list of to-dos and work myself down that list as fast as I can and with as much attention to detail and quality as I can.

But Ben persisted, impatiently: "So what does that mean for our work? What kinds of implications can I draw? What expectations can I have?" The senior banker answered: "What can I tell you? There is too much uncertainty in our work to tell you what to expect – except that you shouldn't try to form expectations about what your day looks like but constantly stay open to rearranging your priorities." Apparently unsatisfied with the senior banker's reply, Ben snapped to the associate sitting next to him: "This feels like grad school all over again, where you can't get a straight answer out of the prof." The senior banker's answer amplified cognitive uncertainty because he withheld abstract scripts and asked the junior bankers to consider more information. The new bankers did not appreciate this.

When new Organization Bankers did learn about their roles and tasks, they often were presented with a broader scope of responsibility and received fewer guidelines than the Individual Bankers. One senior banker told the incoming bankers: "You are trusted to manage effectively an extraordinary amount of the company's and the clients' resources." The only guideline he gave the bankers was: "Manage these resources as if they were your own." Like other speakers, this senior banker withheld abstract guidelines and focused junior bankers on the need to think through each situation.

Despite the trust that senior bankers showed in them, the incoming Organization Bankers were dissatisfied with these "vague" and "confusing" guidelines. One associate told a peer, after being urged simply to "manage these resources as if they were your own:" "This is just bullshit. If I am traveling by myself I would never stay in the kinds of hotels that bankers here stay in regularly. That's because I don't have the bank's amount of resources. Why don't they give us a standard that makes sense? Or just flat out tell us what is acceptable and what not?"

Another associate said: "In any other business that I know of people get specific spending guidelines. Why not here?" A third associate said: "This is really confusing because they make it clear that there are better and worse ways of spending the firm's money but then they don't say what the criteria are." Despite such complaints, the bank gave bankers extensive resources and made them aware of their considerable discretion without offering any guidelines or constraints.

The Organization Bankers did learn some general principles. For example, a managing director presented a mini-case in which a hypothetical associate had been working on an important deal and was the key contact for the client. A deal-related deadline conflicted with a family event. What should the associate do? The managing director asked the newcomers to consider the perspective of their deal team: "You are dancing out the door with light feet, waving, and while you are living it up with your family, your poor schmuck colleague has to do your work. He cannot see his wife and kids all weekend just so that you can go party. Do you think that's right?"

This case had an unexpected right answer, however – to honor the family commitment. The managing director explained this answer: "That's why we are an organization. More than one person can do every single job in this place." Some principles at Organization Bank thus were not subject to uncertainty, such as important family obligations come before firm obligations.

The family example, however, also needs to be considered in the context of other information. This reveals complexity and contradictions. Much of the training had the subtext "be sensitive to your clients and colleagues." Like Dick, the colleague from the capital market desk, the managing director taught in a way that let the bankers experience a situation from different perspectives. Before he offered the general principle, he encouraged the associates to experience this situation from the perspective of their colleagues. In fact, the two new associates who first addressed the case said that "you cannot leave your team hanging" and "I stay here because we are an organization in which people are there for one another." However, in contrast to prior lessons, this example challenged the associates to, on the one hand, understand their colleagues' situation and, on the other hand, prioritize their own family obligations. Despite the fact that he ended with a general principle about the importance of family, then, the managing director made his point by highlighting the tension between conflicting obligations and emphasizing that judgment was required when making such decisions. New bankers were asked to move beyond script-like general principles.

While the Individual Bankers' training was designed to, as their training material said, "simplify your daily decisions," the Organization Bankers' training highlighted inconsistencies and conflicting priorities. Even in the rare instances in which junior bankers received explicit advice it was often phrased as a contradiction, such as: "Make swift, practical decisions and carefully analyze all available information." The senior Organization Bankers who had planned this training believed that contradictions fostered attention to the concrete. As one explained, "They are anti-rules. They tell people that for every plausible rule there is another one that makes just as much sense. They tell people not to get entranced by rules and recipes but to stay alert." Bankers were supposed to make decisions not by applying preconceived rules but by understanding situations in their own terms before drawing on the most appropriate concepts. Another senior banker said that contradictions remind people that logically contradictory things can nevertheless be true, which he considered a fundamental insight. "That is the one thing you always got to keep in mind here. Real life is always more complex than the concepts you have for it. And you have to be super careful not to mix the two up." Thus, Organization Bank's introductory training was designed to help people notice the gap between a banker's abstract understanding of a situation and the situation's more objective attributes. Despite the associates' clamoring for more conventional training, Organization Bank resisted. A director explained that "training can lull people in false certainty or seduce them to use easy recipes. But recipes are dangerous in our business."

Like the junior Individual Bankers, many Organization Bankers did not have relevant background knowledge. Therefore, some bankers were nervous when they saw only a few hours of finance training on the schedule. Toward the end of introductory training, most bankers expressed surprise that they had not been prepared in more detail for their jobs. One associate lamented: "I just learned about everyone else's job but mine." Senior bankers readily acknowledged this and tried to assuage the newcomers' concern: "This is all about getting to know the bank's resources. No one will expect you to know anything when you start." The senior bankers were referring to the practices described in Chapter 3 in which a banker could complement his or her own knowledge with the resources of the organization. Through ad-hoc interactions with colleagues and the use of templates and other resources, junior bankers could find effective solutions to client problems despite their own lack of knowledge. New bankers did not understand this for several months, however.

Uncertainty was amplified when some associates were asked to help out on "fire-drills," which were urgent deals with high stakes, while they were still in training. One junior banker had to complete a complicated leveraged buy-out analysis for the next morning, something he had never done before. The bankers were expected to master such unfamiliar tasks by drawing on the relevant organizational resources. News of these incidents spread rapidly among the newcomers and amplified cognitive uncertainty because they seemed to contradict explicit statements that no prior knowledge was required and because they challenged the newcomers' assumptions that bankers were experts. One trainee said: "I don't know what they are thinking to throw us right on the job. Many of us don't have finance backgrounds. The training didn't do much for us either. And it's not like we are only stuffing envelopes or something. It just doesn't make sense."

At the end of introductory training, 96 percent of the newcomers reported "extremely high" stress levels (see Table 5.2). In contrast, 93 percent of the Individual Bankers experienced only "high" or "medium" uncertainty at that point because they had faith in Individual Bank's comprehensive training system. One Organization Banker explained his rating:

> I was calmer and more confident before this [i.e., the introductory training] than I am now. I am really not sure what I got myself into. I am already staffed on four deals and have deliverables coming out of my ears and the training is over and I still don't really know what a balance sheet is. That kind of freaks me out.

New Organization Bankers, then, began their jobs with the same interest in abstract guidelines and individual traits as new Individual Bankers. But Organization Bank frustrated these expectations, deliberately withholding the knowledge that bankers sought and creating more uncertainty by providing contradictory information and practices. This caused newcomers' stress levels to surge.

THE FIRST SIX MONTHS AT ORGANIZATION BANK

Self-Interpretation

This section describes in more detail how junior Organization Bankers initially preferred to use their personal resources to solve problems. Like

Individual Bankers, they construed learning as a process of accumulating concepts that would help them work more independently. At both banks, new bankers interpreted the self in terms of traits and preferred to rely on their own individual capacities. Organization Bank's uncertainty-amplifying practices were designed to make the bankers aware that their personal resources were often insufficient and to compel them to make use of the bank's larger set of resources. This was not pleasant for the new bankers.

From their first day on the job, junior bankers were expected to contribute substantively to their teams. For example, Mike had to leave introductory training a few days early, on a Wednesday, because a team needed help with a fire drill, an important deal for which a presentation had to be completed over the weekend. When Michel saw him on Friday, he was still wearing the same clothes he had worn on Wednesday and had not shaved. He sat in his cubicle surrounded by documents that he had ordered from the bank's library, entering data into a long spreadsheet. Mike had a degree in finance. But he was unfamiliar with the financial analyses that he was being asked to complete under extreme time pressure. When Michel asked him how it was possible for him to deliver the assigned work product, he explained:

> David sketched the model for me and then basically said "good luck." Well, no not really. I mean that guy has slept even less than I did. He was just running around like crazy himself. . . . He told me to walk around the floor and see whether we have done [similar deals] before and to just cut and paste from that. . . . He calls in from time to time and asks me to tell him stuff like the earnings ratio. . . . And when the numbers sound funky to him, he asks me to go back or to check with whoever is around to see where the analysis went wrong. . . . But people are really good about pitching in. George (a senior vice president, who was not on Mike's deal team) saw me here when he was leaving at 1 [AM] and stayed until 4 this morning to help me out.

Mike judged his stress level as "extremely high," partly because he fell short of his own expectations:

> I feel bad asking people to help me out all the time. I should be able to figure this stuff out by myself. And I probably could, but not in a few hours. . . . I was lucky that George was around. But at the same time I just felt bad making him stay here all night. But I told him I'd return the favor.

Note that Mike interpreted George's help not as routine business but as a personal favor – which sounds like the favor-based exchange system at

Individual Bank. What he thought he learned from this situation was how to do these analyses independently: "I guess I just got a crash course in [financial modeling]. So the next time around I won't do so bad." These excerpts show how, like the Individual Bankers, incoming Organization Bankers also thought of expertise as a personal resource.

David and George, who had been with Organization Bank for years, had a different interpretation of this episode. David said: "If I had been around, I would have helped out more. But this is good practice for Mike. It shows him the ropes. How to get things done. Getting the books, not spinning your wheels, and asking for help. These are all the things that newcomers typically don't do and why they are miserable and ineffective for months."

According to David, it was not so important for Mike to learn how to complete specific types of financial analyses by using his own personal resources, which is what Individual Bank's big buddies would have focused on. It was more important that Mike learned "how to get things done" by using the bank's resources effectively. This kind of learning focused less on developing relevant concepts and more on noticing opportunities for marshaling other resources and becoming comfortable seeking out those resources.

At Individual Bank, George would have had no obligation to help Mike in any but the most rudimentary ways. The Individual Bankers contributed to the bank by completing the tasks assigned to them. Just as Mike interpreted the situation, the Individual Bankers viewed the help they extended to others as personal favors that they tracked and expected to be repaid. Individual Bankers often talked about "chits" that they could "cash in" or about calling in favors from people who "owed them one." It was also not uncommon for Individual Bankers to reach out in vain to their colleagues. For instance, one Individual Bank vice president said:

> When I started, they said all of these things like how teamwork was valued, how we all work for the same firm and how there are no stupid questions. But the more senior you get, the less I found that to be true. People here are busy and they watch out for themselves. You need to have personal relationships to get others to get back to you. . . . Why should I take time out of my day to help you do your job? . . . I left lots of voice mails that never received an answer.

Junior Individual Bankers often found that senior bankers did not return their calls. One senior Individual Banker acknowledged this: "My attitude is that it is an associate's job to support me, not the other way round." Such experiences are not uncommon in the investment banking industry. For example, Knee (2006) reported how, during his first weeks at Morgan Stanley, he believed that his voice mail was broken because his messages to colleagues did not yield replies. He later learned that replies could not be taken for granted. They were a favor that one must earn.

Norms of reciprocity are an important social lubricant in professional service firms. Researchers most often view reciprocity as the basis for a sociocentric way of organizing (Adler and Kwon, 2006). The contrast between Individual Bank and Organization Bank, however, shows that reciprocity still has significant individual-centered aspects. Its basis is the individual, who construes the self and others in terms of personal resources. These resources can be exchanged for the benefit of individual bankers who each do their "own job." When personal relationships do not exist in such a system, bankers are cut off from needed organizational resources.

The senior Organization Bankers had a very different model for interpreting situations such as Mike's:

> You have to make a judgment call. . . . If staying until four in the morning on a project means that you will have to renege on another project you took on, that's clearly a bad choice. On the other hand, if you can help getting something done in three hours that would otherwise have taken a day or that would have been done incorrectly, then this is clearly a good investment of your time.

This excerpt illustrates how Organization Bankers made choices from an expanded perspective. Making sure that a colleague could work faster or more effectively was inherently important, regardless of whether the colleague would reciprocate. Another senior banker explained his motivation for helping colleagues: "There is reciprocity here but it is more of a universal type. You do things for others because you realize that you yourself are constantly receiving help. But it is not tied to specific people. Speaking for myself, I don't keep mental ledgers about who owes whom what."

An Organization Bank vice president added: "Even managing directors return analysts' phone calls within a day or less. . . . That might be partly because many of them have come up through the rank of an analyst and still remember what it's like." Consistent with this attitude, George did not feel that he had done a personal favor for Mike.

> GEORGE: We don't have job descriptions around here. Stuff just comes your way and you get it done. It's not that I have "my" work and Mike has "his" work. I mean sure, we all have projects that we work on. It's not like everyone works on everything. And it might not be the best use

of my time to work on spreadsheets. But I was the only one around and I guess that means I am Mike's man. . . .

RESEARCHER: Mike said that he felt bad that he could not do the work by himself.

GEORGE: That's just ridiculous. He'll get over it.

RESEARCHER: What do you mean?

GEORGE: No one does work by himself. For each deal, a lot of different people have to give their input. People in capital markets tell you what the reasonable assumptions are for a model. People in corporate finance tell you whether this should be a public-market deal. And someone in mergers also gives his or her opinion on whether it should be a public- or private-market deal. The industry analyst judges the market conditions.

George clearly understood the social context differently than did Mike and the Individual Bankers. He did not experience the organization as consisting of people who each fulfill their personal responsibilities, such that the organization's output is the sum of each individual banker's contributions. George had a more systemic notion of interdependence. Even when people do "their" jobs, they depend on a broader set of resources. The contributions of specific individuals cannot be separated out. Expertise is not something that a particular individual possesses and uses to solve a project. Instead of being a property of an individual, knowledge is the outcome of a social process. The organization's output is not an aggregation of individual products, but is fundamentally systemic.

Despite actions like George's, and despite the bank's attempts to teach new bankers that they must draw on organizational resources, we detected no change in new Organization Bankers' individual-centered self-interpretations during the first six months. They felt overwhelmed, but they continued to think of themselves as autonomous individuals, just like Individual Bankers.

Cognition, Emotion, and Motivation

Throughout our observation period, the Individual Bankers understood their identities in terms of traits. They thought, felt, and acted with reference to these traits. In contrast, Organization Bank signaled that identity traits were irrelevant. Whatever one banker did not know could be obtained from others. Senior bankers often said things such as "what *I* know doesn't matter" and "we are all doing the same thing, drawing on the resources of the organization." Such practices made it difficult for bankers to establish a causal connection between individual traits and outcomes. These practices were designed explicitly to orient bankers away from their own traits.

New Organization Bankers nonetheless continued to think in terms of individual traits and tried to infer their own and others' traits from their observations of behavior. During interviews and informal conversations, Michel regularly asked the new associates open-ended questions about what they were learning, how they were learning, and how they thought and felt during learning situations. For both the Individual Bankers and the new Organization Bankers, trait-relevant information was in the foreground. During their first six months, about 80 percent of the junior Organization Bankers' answers referred to identity traits. This compares to about 65 percent for the junior Individual Bankers. At both banks, the junior bankers described how they learned to exhibit valued traits by observing senior bankers. One new Organization Banker explained:

> One of the things I am learning is what kind of personality works with clients and with colleagues around here. I am naturally aggressive and gung-ho. So I am trying to find senior bankers who have a similar style and see how they work that. One of the things I am learning from Jack is that being aggressive doesn't necessarily mean being loud. He sits in meetings and for the longest time says absolutely nothing, just observes. And then he pounces. He comes out with an observation that is so astute and so insightful that it just blows people away. That is what I call power.

Another Organization Bank associate said:

> When you join an organization, it's not only about the work you are doing. You make a choice about what kind of person you are going to be. One of the ways you can gauge the implications of your decision is to look around and see what kind of people are there. There is a good chance that you will end up being like some of them.... I am determined to take charge of this process.... I compare different styles and then pick the one that I want.

Even though Organization Bank focused the associates' learning on how to use the organization's resources, the associates maintained their focus on abstract traits. Instead of trying to emulate senior bankers' resource usage, associates ascribed traits to senior bankers and tried to imitate them. In a more general study of junior professionals, Ibarra (1999) documents how newcomers in various organizations similarly attended to the identity traits of their senior colleagues as templates for constructing a new identity, which suggests that this tendency is prevalent in American professional cultures.

The junior Organization Bankers also observed their own behaviors in order to infer their own traits. When they found that they behaved consistently across situations and that their behavior differed from others in these situations, they sometimes concluded that they had an underlying trait. For example, one banker who had just worked three nights in a row said: "I have always been a fighter, you know, just doing whatever it takes. When I worked on projects in school, I was always the one pushing the hardest no matter how tired I was or how sick I felt. I guess that's just who I am." These inferences are consistent with processes described by traditional cognitive theory (e.g., Bem, 1967), in which people infer their attributes by observing their own behavior.

Once new bankers inferred a pattern of self-defining behaviors and traits, they ignored or discounted memories that would have contradicted this dominant pattern. For example, Michel showed the associate just quoted data from situations in which he appeared to have taken shortcuts. These data included hideouts in the bathroom when the staffer was making his rounds to recruit associates for new projects, leaving his jacket on the chair while going on a date to pretend he was still in the building and working, and going home while a summer associate and an analyst were completing a client presentation for the next day. In response to these data, the associate responded that these were situations in which shortcuts were "completely natural" and therefore did not reflect who he was. He claimed that "everyone tries to avoid getting staffed. It's a game that people play here. That has nothing to do with your personality." Abstract identities thus functioned like general schemas that helped the associates distinguish between relevant and irrelevant information. Because the schema was the criterion for relevance, associates ignored and even resisted information that did not fit the schema. This pattern is predicted by psychological research on self-narratives (White and Epston, 1990) and more general cognitive processing (e.g., Ruble, 1994; Fiske and Taylor, 1991).

Because junior bankers only accepted a limited set of traits as self-descriptive, their identities tended to be narrow, well defined, and internally consistent. The wife of one associate described the rigidity and self-stereotyping characteristic of such trait-based identities:

> When he talks about the kinds of situations he is in, the stories always have similar kinds of punch lines and he is always in a similar kind of role. He is always the one who sees things that do not work well or that

are not right, and a bit of an outsider. When he was in law school, he had that same kind of role. He was always the one who was informed about politics and had an opinion about it and couldn't understand why others didn't read as much as he did or just didn't care. And when I point out to him that he is pigeonholing himself, he doesn't see it. He says: "That is who I am and I have to be true to that."

When individuals observe their behavior and believe that they detect a pattern, they might conclude that this pattern represents who they are. Rigidity results when, in the name of authenticity, individuals feel compelled to exhibit loyalty to this trait and engage in self-stereotyping (Mael and Ashforth, 1995). This sort of identification involves depersonalization. People experience themselves as interchangeable members of a type defined by attributes and socially expected behaviors (Turner et al., 1987).

New Organization Bankers doggedly sought trait-based information despite the fact that it was not readily offered. But senior Organization Bankers persisted and eventually counteracted what appears to be a deeply rooted tendency in Western cultures (e.g., Baumeister and Leary, 1995). Organization Bank accomplished this partly by overloading new bankers with work. Organization Bank was known in the industry for staffing its teams leanly, so much so that competitors were incredulous: "I don't know how they can pull this amount of work off with teams that size." On comparable transactions, Organization Bank had up to 75 percent fewer bankers on a team than Individual Bank. Organization Bank's industry groups also often had only a fraction of the members that similar groups had at Individual Bank. In one case, a sixteen-member Individual Bank group did the same work as a four-member Organization Bank group – with similar success in terms of industry rankings. These practices earned Organization Bank the reputation of being a "sweatshop" or "bone-grinding mill." As one competitor remarked, "Something's gotta give. Their client service clearly doesn't suffer. So my guess is that they work their bankers to the bone. At least that's the rep."

One effect of the excessive workload was that bankers simply could not work independently. After observing their collaborative behavior, junior Organization Bankers eventually had to conclude that a trait-based identity was not plausible as an explanation for performance. They had to acknowledge that the organizational outcomes they achieved could not be attributed to their own traits, but depended instead on the contributions of organizational resources. In the next section, we describe how this developmental shift occurred.

The unusually heavy workload had a pronounced effect on Organization Bankers during their first six months. While newcomers held the view that their traits caused important outcomes, they did not yet know how to display these traits in the new context. Because of the enormous workload, junior Organization Bankers were too pressed for time to engage in the informal social conversations that facilitated identity formation at Individual Bank. This time pressure was different from Individual Bank's norm of staying at work for a predetermined period of time even when there was no work to do. For the Organization Bankers, working hard was not a choice they made to satisfy social norms. It was a necessity dictated by urgent deal deadlines. The difference became visible when there were unexpected lulls in the Organization Bankers' deals. In such cases Organization Bankers felt free to leave at any time of the day, even in the morning, which would have been unthinkable at Individual Bank.

Organization Bankers consequently had less opportunity to engage in the gossip and social comparison that made their Individual Bank peers so self-conscious. The Organization Bank associates said they often "cringed" when they saw a peer leisurely approaching their cubicle because they felt too pressured to "chit chat": "Most of the time I am just running around like a chicken with the head cut off, trying to get everything done in time." Gossip was also actively frowned upon at Organization Bank. When junior bankers were caught gossiping, senior bankers said such things as "you should be worrying about your work instead" or "these [personal] issues are of no concern here." When blunders in attire or behavior were severe, senior bankers corrected junior bankers privately. The bank's chief operating officer explained this practice: "There are norms in our society concerning what the kinds of people whom you entrust money to should look like. But beyond that you don't want people to spend time and energy fussing about this and becoming all self-conscious."

This intense focus on work encouraged bankers to encode information at the level of the task or activity and to downplay trait-relevant concerns. Similar dynamics have been reported in accounts of natural disasters and other crises when people, preoccupied with matters of survival, forget to classify themselves and others using traits and identities that previously influenced their interactions (e.g., Char, 1995, 1996).

Ironically, however, the short-term effect of Organization Bank's sociocentric culture was to focus the junior bankers even more on their trait-based identities. While the Individual Bankers could competently participate in their bank's activities early on, the junior Organization Bankers struggled for at least six months. The following example illustrates the difficulties that junior Organization Bankers had. One new banker gave the following example to illustrate his "task-orientation," a highly valued characteristic at Organization Bank. He described how he had worked all night, despite severe pneumonia, and continued to work while vomiting blood into a garbage can (an episode that Michel witnessed). He explained his behavior with a desire to "prove myself and show that I can get the task done." The banker here showed the same type of performance-based motivation that Individual Bankers showed after six months, only earlier. Like the Individual Bankers, his goal was to use his performance to establish his valued traits, such as dedication. The resources the banker focused on were his own, and his underlying question was: "How will *I* complete the tasks that are assigned to me?" Thus, despite the bank's more sociocentric culture, trait-relevant concerns were very much in the foreground of the newcomer's focus.

Senior bankers judged the behavior of this sick banker as "stupid" and "unnecessary." One senior banker rated the behavior as "the opposite of task-orientation – a pure ego trip. What he doesn't get is that tasks get done by an organization, not by people." The bank's practices shifted the cause of action from the individual banker to a larger social system. For the more task-oriented senior bankers, self-interpretation had shifted to a focus on "*How* will I complete the tasks that are assigned to me?" In contrast to the newcomers, the focus of senior bankers was on the *how*, not the *I*. This young banker would have been better served to have others do the work, both for his own and for the bank's interests.

New Organization Bankers' lack of experience and training, and the firm's availability-based staffing practices, made independent work difficult. The bankers also received explicit instructions to draw on others. Nevertheless, newcomers tried to complete the staggering amount of work assigned to them by themselves. During the first six months on the job, junior Organization Bankers worked 118 hours per week on average, while their counterparts at Individual Bank worked 94 hours per week on average. These individual heroics created severe personal hardships, such as stress-related illnesses and rifts with friends and family. Many associates gained significant amounts of weight. One gained sixty pounds during his first year, and another gained about twenty pounds during her first six months. She explained:

> I would describe myself as someone who is highly health-conscious and disciplined. Before I started working here, I worked out every single day, no matter what. And I watched what I ate to the extent of writing down every single calorie. But these habits that I cultivated over years

and years are out the window here. You cannot help it. What are you going to do when midnight comes around and you still have an eight-hour workday ahead, on top of the sixteen hours that you just worked? The answer is: A steady stream of caffeine and sugar.... You literally have to bludgeon your body into submission.

Other associates complained about what felt like permanent colds or allergies. One associate's cube was littered with vitamins, homeopathic remedies, tea boxes, honey, and used and unused tissues: "I am usually pretty resilient. But for the last few weeks I have been sniffling and sneezing nonstop. I also have a sore throat, fever. But I have to keep going." Even though the bank stressed the importance of family, most associates said that they had no time to see or even speak to their family on the phone:

> My wife is pretty upset. She feels that I am treating our home like a cheap motel where I go to shower and change. I try to make up for it by calling her, but the only time I can do that is when I am having lunch in front of my computer and checking e-mail at the same time. I don't tell her that, but she says she can hear me eat and that I am not listening to her because I don't answer quickly enough or because I don't initiate long conversations but just say "yes" or "no."

The associates' families and friends were also disappointed because the bankers regularly broke commitments:

> One of the drawbacks of this job is that you cannot make plans. My family is in town this week. They came over from India to see where I work and live. And I told everyone on my deal teams that I needed to at least have dinner with them. But then I got staffed on this hostile take-over and the presentation is Thursday and I have to get the presentation done and then fly out to the client. So the only time I am going to see them is when I go home to pack for the trip. I'll try to make them understand, but they probably won't.

Similar things happened at Individual Bank, especially the broken commitments, but much less often. Individual Bankers who were sick usually took time off. Individual Bankers also worked fewer "all-nighters," and many associates maintained a regular exercise schedule. For one Individual Bank associate this meant going to the gym twice a day: "I do cardio in the morning on an empty stomach, because that burns more fat, and then weights in the evening."

All Organization Bankers worked hard. Even after the six-month period associates averaged around one hundred hours per week. Most of the senior bankers who reviewed the above data did not think that the associates' work hours were excessive. One director said: "If you have a deal that needs to get done, you have to do what it takes and that might include working several nights in a row and keeping up that pace over the period of a few months." The senior bankers nevertheless said that the associates' behavior was not consistent with Organization Bank's task-oriented culture because their hard work often was not required by deal demands and because bankers did not attend to family events in the way that Organization Bank encouraged them to. One vice president said:

> Whenever you are new somewhere, people tell you about how you should draw on help and how no question is too stupid and so people come in here and think this is like any other place and don't understand the radical shift they have to make. When we tell people to draw on others that is not a friendly gesture or a signal of how welcoming our culture is. That is the essence of how we work and we depend on people to do so. But until people really get it, they do what they have always done, work as an individual performer and spend many agonizing hours in the office that they could spend with their family or in bed.

By their fifth month with the bank, 100 percent of the junior Organization Bankers rated their stress levels as "extremely high" (see Table 5.2). Many said that these were the "most grueling" times of their lives. Most of the bankers rated their highest stressor to be their uncertainty about whether they had "what it takes" to succeed at the bank. Michel asked the associates to rate their stress levels on a weekly basis and to explain their responses. Organization Bank associates referred to a range of stressors, including lack of sleep, isolation from family and friends, and their declining health. But associates tended to experience these stressors as less severe than uncertainty about their competence because these other stressors resulted from their own choices. One associate remarked:

> Of course it gets to me that I average about three hours of sleep these days and that I haven't seen my fiancé for more than a few minutes here and there. But this is something that I choose to do. It is a commitment that I have made and that I can stand by. What really gets to me is that all of this may not be worth anything. I sometimes have the feeling that there is only so much you can make up for with hard work. You also need to have talent and maybe I don't have the kind of talent you need to perform at an Organization Bank level. That is what gets to me. That I might not have what it takes and that there is no way to tell right now.

Others blamed Organization Bank's "bad training system" for their predicament. After four months on the job, one associate said: "If you ask me, the introductory training here just sucks.... I am smart, capable, and highly motivated. The fact that I still don't know how to do my job means that the system here simply doesn't work."

Like the Individual Bankers, these new Organization Bankers felt self-conscious emotions. However, as compared to the Individual Bankers' first six months, junior Organization Bankers talked more frequently about their emotions, had a more elaborate vocabulary for these emotions, and expressed greater emotional intensity. As a result, they experienced a heightened preoccupation with their inner states and a concurrent disconnection from the immediate context.

One of the few reasons that new Organization Bankers took time away from work was to get emotional support. Associates typically did not seek support from their family and friends, but instead from peers – because family and friends "just don't understand what we are going through. If you have never worked around the clock for days under the kind of pressure we have you simply cannot relate." Moreover, family and friends often were affected negatively by the bankers' hard work and told them things that they did not want to hear: "When I try to talk to my wife, she just takes this as a welcome opportunity to persuade me to change jobs so that we can spend more time together. But that's not what I want to do. I need someone who can build me up so that I can get through this, not seed more doubt."

Bankers rarely wanted advice from their peers. They just wanted someone to listen and to "vent to." One associate said:

> I am usually not like that. I am usually a doer. I don't get caught up in emotions. But I have never been in a situation like this before that pushes me to the edge like this. You just feel this knot in your stomach and your entire system goes haywire and you cannot stop and think about it because you have to go on and do your work.... It's like you are someone else.... Just figuring out what it is that you are feeling is actually a big help.

Another associate described how a peer initially provided unsolicited suggestions for how she could change things that troubled her. Irritated, she told him that she would henceforward provide him with a clue before they started the conversation: "red wine" signaled that she merely wanted a conversation, and "blue overall" was a reference to a handyman's attire, which signaled that she wanted the peer to help fix things.

Looking back on their first six months, associates sometimes referred to these conversations as episodes of "wallowing," "indulging," and "being caught up in self-pity."

New Organization Bank associates' informal conversations with the researcher also allowed them to vent and try to work through their experiences. During these conversations the bankers tended to talk about agitation and anxiety-related emotions. In informal conversations at both Individual Bank and Organization Bank, the researcher probed with such questions as "how would you describe what you are feeling?" and "what kinds of emotions do you feel most frequently?" The Organization Bankers responded with more interest and elaboration than the Individual Bankers, producing a wider range of emotions – including confusion, worry, uneasiness, despondency, hopelessness, lack of courage, fear, threat, indecision, nervousness, anxiety, irritation, frustration, tension, agitation, distractibility, paranoia, being wired, being on the edge, impatience, annoyance, and restlessness. Like the Individual Bankers, the young Organization Bankers alternated between these self-conscious emotions and "anger," "rebellion," "outrage," "unfriendliness," and "fury" directed at the bank context that "makes me feel this way," "has made me become this kind of person," and "treats me like this." New Organization Bankers' emotions often presented themselves as syndromes – comprehensive patterns of feelings, disruptive cognitive states, arousal, and behavior (Beck, 1976).

Even though these emotions connected bankers to their peers in commiseration sessions, they disengaged bankers from their work. The Organization Bankers often experienced emotions so intensely that they "could not stop obsessing about something," "had a hard time concentrating," and "found it impossible to sit still and listen." The physical symptoms that accompanied these emotions included sweat, sleeplessness, eating disorders, heart-pounding, mind-racing, nervous tics, and muscle tensions ("shoulders up to the ears") or spasms under the eye or in the back. One banker said: "I cannot walk around without a jacket because I constantly have these huge sweat marks under my arms that tell people right away how nervous I am." Another banker said: "My wife keeps mocking me with this nervous tic that I have developed of fidgeting with my hair unless I really discipline myself not to." A third associate found himself chewing on his nails, a habit that he had thought under control since childhood.

During this time, senior bankers believed that junior bankers made "a lot of avoidable mistakes." In one case a newcomer, Lara, had stayed up all night to complete a memo. Even though the memo was not a critical component of the deal, and even though the deadline was not a "hard" one, she felt compelled to get it done by herself and in a timely manner because she "did not want to look stupid." Lara thus interpreted her behavior as reflecting underlying traits, such as competence or intelligence. When the vice president reviewed the memo the next morning, he found that it was of low quality. He told Lara:

> You are trying too hard. You've got to be more task-oriented. Don't worry about what I will say or what the client will think about you. Then you are making bad choices. Here, look at this section. Once you made [that decision], the [other section] should have followed by itself. Take one step and then see where it takes you. Have some fun!

This quotation describes the two cognitive, emotional, and motivational patterns that we observed at the two banks. Lara's pattern represents the individual-centered psychological functioning that we also observed at Individual Bank. She experienced anxiety because she feared that she might fall short of traits that she aspired to, and this motivated her to make bad choices such as "trying too hard." It also distracted her from noticing cues present in the unfolding task. The vice president juxtaposed Lara's behavior with a task-oriented, sociocentric approach. He discouraged her from construing behavior in terms of identity traits ("don't worry about what I will say or what the client will think about you"). He told her to encode behavior at the level of the activity instead, literally pointing her toward concrete information ("Here, look at this section"). He explained how this situation-specific information could motivate and guide behavior. The vice president associated this sociocentric cognitive-motivational pattern with a more positive emotion that would reflect engagement in the task.

The vice president's comments also illustrate how the focus on task-orientation at Organization Bank involved a distinct theory of action. On Individual Bank's trait-based account, traits cause behavior. Lara acted using such a theory. She made choices because she wanted to establish an identity for herself, whereas she should have let the task make decisions instead ("take one step and see where it takes you"). Other senior Organization Bankers also talked about task-orientation in terms of "letting the task take over" or "being guided by the task." These comments suggest that situational cues and constraints can cause action – when people notice them. Task-orientation at Organization Bank was not primarily a property of individuals, but indicated instead that cognition is distributed across people and material resources such as task-structures.

Across their first six months, then, new Organization Bankers exhibited a similar type of individual-centered orientation as Individual Bankers, but earlier in their time at the bank and more intensely. The heightened intensity resulted from the discrepancy between the identity traits that new Organization Bankers aspired to – looking intelligent and competent, producing excellent work, appearing promising and talented – and the actual situation at Organization Bank in which the bankers could neither fully understand what it meant to exhibit these traits nor live up to their aspirations. The bankers' chronic and intense uncertainty about their identities impeded effective engagement with tasks and thereby undermined their goals.

AFTER SIX MONTHS AT ORGANIZATION BANK

Self-Interpretation

Starting at around six months, the junior Organization Bankers began to use more diverse resources and use them more creatively. For example, junior bankers were usually responsible for producing the client presentation book. They gathered analyses and hand-written comments from team members, structured them into a presentation format, submitted the marked up documents to word processing, checked the accuracy of the word-processing work, put this material into separate tabs, instructed document production on how to bind and reproduce the books, checked the final books, and sent them to team members before the client meeting. Initially, the junior Organization Bankers and the Individual Bankers completed all of these steps by themselves. Over time, however, many of the Organization Bankers found ways to make better use of the bank's resources.

Chloe, an Organization Bank associate, went to word processing herself one day and talked to the word processors, who were all employees of a temporary personnel agency. Individual Bankers never did such things, instead relying on their secretaries to make deliveries. While talking with the word processors, Chloe learned about their backgrounds and she leveraged their skills for her purposes. One word processor, Bill, was an unemployed writer. Chloe subsequently drafted her documents in bullet points and let Bill formulate full sentences and edit the presentation. Another word processor, Cindy, was a graphic designer. Chloe gave Cindy the raw numbers and let her design the graphs. No one used the word processors as efficiently as Chloe, but other Organization Bankers did train their secretaries to do basic spreadsheets.

This creative use of word processors and secretaries shows how Organization Bankers began to construe their environment differently six months after joining the bank. Instead of orienting toward abstractions – such as role occupants with role obligations – they now thought of others more concretely, as resources that could substitute fungibly for one another, independent of the role occupant who "owned" these resources. From this perspective, a resource was defined only in reference to a particular task, not with respect to a role that persisted across situations. "Fungibility" was a term that Organization Bankers used frequently to talk about how the specific attributes of particular individuals did not matter. In fact, fungibility usually did not refer to an integral person but to contributions that people and objects could make. For example, when a senior banker was not available to talk to an associate about the deals that the firm had done in a particular industry, the associate could get this knowledge from a combination of the bank's databases, research reports, books, and bankers in other departments. This combination of resources was fungible with, or could substitute for, the advice of an expert. Because of this fungibility, junior bankers without relevant knowledge could offer advice to clients in ways that never happened at Individual Bank. The junior bankers often brought together a combination of organizational resources in order to serve the client.

In contrast, junior and senior Individual Bankers thought of secretaries and word processors in terms of their roles – thus adopting an abstract orientation – not in terms of resources that they could contribute to a particular task. When one junior Individual Banker heard about how his Organization Bank counterparts leveraged their secretaries by letting them design spreadsheets, for example, he shook his head in disbelief: "My secretary has been working with me for three months now and still cannot remember my last name. And answering the phone is the best I can get her to do. I have to do my own expenses.... I just don't think this [the Organization Bank arrangements] would be possible here." Yet these junior Individual Bankers acknowledged that it had not occurred to them to ask their secretaries or word processors to fulfill anything but their role obligations. When one senior Individual Banker heard about how the junior Organization Bankers used word processing, he simply assumed that Organization Bank had the more effective temp agency:

INDIVIDUAL BANKER: Wow, you got to give me the name of that temp agency.
RESEARCHER: It's called Dragon Temps.

INDIVIDUAL BANKER: That's funny. I bet we have Turtle Temps. I could use some dragons on my word processing. That's for sure.

Because the Individual Bankers acted as if resources were located in individuals, not in a system, they assumed that the Organization Bank secretaries were more motivated or that Dragon Temps had more effective employees. The Individual Bankers did not imagine the alternative explanation: that Organization Bank might have a system that helped bankers use similar secretarial and temp resources more effectively.

We also observed more flexible resource usage among senior Organization Bankers, but not among senior Individual Bankers. Organization Bankers used different types of resources in different situations, and their behaviors were informed by the specific demands of the situation. They did not bring preconceived, internalized concepts to the situation in the same way as the Individual Bankers did. For example, in one meeting the Organization Bankers did not use the customary spreadsheets or presentation books but presented analyses on colorful posters. The team's director explained this choice:

> During my phone conversation with [the client], he used the word "creative" at least eight times. He said that his business was all about creativity and that he wanted us to show that we understand creativity.... This [process of assembling pitch books or less conventional poster presentations] is not about how we are used to presenting information but about how the information is most useful to the client.

This example shows the Organization Bankers using the concrete preferences of a client as a resource for structuring their activities instead of relying on concepts that the bankers brought to the client from their prior experience. Organization Bank did of course have routines, and not every single aspect of these routines was reevaluated for every situation. As compared to the Individual Bankers, however, the Organization Bankers were more alert to situational cues that indicated that a fresh approach was required.

Cognition, Emotion, and Motivation

After six months, junior Organization Bankers began to find resources outside themselves, in the larger organization. They brought together various resources to address concrete problems, without relying on abstract concepts that restricted resource usage. This section shows how the bankers' psychological processes consequently shifted from internally to externally oriented, from individual-centered to sociocentric. Because the bankers believed that work outcomes did not depend on their own resources, but instead on how organizational resources came together, they focused less on themselves and more on assembling resources appropriate to concrete tasks. When psychological processes focus not on identity traits but on the concrete situation, they function differently.

One indication that the junior Organization Bankers had entered a different phase was lower self-reported stress ratings (see Table 5.2). After seven months, 40 percent rated their stress as "high," while 60 percent continued to rate it as "extremely high." At the same point in their development, 22 percent of the Individual Bankers rated their stress level as "high" and 78 percent rated their stress levels as "extremely high." The Organization Bankers' ratings changed to 80 percent "high" and 20 percent "extremely high" after a year, where they stayed for the rest of the two-year observation period. This contrasts with the Individual Bankers, 85 percent of whom rated their stress levels as "extremely high" during the same period.

> One junior banker, Anton, explained the change in his stress level:

> You know, I eventually figured it out. This is not about me, it's not about how smart I am. This is about what you can do when you pull extraordinary resources together. I might not know whether the client should sell the business, spin it off, whatever. I might not even be able to do half of the analyses that I am responsible for. But I can still get it done and get it done well every single time because of the resources here.

Another associate described how he experienced challenging situations as less stressful than he had in his first six months:

> Before, I used to have this knot in my stomach in each and every meeting because I was just waiting for someone to ask me something that I was clueless about and worrying about what to say and about losing credibility.... Now these are the moments I live for.... I ask tons of questions to really understand this client... then I literally say it flat out: I don't have the answer for you right now. But we'll get our heads together and make sure you get the best advice possible.

The associates continued to experience high cognitive uncertainty about tasks ("I don't have the answer"). But they did not interpret their lack of knowledge as being about them and their lack of expertise. Instead, they took it as a cue for action. Instead of disengaging from the situation in an attempt to hide shortcomings, the associates openly displayed their lack of knowledge through the questions they asked ("I ask tons of questions") and used these questions to understand situations more deeply. The answers they received helped associates engage appropriate organizational resources to serve the client.

As the previous two excerpts illustrate, the demands on junior Organization Bankers stayed high, and their personal resources continued to fall short. But the bankers experienced lower stress because they became comfortable drawing on a larger resource system, which they used fungibly with their own resources ("this is about what you can do when you pull extraordinary resources together"). This integration of personal and organizational resources changed the perceived ratio of demands to resources and thereby lowered the bankers' stress levels.

Associates still disliked the persistent uncertainty: "You just never get used it. And you can't because there is just no pattern to get used to. So I still do have all of these negative emotions. But it is just that other things are more important." A director concurred: "We are not different from anyone else. No one here likes uncertainty. But uncertainty is just a fact that you cannot afford to forget. And this place reminds you all the time." These excerpts suggest that the Organization Bankers did not simply habituate to cognitive uncertainty, which would be another explanation for the reduction in stress. The bank did not cultivate a "tolerance of ambiguity" in bankers, encouraging them to perceive ambiguous situations as desirable (Budner, 1962). Neither bank selected bankers based on their tolerance of ambiguity, despite the prominence of uncertainty in their business. Nor did we find any evidence that the banks created a different tolerance for ambiguity in their bankers. Bankers in both banks regularly complained about their unpredictable working and travel schedules, about deals that become active or inactive unexpectedly, and about to-do lists that changed many times an hour.

After six months, about 70 percent of the Organization Bank associates responded to open-ended questions about what they were learning by mentioning such skills as "listening closely," "paying attention," "detail orientation," and "staying alert." For example, one associate answered: "I learned how to listen closely because I had to.... When I come out of that client meeting, I have to reproduce this information in exact detail to get the input I need." Another associate said: "When you are going to someone for input, they typically ask for a lot of background." Associates also listened attentively to clients because teams often reviewed available information about a deal and relied on associates for input:

> Whenever we meet as a team, people reflect on the meetings we had with clients. They ask such questions as: "What did we learn during the meeting?" "What matters to each decision maker?" "How do we know this?" Sometimes you are the only one who has met with some of the lower-level executives and the team relies on you for insight.

In addition, bankers needed to listen closely to their colleagues because they needed to integrate colleagues' input into client presentations and they often needed to draw on further resources as a result of a colleague's ideas. Senior Organization Bankers confirmed that listening and alertness were important skills. One managing director explained: "What you think holds true one day can radically change the next. Securities that move together today won't have any connection tomorrow and, instead, completely unrelated securities might move together. You just can't make assumptions."

In contrast, the majority of the Individual Bank associates stressed the importance of learning concepts, such as various financial-modeling techniques or industry information. Like the Organization Banker just quoted, senior Individual Bankers also believed that their environment was uncertain, but they drew different conclusions about how to deal with this uncertainty. Instead of stressing the importance of alertness, they stressed the importance of expertise. For example, one Individual Bank vice president said: "Your experience is always the best predictor. Even with something as random as the weather you are best off when you expect that tomorrow is somewhat like today."

As suggested by their emphasis on listening and alertness, after six months Organization Bank associates had switched from deduction to abduction. They attended to the concrete aspects of particular situations instead of supplying preconceived abstractions. Like inductive cognition, abductive cognition involves attention to concrete, observable information. Both abduction and induction aim at the situation. In contrast to inductive cognition, however, the Organization Bankers attended to concrete information and not to the retrieval of existing solutions from memory. They often did not know the relevant solution. Instead, they attended to details in order to generate new solutions through interaction with other people and objects. In contrast to inductive processes, they did not expect these solutions to hold across all similar instances. The Organization Bankers used abductive cognition to establish an ongoing direction for action that did not necessarily require abstract concept formation. Like the associate who "loved to ask questions" described above, Organization Bankers attended to concrete information about the client situation so that they could decide where to go next for input.

One might argue that the Organization Bankers' abductive cognitive style was a decontextualized tendency that they brought to a situation, a kind of norm that Organization Bankers internalized and applied to each situation. It may be that task-orientation in this sense is a kind of norm, but it appears to be a norm of a different type. Instead of invoking general standards (e.g., "don't leave work before 11 PM"), it is a norm that reminded bankers not to have general standards and to orient to the situation instead. When clients asked senior Organization Bankers what their deal strategy was, for example, the bankers sometimes replied that their strategy was not to have one but to analyze each new event and respond accordingly.

The task-orientation norm itself consequently was less influential in guiding behavior than abstract Individual Bank norms because Organization Bankers' norm dictated that they needed to consider situation-specific factors. The difference between these two types of norms can be understood in terms of their distinct intentions and effects. In contrast to the uncertainty-amplifying effect of task-orientation, the norms at Individual Bank (about appropriate work hours, revenue goals, and spending guidelines, for instance) reduced cognitive uncertainty. They aimed to simplify the bankers' cognition by restricting the need to consider additional information.

After their first six months, Organization Bankers also experienced fewer identity-focused emotions and more task-oriented emotions. Like the abductive cognition they exhibited, the bankers' task-oriented emotions helped them engage diverse resources as they became less preoccupied with identity traits. In their first six months the new Organization Bankers mostly experienced anxiety and other self-conscious emotions. These emotions had two crucial aspects: they indicated that an important identity goal (e.g., looking intelligent) was being threatened and they motivated the person to defend the threatened identity trait. Because of the resulting preoccupation with identities, bankers became disengaged from concrete situations. Emotions thus served an individual's interests by orienting him or her toward an abstract identity trait and using this trait to construe a situation.

Task-oriented emotions, in contrast, served different purposes. They indicated the extent to which a task-related goal was progressing and they motivated the person to act on behalf of that goal. These emotions involved the person more deeply with the situation. Unlike identity-focused emotions, which are best understood as properties of individuals, task-oriented emotions are better understood as attributes of a social system that includes but is not limited to the individual. They react to systemic dynamics, reflect these dynamics, and serve the system's interests by focusing individuals on collective activities and goals. Task-oriented emotions go along with an abductive cognitive style because they orient participants to the situation instead of toward their own identities. In contrast with the identity-induced involvement that includes deductive cognition and identity-focused emotions, abductive cognition and task-focused emotions facilitate direct involvement with a situation, unmediated by abstract cognitive categories and conceptions of one's identity.

In one of the excerpts given above, an Organization Bank associate described how he felt energized while gathering information about a task ("these are the moments I live for"). This energy came from the momentum of the task. Very similar situations, when experienced with reference to their own identity traits, had previously paralyzed the same junior Organization Bankers with worry, as they imagined a client's disapproving response to their lack of knowledge. After six months, however, they focused more on what to do next – understanding the situation at the concrete level of task goals ("I ask tons of questions to really understand this client") – and less on implications for their own identities. The energizing emotions did not distract associates from the situation but instead facilitated the task of gathering information, a task that required intellectual stamina and attention to detail. In similar situations, other Organization Bankers described their emotions as "completely absorbed" and "tense but in a good way." The Individual Bankers also experienced absorbing emotions, but usually not in situations that were so unfamiliar that the bankers could not handle the situations by themselves. They felt this absorption when they were "in the zone," when they experienced situations that challenged but did not exceed their level of ability.

Senior Organization Bankers who have read and commented on our account said that the associates described in this section exemplified high task-orientation. One director said: "I think this is task-orientation because it was more important for the banker to solve the client's problems than his ego problems." Thus, after six months, the junior Organization Bankers' emotions were becoming more aligned with the bank's task-oriented culture. A vice president explained how the bank's culture facilitated this alignment:

> Most of the time people cannot listen in situations because of the fear that they are inadequate. But once you understand that there is a whole organization supporting you, this fear just falls away and you can actually enjoy the kind of work that we do and appreciate the excitement and not always cringe when something new and unexpected comes up.

This banker points out that the anxiety-related emotions new Organization Bankers experienced disconnected them from situations in part because they suppressed emotions that could have facilitated their work.

Task-oriented emotions were not always positive, however. One associate talked about a meeting with members of another department:

> I just couldn't keep myself awake even though I had not slept less than before. And this meeting was really important for the deal. And at first I kept badgering myself and I kept notes just to keep me awake. And as I was looking at what I was writing down, I noticed that we were not making any progress at all. There were a lot of big ideas floating around and that's why I might not have noticed it before but they were all not what the client was interested in. . . . That's when I thought that it wasn't me. I wasn't bored because I had slept too little. I was bored because we were not getting anything accomplished.

The associate subsequently excused himself and found a more senior member of the deal team to intervene and get the situation back on track. Other associates talked about how they felt anger when participants neglected joint goals:

> I was frustrated when they started to get bogged down in politics and not focus on what we were here to do. And it was frustrating because I was the most junior person in the room and so I couldn't really say anything. And at first I felt bad about being so annoyed. But I guess this frustration also emboldened me; it must have. Whenever we were getting off track again, I just started making coughing noises or tapped my pen really loudly and I tried to send signals that way. . . . I couldn't believe my own chutzpah.

These excerpts illustrate how task-oriented emotions are more sociocentric. Both of these associates interpreted their emotional states not in terms of their own identity traits but instead as information about the situation, and they used this information to improve the performance of their teams. The emotions thus oriented bankers toward a social system and served the interests of that system.

As Organization Bank associates made the transition from more identity-focused to more task-oriented emotions, they began to frame their identities differently. In the first excerpt above the associate said: "That's when I thought that it wasn't me." In the second excerpt above the associate talked about his behavior as if he were observing and scrutinizing it for information ("I guess this frustration also emboldened me; it must have. . . . I couldn't believe my own chutzpah"). Anton, who was quoted earlier, similarly reminded himself that "this is not about me." These excerpts show a new, self-observing attitude that involves distance from one's behaviors. The associates no longer interpreted their behavior as evidence of underlying traits, but instead observed their own reactions as cues to what was happening in the situation. As the associates came to recognize their emotions as part of a larger system – both as called forth by the system and as contributing to the system – they began to use their emotions to gather information about situations and possibilities for action.

Previously, junior Organization Bankers had attended only to behaviors that they found consistent with their identity, ignoring behaviors that did not fit this identity. In contrast, the two associates just quoted paid attention to their boredom and frustration precisely because they realized that these emotions were not typical for them. The first banker usually was not bored in meetings and the second banker was known for behaving in a shy and unassuming way. After six months, Organization Bankers thus broadened the range of emotions and behaviors that they attended to. Their emotions also became more diverse. Instead of being generated by the associates' own preoccupations with identity, their emotions were generated more with reference to conditions in the heterogeneous situations they experienced. When the bankers recognized that their emotions could serve as cues about the situation, they began to act differently. They initially felt the typical urge to turn inward and berate themselves ("I badgered myself;" "And at first I felt bad"). But they then resisted this impulse and turned their attention toward the situation for information on possible actions. The associates' newly discovered distance from their identities allowed them to suspend habitual reactions and keep themselves open for new emotions, information, and possible actions. This ability to embrace novel cues and imagine other actions is one important attribute of an abductive style.

As they moved past six months at Organization Bank, associates were increasingly able to suspend distracting emotions. Even after one year, associates still experienced the anxiety-related emotions that preoccupied them during their first months with the bank. But now they were able to "drop," "ignore," and "turn away from" these emotions. One associate said:

> Old habits are hard to break. There are still times when I want to prove myself or gain the respect of someone I admire or want to work with. In these situations it is easy to be hyper-vigilant about how everything you do or say sounds and to become completely wrapped up in frustration over minor things that didn't go so well. But here you cannot afford that kind of indulgence. There are more important things that you have to take care of.... I would say that the main difference is not that I don't have these kinds of emotions but that I can drop them quicker and return to what I really want to do.

Another associate who overheard this comment agreed: "I think we can do this because we have been conditioned to be hyper-vigilant about every situation we are in.... No one really cares about what you are thinking or feeling if it doesn't promote what you are doing." As this second associate argued, the bank's culture influenced bankers by directing their attention toward different concerns than those that preoccupied Individual Bankers. Individual Bank helped its bankers to elaborate an inner realm of abstract concepts and traits, and these abstractions mediated the bankers' reactions to situations. In contrast, Organization Bank discouraged bankers from thinking about such abstract concepts and traits. It elaborated an outer realm consisting of tasks, situations, and concrete cues and asked bankers to attend to these as they developed solutions tailored to the situation. Through this focus, Organization Bank gradually redirected their associates' attention away from the inner realm and toward the outer realm. As a vice president said:

> I think emotions are always present in any kind of human situation. And if you look closely you can see all kinds of emotions here, ranging from the thrill of chasing the deal to impatience when things don't happen fast enough and bitter disappointment when deals fall apart. But in all these situations what people focus on is the deal. And in most of these situations that is precisely when you have to focus most closely on the deal to stay on top of things.... People have all kinds of emotions but we cannot really afford to think much about them.

A director said: "I guess we have more of an action-oriented culture where the articulation of emotions is not really common or encouraged."

The transformation in Organization Bankers after six months of socialization, and the contrast with Individual Bankers, suggests that habitual emotions can vary across social contexts. Emotions are culturally informed, registering aspects of situations that matter in a culture while backgrounding other aspects. With cultural reinforcement across a socialization period, people's emotions can come to register different aspects of the environment and people can learn to monitor their emotions differently. At Organization Bank, the new bankers' commitment to a narrow range of identity-focused emotions loosened because the bank discouraged attention to identity and encouraged attention to concrete situations. As a result, Organization Bankers' emotions functioned less to express an inner self and more as another means of access to situational cues.

After six months, junior Organization Bankers continued to work more hours on average than the Individual Bankers. Individual Bank associates averaged ninety hours per week while Organization Bank associates averaged around one hundred. After the first six months, however, the Organization Bankers showed fewer self-sacrificing behaviors than they had exhibited earlier and fewer than comparable Individual Bankers. During the first six months, as we described above, new Organization Bankers persisted at tasks even when this damaged their health. One example of this was the banker who continued to work around the clock despite pneumonia. The following excerpt illustrates how an Organization Bank vice president avoided such self-sacrifice while still acting on behalf of the task. We observed similar behavior among Organization Bank associates after six months with the bank.

> At twelve last night, I was just beat and I stopped writing [on a document for a client presentation]. I thought to myself that I won't get this into any reasonable shape tonight. So I started to think about the consequences for the meeting tomorrow morning and how we [the participants in the meeting] can deal with this in a different way there.

Like the stressed junior bankers, this vice president worked very hard to complete the task. However, unlike beginning bankers, he remained sensitive to other components of the task system and he noticed how his declining performance would affect the overall task. Individual Bankers aimed to produce high-quality work because it expressed their underlying traits, such as being meticulous or excellent. In contrast, this Organization Banker used a task-related standard ("reasonable shape") as a relatively dynamic and concrete standard that could guide his efforts, together with the cues that his own physical state provided. Instead of working all night, he stopped when his physical state made a quality work impossible. His emotional state ("I was beat") provided information about himself in relation to the task. It indicated that trying harder would not have been beneficial to the larger system that included him, the team, and the larger task.

When asked how he had felt during that night, the vice president shrugged his shoulders and said that it was a "nonevent." In similar situations, new Organization Bankers and more seasoned Individual Bankers exhibited intense emotions, including worry, anxiety, and shame that they were not living up to an abstract image of their identities. Because of their intensity, these emotions degraded task performance. In contrast, the vice president did not focus on implications for his identity. He was not interested in how his performance was being perceived, but in locating the best set of resources for the task. This allowed him to see possibilities for action that were less apparent to bankers who took an identity-based perspective. In this case, he shifted the role of the client from an evaluator to a potential resource and he devised a plan to gather more information from the client team and have them collaborate in the production of the task solution. Instead of experiencing strong negative and disengaging emotions, then, this banker's reaction allowed him to draw in other resources.

The decline in self-sacrificing behaviors after six months at Organization Bank reflects Organization Bankers' shift away from identification with an abstract image of the self as an Organization Banker. Focusing on their own organizational identities led Individual Bankers and new Organization Bankers to sacrifice their own interests for the good of the collective with which they identified. They adopted the bank's interests as their own and then thought, felt, and acted with reference to an abstract conception of the bank and being an Individual Banker or an Organization Banker. More seasoned Organization Bankers also oriented toward the bank, but they saw the bank not as a set of abstract standards and identities but as a collection of resources for action. The Organization Bankers experienced unity not in terms of abstract concepts, but in concrete actions that involved coordination among subsets of the bank's resources. Bankers had no personal stake in using their own or others' resources, but instead selected resources based on the demands of the concrete task. The notion of self-sacrifice implies that the unity experienced as part of typical organizational identification is incomplete because the individual subtly continues to differentiate between the person and the organization, ready to sacrifice the former for the latter. In contrast, the Organization Bankers' perception of unity with the bank was more complete. Bankers contributed resources toward a pool and treated the personal resources that they contributed as fungible with other organizational resources. They did not make an ongoing distinction between what was the bankers' and what was the bank's. The bankers did not sacrifice the self because the larger system on behalf of which they acted, the resource pool, included the self. When Individual Bankers and new Organization Bankers identified with their bank, they experienced an identity that could be threatened, humiliated, or fed. As identities moved into the background of more seasoned Organization Bankers' experience, so did these self-conscious emotions.

The difference between the task-orientation practiced by seasoned Organization Bankers and the organizational identification experienced by newcomers and Individual Bankers also became clear when clients criticized the banks. We described above how senior Individual Bankers sometimes responded with indignation and agitation when a client asked about Individual Bank's commitment to a line of business. The Individual Banker quoted above interpreted this as a challenge to the bank's commitment, and by implication a challenge to him. In contrast, Organization Bankers were remarkably insensitive to harsh criticism of both the bankers and the bank. In one meeting a client CEO complained: "Looks like I got the B-team. Is our organization not big enough to merit more attention from Organization Bank?" Another CEO sneered about a young Organization Bank team: "There must be some kind of misunderstanding. This is not the interview for internships. This is about discussing the strategic direction of a major, multinational corporation." Another client claimed that Organization Bank had misjudged the seriousness of the client's situation ("My ass is on the line") and the competitive environment ("These banks send in their superstars") by sending inappropriately junior bankers ("What is this? The high school science project team? I have a granddaughter who is older than you are"). Instead of treating these comments as personal attacks, however, Organization Bankers interpreted them as legitimate concerns about the resources that would be available for the task. In response to the last criticism, the Organization Bank director answered:

> Think of it [the deal process] like one of these sausage machines. I think of myself as putting things into the machine. Once this machine is set in motion, it inexorably grinds toward the end. This means that when you hire [Organization Bank] there is no stopping. Your deal will get done, independently of what any one of us does or doesn't do.

In another case, responding to a similar challenge, an Organization Bank vice president answered: "We are just the arms and the legs of the organization. We access for you the resources of [Organization Bank]." He then started asking about the client's specific situation and explained how Organization Bank would allocate resources at each step in the process.

Individual Bankers became overwhelmed by negative emotions when they were criticized like this, and they often disengaged from the situation. In contrast, Organization Bankers interpreted the clients' criticisms as invitations to a problem-solving dialogue and they responded by engaging more deeply in the situation – searching for information about the specific task and providing strategies for deploying the bank's resources to accomplish this task. The Organization Bankers focused not on who they were but on what to do next, and thus distracting emotions did not occur. Other Organization Bankers characterized these reactions as involving "high task-orientation" because their colleagues had responded solely to what was "relevant to the task," working to "advance the deal" and to avoid getting "sidetracked."

The deductive and abductive styles that we have described, the first adopted by Individual Bankers and new Organization Bankers and the second by more seasoned Organization Bankers, are systems of interdependent psychological processes that orient toward the same reference point – either toward abstract identities or toward concrete situations. We have described how bankers' cognition proceeded deductively, from abstractions to situations, or abductively, from concrete cues to new understandings of situations. We have described how emotions either oriented bankers toward abstract identity traits or served as cues about concrete situations. And we have described how motivation came either from a desire to live up to abstract ideals or from engagement with concrete tasks. Now we give one more example of the contrast in motivation between the two types of bankers. We describe how money, in the form of yearly bonus payments, functioned differently for bankers with the two different orientations. In order to make the contrast clear, we also include data from Individual Bank in this discussion.

As Table 6.1 indicates, bankers at both banks earned most of their income as a performance-contingent bonus. Because the banks were direct competitors for personnel, they paid similar bonuses to bankers with analogous seniority and performance levels. The base salary was paid in monthly increments, while the bonus was paid as a lump sum at the end of the year. At both banks, each banker cohort was divided into four tiers with respect to relative performance. The difference in pay between the highest paid banker in a cohort and the lowest paid banker was substantial. Because many bankers were married and lived in an expensive

TABLE 6.1 *Banker compensation*

	Base salary	Discretionary bonus
First-year associates	$85,000	Lowest tier: $0 Second and third tier: $85,000 Top tier: $150,000
Second-year associates	$95,000	Lowest tier: $0 Second and third tier: $135,000 Top tier: $230,000

metropolitan area, they depended on the bonus. These bonus payments represented a challenging test for the Organization Bankers' task-orientation. The bankers' personal financial dependence on the bonus increased the likelihood that they would focus on their own individual situation in this context. There is also no clear "task" involved in reacting to one's annual bonus.

Bankers at the two banks nonetheless differed substantially in how they interpreted their annual bonuses. The Individual Bankers interpreted the size of their bonus as an indication of their traits. They believed that "money is the best measure of what you are worth" to the firm and that the size of a bonus was an important indicator of their identities as bankers. To discover the identity-related implications of their bonus, Individual Bankers furiously worked their telephones on bonus day, calling colleagues whom they considered comparable.

ASSOCIATE: David, Jim, and I have an agreement that we tell each other what we made. . . . I think that I am at least as good as they are and want to know how I am doing compared to them. It would just bug me to know that they are making more than I do.

RESEARCHER: But David is a year ahead of you. And Jim is in another department. Are these numbers comparable?

ASSOCIATE: Maybe not objectively. But that is not what matters to me. Haven't you ever been envious when the neighbor has a better house or a car? When you feel that way, do you think about all the mitigating factors? No. You just want to do as well as the person who is most salient to you, right?

RESEARCHER: But if they did make more, that would not necessarily be a statement about you. It might mean that the other departments have had a better year than yours. And the more senior you are the more you earn.

ASSOCIATE: I disagree. Money here is the ultimate statement of what they think of you. I don't care about titles or performance evaluations. All of this stuff is cheap. For all I care, my business card can say "asshole" as long as they pay me well.

As we would expect, the Individual Bankers' emotions and behaviors at bonus time were also oriented toward money's identity-relevant implications. When bankers thought that the bank did not appreciate their worth, they expressed identity-focused emotions such as shame ("It's embarrassing. I feel like I am publicly marked as a loser") and anger ("I am not stupid. They screwed me over this year, but I am not going to take it lying down"). These bankers also spent much of their time during the following weeks acting on behalf of their slighted identity – by, for example, trying to reinterpret the meaning of their bonus in conversations with colleagues ("There is so much noise in this process that it ends up being kind of random") or by soliciting external job offers that only a few bankers intended to pursue ("That's the only way they start to respect you. You've got to show them what you are worth on the market"). One banker described how all this bonus-related activity took a toll on work: "Bonuses really get the egos around here going. . . . During this time, all people really care about is who has the biggest dick. Work just has to wait until that is sorted out." Thus Individual Bankers' focus on the identity-related implications of their bonuses directed their energy toward abstractions and disengaged them from concrete tasks.

Traditional cognitive theories would predict this sort of behavior – including social-information processing theory (Salancik and Pfeffer, 1978), social-comparison theory (Festinger, 1954; Deutsch and Gerard, 1955), and theories of shared reality (e.g., Hardin and Higgins, 1996).

> When physical evidence is unavailable and judgment is uncertain, Festinger argued that people are motivated to communicate with others, and through this communication, develop stable, socially derived interpretations of events and their meanings. Festinger also suggested that people evaluate information sources in terms of personal relevance, using similar others for comparison: the more similar someone is, the more relevant his or her views for understanding one's own world. (Salancik and Pfeffer, 1978: 228)

Judgment about a bonus is uncertain because bonus numbers do not speak for themselves. They must be contextualized before one can draw conclusions. The Individual Bankers sought out contextual information relevant to their own identities, comparing themselves to a reference group of peers whose abstract identities they knew. As the cognitive theories would predict, Individual Bankers framed this comparison in terms of their own and others' personal "worth." Relative power and status were crucial in these judgments, as shown in the following comment: "Mike raked in two million this year. I guess that makes him a hitter now." Cognitive theories also argue that people experience the self as an "object among other objects" (Heise, 1979, 1989; Higgins, 1996; Piaget, 1967). Consistent with such a construal, Individual Bankers acted as if their selves had an objectified worth in relation to comparable kinds of people.

The bankers received their first bonus after about a year with the bank. We thus have no information on how new Organization Bankers responded to money during their first six months, which would have been a useful comparison. The data presented above show that new Organization Bankers had interests and behaviors similar to Individual Bankers. By the end of the first year, however, the Organization Bankers acted differently. On bonus day, a group of Organization Bankers, including some of the first-year associates, went to a nearby pub. Each banker wrote his or her bonus number on a piece of paper, with no name or other identifying information, and placed it into the same hat as colleagues from the same cohort. Under hollering, shouting, and joking comments, each cohort unfolded the papers and arranged them from lowest to highest bonus number.

Because the banks determined bonus numbers separately for each cohort, the Organization Bankers' chose a more objectively relevant comparison than the Individual Bankers. The Organization Bankers sought information not about the individual in relation to a personal competitor, but about each individual with respect to the whole compensation system. One banker described the purpose of this exercise: "By pooling our numbers and arranging them in this way [from lowest to highest], you are generating more information. You can get at statistical data about the whole cohort – standard deviations, frequency distributions." Because bonuses were partly contingent on the performance of the bank and the given department, this data also allowed inferences about these larger factors. As one banker said: "It gives you information not just about you and one or two other people. You can get more directly at how healthy the department and the rest of the organization are. It is one thing to get management updates about this. But in the end, money is always the best indicator." The Individual Bankers made no similar efforts to obtain information about the whole compensation pool.

This broader, systemic frame of reference, in contrast to the Individual Bankers' more narrow focus on self, influenced how the Organization

Bankers thought, felt, and acted about the bonuses. For example, when asked what his relatively low bonus number meant, one Organization Banker answered crisply: "That I need to pay more attention." Another banker with a low bonus number said: "It is information. It is a wake-up call." When these bankers were asked how they felt, the first one said: "Disappointed, that's for sure. But that's not really the point. The point is focusing on what to do." The other banker said: "I probably have all the kinds of emotions that one would expect: anger, shame, embarrassment, and self-reproach. I just keep telling myself that there are other things that are more important. What matters is to not get caught up in these emotions and to use this information as information and to keep moving." Thus Organization Bankers used bonus numbers mostly as information about courses of action, not as indications of their underlying identities. For this purpose, the data they gathered were more informative than the Individual Bankers' personalized comparisons.

The Organization Bankers also conducted their bonus comparison as a social event, as something that they collectively decided to do, not as something motivated by an individual's personal interest. The event had norms about what to do (writing down numbers, throwing them into a hat) and how to respond. Bitterness and emotional outbursts were clearly inappropriate, given the pub setting and the relaxed, lighthearted atmosphere of the conversation. The Organization Bankers, as a group, together accomplished a task that benefited everyone involved – bringing performance information out into the open so that they could draw inferences about themselves and the bank – without requiring anyone to divulge his or her own bonus. The group thus made creative use of the resources that were at hand.

The Individual Bankers compared bonuses in a much more individual-centered way. They construed their fellow bankers as a set of abstract social positions, and they wanted to locate themselves in comparison to others. The Individual Bankers narrowed their focus to their allies, with whom they exchanged information. These bankers used the comparative information to advance their own career goals without regard for the group's overall benefit. Even though the Individual Bankers defined themselves in terms of social positions, they acted on behalf of their own individual interests. They worked in the privacy of their offices, trying to reach selected others on the phone. This isolated setting reinforced the bankers' sense that they were enacting their own plans and tendencies. They thus enacted a trait-based identity and disregarded the larger system that influenced their bonuses.

These data on bonuses further illustrate how, after their first six months, Organization Bankers' cognition, emotion, and motivation focused less on their own trait-based identities and more on concrete tasks and situations. As a result, the Organization Bankers developed a more contextualized identity. Such identities had two main attributes. They were not organized around abstract traits that have cross-situational stability, but were instead evoked by concrete cues in context. And they were not perceived as causes of predictable behavior, but instead contributed resources to a larger system that generated outcomes.

The first attribute of such contextualized identities – the relative absence of abstract self-descriptive traits – became salient after about a year, at which point the Organization Bankers began to have trouble responding to self-descriptive questions. Following up on the bankers' initial focus on their identities, we regularly asked them to describe their identity attributes. At entry, both the Individual Bankers and the Organization Bankers answered these questions without delay and with much elaboration. During his first month with the bank, for example, one Organization Banker answered: "I would describe myself as a quant jock. I am great with numbers.... I also tend to be somewhat reserved." Another associate said: "I am your typical extrovert. I love being surrounded by people and I hate to be by myself, absolutely hate it." As described above, during their first few months the new bankers often spoke about identity-related issues with their peers and started conversations about their identity with the researcher, especially when they experienced strong emotions about a threat to their identities. After about a year, however, such conversations became less frequent and bankers found it difficult to answer self-descriptive questions. They sometimes stammered and took a relatively long time to answer such questions.

When the researcher persisted, bankers replied with such comments as "I guess I just don't think about these issues [my own attributes] a lot" and "I don't have the time to reflect on this [my traits]." One associate answered: "Hmmm, I think you asked me that question before. What did I say the last time?... You just don't have that much opportunity to think about these things [one's self] around here." A director helped explain these responses: "I know you are interested in identities. But you just have to accept that people here don't think in these terms.... People think of themselves in the context of the deal they are working on and what they have to do next." Similarly, an associate said: "This job glues your attention outside of yourself, to what you do. No one cares about who you are. It's just not practical information."

The last two quotations show how Organization Bank's work environment shifted bankers' attention away from an inner realm of abstract concepts, including identity traits, toward a practical realm of concrete, deal-relevant information. An Organization Bank trainer, who was skeptical about the bank's approach, explained the rationale behind the bank's work practices:

> No one here is interested in using personality profiles. We [the training department] have broached this with the bankers again and again. Many of our competitors use personality profiles for either hiring or promotion. Or you could just use them to generate some self-awareness in people, like [prominent consulting firm] does. They use the Myers-Briggs. But people here believe that if you tell someone that they have such a thing as a personality, they'd actually come to believe it. Seriously, the idea is that the more time you spend talking about personality traits, the more people start to behave that way and the less likely they are to just roll with the punches.

According to the Organization Bankers, a personality or a set of abstract identity traits is not something that people naturally exhibit. It *is* something that people exhibit when they are in a context that encourages them to think and talk about their traits. But a work context need not be organized this way. At Organization Bank, thinking and acting in terms of stable traits was undesirable because it prevented one from being responsive to the situation, from "rolling with the punches."

Organization Bank's practices deliberately counteracted the formation of a trait-based identity. The bank blocked categorizations of individuals' identities and thus interfered with their sense of themselves as having stable traits. In contrast to Individual Bank, Organization Bank did not tell bankers what it meant to be an effective or excellent banker. It also withheld information from which bankers could infer such descriptions, such as explicit role expectations. Because of these practices, after six months with the bank Organization Bankers reported that they were "not thinking much" about their identities, and this explains the relatively long response latencies when they were asked about their identities.

The bankers' infrequent attention to their identities yielded an unusual type of identity. Cognitive researchers who study identity call a person "schematic" on an attribute (such as independence) if the person has been repeatedly categorized by others, or has self-categorized, along that dimension. By frequently thinking about one's identity in terms of "independence," the person builds up abstract mental representations that summarize the various situations in which he or she has behaved like an "independent" person. In contrast, a person is said to be aschematic on "independence" if the person does not think much about dependence or independence (Markus, 1980). In this case, abstract mental representations of "independence" are less likely to form and the person will take a longer time to self-report on this attribute.

Our work at Organization Bank suggests that people might also be aschematic on their *identity as a whole*, not only on particular attributes. Organization Bank's task-oriented culture encouraged people to think less about who they were as people, not only less about certain personality attributes. Abstract mental representations of identity traits were thus less likely to form in the Organization Bank context, and existing representations of self from other contexts were less frequently activated and put into use. Organization Bankers became less likely to experience situations in terms of any identity traits. We do not claim that the Organization Bankers had no sense of identity. We merely suggest that this identity was situation-dependent and thus that it was difficult for them to form an abstract description of self that could be activated and applied across contexts.

We refer to this novel type of identity as a *contextualized identity* and we argue that it developed about a year after bankers came to the bank. When Organization Bankers did respond to questions about their identities after a year at the bank, they did not use abstract traits but instead placed attributes within the time and the place when they exhibited them: "Just yesterday, I was in a phone conversation and when the vice president pushed me on something, I got back way too aggressively." At about the same time, the bankers also described others in a more contextualized way, which suggests that bankers reconceptualized persons in general, and not only themselves. For example, one performance review written by a second-year associate read: "When Sally was overworked and when the time frame was rushed, she overlooked input from team members." In contrast, the following is a typical excerpt from a performance review at Individual Bank, in which the banker describes his colleague in context-free, trait-based terms: "John is highly intelligent. But he is also shy and does not have the personal presence expected of a banker at his level."

A contextualized self fits with an abductive cognitive style because it is tailored to the concrete situation. As compared to a trait-based self, someone who thinks in terms of a contextualized self is less likely to perceive behavioral stability and is more open to new insights about the self and others. One senior Organization Banker, who read versions of this manuscript, explained how a person can experience new insights about the self when he or she stops attending to traits:

> Just like people have preconceived notions about business situations, they have preconceived notions about who they are and what is possible for them. But this is largely a limitation we impose on ourselves and it usually holds us back from unfamiliar situations. Either because of some kind of aversion – some people think that selling something is just beneath them – or because of fear – they might think that they just don't have the resources to cope with a situation. But the fact is that if you throw yourself at each situation, you'll learn new things about yourself and about how flexible and resourceful we all are.

This banker argued that trait-based identities could prevent people from engaging in situations that would allow them to act in unexpected ways. In this way traits can become self-fulfilling prophesies, as they lead people to restrict their environments in ways that confirm and maintain their familiar identities – even at the expense of an enriched life. This banker recommends that people should engage in whatever situation they are presented with, knowing that the bank's resources are available for support, and he predicts that this will yield behavior one would not have expected. Identity, then, can also be abductive in the sense that identity need not be an abstract trait deductively applied to a situation, but instead can be a response potential that the person discovers from observing his or her behavior in new situations. The relevant agent in such a case is not the individual and his or her properties, but the situation that evokes sometimes-unexpected behaviors in the individual. As another senior Organization Banker said, "I think of this kind of self as almost like a chameleon. You are in a new situation and it just brings out different things in you."

As Organization Bankers moved beyond six months with the bank, then, they thought of themselves less in terms of abstract traits and more in terms of contextualized attributes. The bankers reminded themselves and others that bankers' own attributes were not important for understanding the kinds of outcomes the bankers could bring about. When junior bankers started to worry about their lack of expertise when working with a client, they reminded themselves that "this is not about me." When clients worried that they would receive inferior advice because Organization Bankers lacked experience, the bankers corrected this trait-based understanding of outcomes: "you are not hiring my expertise, but the resources of the organization." Their more contextualized identities help explain why Organization Bankers experienced less stress in situations that formerly had been extremely stressful. They no longer worried that success or failure depended on their own enduring attributes, and this freed them to find relevant resources to address the task at hand.

Organization Bank enacted a different account of how knowledge-based organizations accomplish their tasks. According to a trait-based, deductive account, success comes from good general principles and the expertise of individuals who possess relevant knowledge and apply it to a situation. This account fits well with traditional cognitive theory. In contrast, for Organization Bankers action was a more collective, emergent process in which individuals made contributions by drawing on various resources, not by applying principles deductively. This account, which is more compatible with sociocultural theories, holds that the entity that possesses the relevant knowledge is the whole system of resources and that individuals shape their contributions depending on the concrete task and the other resources available.

We have described how new Organization Bankers developed this alternative perspective in a paradoxical way. In their first six months, junior Organization Bankers took even more personal responsibility for outcomes and exhibited even more robust trait-based identities than their Individual Bank counterparts. Over time, however, Organization Bank's work practices – such as the fungible staffing of bankers and the absence of abstract guidelines – made this type of behavior unsustainable. Organization Bankers were forced to draw on other resources. One associate explained how these practices brought about a change in his perspective on action:

> Think about it this way. If you had no clue about finance, you have never even seen a number in your life, which incidentally is not too far from where I was when I came in as an English major, and you don't have any training, on-the-job or otherwise, and then you notice how you can produce these complicated high-finance transactions. Hmm. At that point it should dawn on you that your own capabilities are less critical than you initially thought.

The associates became conscious of their preexisting, individual-centered theory of action because they vigorously enacted it in a context where this theory did not apply. One associate complained during her first six months: "I don't understand how I am supposed to do all of this without any training and without any experience in finance." Another associate said: "On the one hand, this is one of the most successful firms in the industry but, on the other hand, they don't even seem to have the basics of banker training right." The bank's practices forced newcomers to confront their beliefs about how knowledge outcomes ought to be generated – namely, by knowledgeable individuals – and to recognize that these beliefs could not account for the successes they saw around them at Organization Bank. Over time, the bankers came to embrace the bank's alternative account and concluded that their individual-centered theory did not apply in the Organization Bank context.

SUMMARY

This chapter has described the transformation from individual-centered to sociocentric selves that Organization Bankers experienced over their first year at the bank. Traditional accounts of socialization describe how people build up concepts relevant to a new situation. In contrast, our description of Organization Bank highlights the importance of *suspending* one's habitual concepts. Instead of internalizing the bank's concepts, Organization Bankers learned to rely less on preexisting concepts and attended more to concrete situations. At Individual Bank, which worked hard to reduce uncertainty and match bankers with more familiar situations, it made sense for bankers to build up a repertoire of concepts. At Organization Bank, however, the bank deliberately created persistent uncertainty, even for experienced bankers. In this context, junior bankers learned to create more concrete, situation-specific solutions by assembling heterogeneous resources.

We refer to the psychological and relational pattern that the Organization Bankers exhibited as direct involvement. This construct captures the psychological processes that allowed more seasoned Organization Bankers to behave as they did. Identity, cognition, emotion, and motivation worked together, as we have described, all focused on situation-specific, task-related concerns. The Organization Bankers' notion of task-orientation, which was the basis for our concept of direct involvement, captures the most important change: after six months Organization Bankers reoriented their attention from identity-related to task-related concerns. This change in attention involved what we have called a sociocentric self-interpretation – in which the bankers attended to a broader set of resources for action – and what we have called sociocentric cognition, emotion, and motivation – the focusing of psychological processes on concrete tasks.

Sociocentric self-interpretation involves a distinct conception of how a person relates to social context. Organization Bankers with this self-interpretation no longer thought much about their abstract identity traits, and they attributed outcomes to a system – a system to which the person contributes resources, but which also includes many other resources. They also no longer thought of themselves as separate from the context, but instead exhibited a more contextualized identity in which their relevant attributes were evoked by a particular situation.

When cognition, emotion, and motivation operate in a more sociocentric manner, these psychological processes work together with social resources to generate outcomes. Experienced Organization Bankers changed from a deductive cognitive style to an abductive cognitive style. They moved away from understanding people in terms of abstract traits and situations in terms of general guidelines, and they attended more to situational cues. They no longer focused on the mental faculties and individual interests of a person, but attended instead to more situated processes and the interests of the larger organization. As they focused on situational cues and social resources, the bankers came to believe that successful action resulted from a social system that included, but was not limited to, the bankers' resources. Because of this change in attitude, the bankers allowed social resources such as objects and task structures to participate more actively in the knowledge-generation process. Like other people, objects and task-structures could offer cues on what next steps might be taken. Organization Bankers noticed the contributions that resources could make because they stopped being preoccupied with abstract identity traits.

Organization Bank was able to reorient new bankers in this way – away from identity and toward tasks – by making identity traits implausible and irrelevant. They became implausible as explanations for success because bankers could accomplish many tasks despite their painfully obvious lack of personal knowledge. They became irrelevant because the outcomes that a banker valued did not depend on the banker's identity traits, but instead on social resources. As bankers came to understand that they should monitor social resources instead of attending to abstract scripts and identities, identity concerns moved into the background and they were able to participate more seamlessly in the higher-capacity organizational system.

7

An Alternative Approach to Organizational and Psychological Transformation

Table 7.1 provides an overview of the central findings of this study, summarizing the empirical patterns and central concepts developed in the preceding chapters. This chapter first reviews these findings, drawing together our central claims about Individual Bank and Organization Bank. It then describes the central contributions of the book – the counterintuitive but productive strategy of *uncertainty amplification*, the benefits of *persistent uncertainty*, the unusual cognitive and developmental approach of *clearing away the self*, and our treatment of psychological *theories as practices* in the world. Throughout our discussions of these topics, we offer advice to practitioners who are working to manage uncertainty in their organizations.

The two banks had different business models that required them to manage bankers' cognitive uncertainty differently. Individual Bank sold the idiosyncratic expertise of its individual superstars. Because high uncertainty overwhelms the cognitive resources of an individual and can impede decision making, the bank had to reduce cognitive uncertainty. New Individual Bankers thus experienced cognitive uncertainty as transient, with significant uncertainty over their first months declining to manageable levels by the end of their first year. An integrated system of carefully articulated role expectations, matching training trajectories, supportive mentoring and feedback, and banker assignment to familiar projects ensured that bankers could solve problems in the independent manner demanded by the bank's superstar culture. This system further reinforced the bankers' orientation toward abstractions, a tendency that they brought with them from prior experience in schools and other workplaces. Individual Bank provided its bankers with abstract concepts – strategies, role definitions, concepts to represent types of client situations, models of possible client solutions – that they could apply across different decision making situations.

TABLE 7.1 *Overview of findings*

Topic (chapters)	Individual Bank	Organization Bank
Work practices (2 **and** 3)	**Uncertainty reduction** (common) Orientation toward abstractions	**Uncertainty amplification** (counterintuitive) Orientation toward concrete
Bankers' cognitive uncertainty duration (5 **and** 6)	**Transient uncertainty** (high at bankers' entry, decreases subsequently) Experience allows bankers to use abstract concepts in new situations, including identity concepts, and to rely on their personal resources.	**Persistent uncertainty** (ongoing throughout bankers' tenure) Bankers' abstract concepts are not applicable, including identity concepts. Bankers are forced to rely on resources of organizational system.
Involvement (5 **and** 6)	**Identity-induced involvement** (enacts traditional cognitive theory) **Individual-centered self-interpretation** (dualistic): Being a person means (1) having an abstract, trait-based identity that (2) causes action (the person is the relevant agent) and is (3) separate from context. **Individual-centered cognition, emotion, and motivation** (dualistic): Cognition, emotion, and motivation are regulated by the abstract trait-based identity (deductive style). Knowing means a person mentally represents context with abstract concepts (focus on person). Objects are passive.	**Direct involvement** (enacts sociocultural theory) **Sociocentric self-interpretation** (nondualistic): Being a person means (1) clearing away abstract identity categories and (2) participating in a social system that causes action. Identity is (3) contextualized – defined by evolving goals of specific activity. **Sociocentric cognition, emotion, and motivation** (nondualistic): Cognition, emotion, and motivation are regulated more directly by the concrete cues in situations (abductive style). Knowing is an attribute of a system. Objects actively contribute.

Organization Bank, in contrast, sold the resources of the organization. Organization Bankers were asked to bring the best resources available to each client situation. This business model required bankers to be alert to the unique aspects of new situations so that they could identify suitable resources. Past experience had taught the bank that such alertness and use of organizational resources was difficult to accomplish and sustain. As soon as individuals feel familiar with situations they tend to rely on their own resources, especially on preconceived notions of what a situation involves. To make bankers aware of situational uniqueness and to make them more prone to bring together creative configurations of resources, Organization Bank amplified cognitive uncertainty. Both new and experienced Organization Bankers thus experienced persistent cognitive uncertainty throughout their time at the bank. Organization Bank used the same work practices as Individual Bank to influence banker cognition, but it arranged these practices in a different way. To reduce the cognitive load on its bankers, Individual Bank limited the information that bankers had to process, gave clear and detailed guidelines, and made sure that information was internally consistent. Organization Bank, in contrast, sought to counteract the bankers' feelings of familiarity and comfort by constantly exposing them to unfamiliar situations and to a surfeit of frequently contradictory information while also withholding abstract guidelines.

INVOLVEMENT

When bankers worked within these different uncertainty-management practices over months and years they became different kinds of people. We conceptualize the bankers' development as changes in how a person's psychological resources – self, cognition, emotion, and motivation – work together with the resources in a situation, including other people and artifacts, to generate cognitive accomplishments. Individual Bank's practices encouraged bankers to rely on their own psychological resources. The bankers' self, cognition, emotion, and motivation formed one system such that changes in one resource encouraged a change in the others, forming a pattern that we have called identity-induced involvement. Organization Bank's practices encouraged bankers to rely on their own resources together with resources provided by social and material aspects of the situation. In this case the relevant system was larger, including the banker's self, cognition, emotion, and motivation, together with others' psychological resources and artifacts available in the setting. We call this pattern direct involvement.

Self-interpretation

A person's self-interpretation is often the central element in such a system, shaping how it functions. A self-interpretation is not merely a person's self-concept – which answers the question "who am I?" – but also a more fundamental, often tacit sense of what it means to be a person and how a person relates to social context. When the new bankers began their jobs, they all exhibited the same self-interpretation, namely, a trait-based identity. They believed that there was a set of abstract identity traits (e.g., "I am smart," "I am an Individual Banker") that defined one's self and that explained why the person behaves in a particular way. For example, bankers believed that making a mistake could be explained by a relatively enduring, underlying attribute (e.g., "being stupid"). New bankers at both banks also believed that a person's own resources, such as expertise, were most important for accomplishing tasks.

During their first six months, new Individual Bankers' self-concepts changed primarily in their content. They refined their identity traits by adding organizational concepts provided by the bank. They learned, for example, about the bank's standards and what behaviors counted as being "smart" there. The bank articulated such standards and behavioral expectations clearly. New Individual Bankers added to their self-concepts or replaced prior contents with new ones more appropriate to the bank, internalizing traits and expectations. They did not, however, change the basic organization of their self-interpretation. They still conceived of themselves as a set of relatively context-independent traits, even though they changed some of the specific traits to fit their new context. This form of self-interpretation is dualistic because it separates the person from the world by conceiving of the person as a bundle of enduring attributes that do not depend in any significant way on the situation.

In contrast, after their first six months Organization Bankers experienced a more profound change in their self-interpretation. The bank deliberately foiled their persistent and increasingly desperate attempts to formulate identity traits that matched their new work context. Because the new bankers' existing identity traits were not relevant in the new context, and because the bank did not offer a more relevant set of traits, after about six months new Organization Bankers engaged their abstract self-concept less frequently. When concepts are activated less frequently they become less accessible to the person. As a result, bankers experienced situations less frequently in terms of their abstract identities. Identity concepts, which had previously organized the bankers' experience, were "cleared away."

Organization Bank's uncertainty-amplification approach also consistently placed bankers in situations that required them to draw on the bank's resources to accomplish their tasks. Organization Bankers consequently experienced themselves less as agents who accomplished tasks based primarily on their personal resources, and more as participants in a broader social system. Over time this created a more relational and contextualized self-interpretation for the new bankers, one in which they defined themselves based on the resources that they could bring to a situation (e.g., "I am here to understand how to connect you with our collective expertise on healthcare"). They consequently worried less about who they were as socially recognizable persons, as individuals identified with respect to their own resources, and more about what they could do with the help of a larger set of resources. This less common type of self-interpretation at Organization Bank was nondualistic because it did not separate the person and the situation. Who the banker was depended less on context-independent traits and more on what he or she could bring to the particular situation.

Cognition, Emotion, and Motivation

When the two sets of new bankers enacted, these two different kinds of self-interpretations, their cognition, emotion, and motivation also changed in systematic ways. For the Individual Bankers, abstract identity traits served as the primary referents for psychological processes. Bankers cognitively framed situations using identity concepts, including goals, wishes, scripts, and behavioral expectations. Emotions registered the discrepancy between an actual situation and identity aspirations. For example, bankers felt pride when they performed more successfully than was expected of them, given their role. More frequently, however, discrepancies were negative. Bankers often felt that they were not as good as they would like to be or as they thought they ought to be. These negative discrepancies occurred when clients made requests that the bankers could not respond to independently, when a colleague performed better, or when clients challenged the bankers' claims to competence. In such situations, the bankers oriented away from the concrete tasks at hand and focused on protecting or asserting their threatened identities. We refer to this pattern as identity-induced involvement because the bankers experienced situations as mediated through their abstract identities. Emotion, cognition, and motivation all oriented to the banker's identity first, before engaging the situation, and only engaged the situation in terms shaped by the banker's relatively context-independent traits, roles, scripts, and concepts.

Identity-induced involvement uses a deductive style for engaging situations. We call this a "style" because we do not claim that Individual Bankers inevitably took a deductive approach, nor that they could not engage more directly with situations. A style is a preferred way of engaging with situations. A deductive style means that a person mentally represents situations and individuals, including his or her own identity, in terms of abstract concepts that the person supplies to a situation. These abstract concepts then guide the person's thinking, feelings, goals, and behaviors. Other terms for such a deductive style are *schema-driven* or *top-down*. Because Individual Bankers approached situations with the self-concept of being an expert, for example, they generally developed solutions before talking in detail with the client and they often neglected to ask questions about the specifics of the problem. They were also sensitive to whether or not clients accepted their claims to expertise. Because of these emotional sensitivities, Individual Bankers were more likely to interpret the clients' questions as challenges to their expertise, they often responded with strong negative emotions such as anger, and they sometimes attacked or ignored the client.

The Organization Bankers also exhibited identity-induced involvement when they began working at the bank. However, after about six months, they tended to adopt the nondualistic direct involvement pattern. They rarely experienced their identities in terms of abstract traits, and situational cues became the primary touchstone for their psychological processes. We refer to this pattern as direct involvement because the mediating influence of abstract, trait-based identities was cleared away and bankers responded more directly to what was needed in a particular situation. Organization Bankers did not, for example, inevitably approach client situations with an expert identity. Individuals stepped forward as experts if they had knowledge on a particular question, but they also withdrew into the background when someone else was more qualified. Even Organization Bank directors deferred to analysts when the analysts had done research on a particular issue.

As the new Organization Bankers' abstract identities loosened their grip over other psychological processes, the bankers' cognition, emotion, and motivation came to reflect situational cues. With identity traits less salient, Organization Bankers were able to use concrete concepts that emerged from a particular situation. For example, because merger bankers did not approach situations as merger experts, they did not frame client problems in terms of the generic concepts that an abstract identity would compel, such as "this is a sell-side merger assignment." As they interacted with the client, better ways of framing the specific situation often emerged. What initially looked like a merger deal sometimes turned out to have important corporate finance components, and the Organization Bankers were able to imagine alternative strategies much more easily than were their counterparts at Individual Bank.

Organization Bankers' emotions registered the relative progress that they made toward situational goals, not the implications of a situation for their own identities. Organization Bankers were thus less focused on how clients perceived them as persons. They even responded to harsh criticisms in task-oriented ways, without showing any of the anger that Individual Bankers exhibited in similar situations. Strong emotions occurred when situations were moving better or in more interesting ways than expected ("what a thrill!") or when something blocked task progress ("I am so frustrated about these political processes"). These differences in the target of banker emotions between Individual Bank and Organization Bank – as the emotions focused either on things about the self or on things about the situation – propelled bankers toward different types of behaviors. Instead of trying to fix their identities, the emotional Organization Bankers focused with renewed vigor on the task. This meant that cognition, emotion, and motivation were resources that the bankers marshaled on behalf of the task, not on behalf of an abstract self-concept.

In identity-induced involvement, bankers experienced emotions that were typical for the individual no matter what the situation. For example, one Individual Bank associate said about a director: "He is just the uptight type. It doesn't matter what the situation is, he always sees reasons for being anxious or panicked." In contrast, more experienced Organization Bankers often were surprised by their own emotions. Bankers who in the past had behaved in meek ways might find themselves being assertive in order to move a task ahead, and they were sometimes surprised at themselves. The situation-specific nature of Organization Bankers' emotions meant that they experienced a broader range of emotions, including emotions that were unfamiliar. The relative lack of familiarity with their own emotional and behavioral responses further reinforced the bankers' contextualized identities. Bankers recognized that being a person does not necessarily involve a characteristic way of thinking, feeling, and acting because new situations can bring out new ways of acting and being.

The Organization Bankers' direct involvement was characterized by an abductive style. Who a person was and what a person thought, wanted, felt, and said were all shaped by the specific aspects of particular situations. This differed from the deductive style of identity-induced involvement in which these aspects were shaped by a person's abstract identity and supplied to various situations. It also differs from the inductive style, which both sets of bankers exhibited at entry, in which they tried to infer the concepts and traits that would be appropriate in their new settings. The goal of induction is to formulate a more general understanding that one can use across different situations. The goal of abduction, in contrast, is to figure out whom else to involve and what to do next in this situation. Abstract representations were neither the starting point nor the goal for Organization Bankers. They aimed to collect appropriate resources for each specific situation, not to supply or induce decontextualized principles. The notion of an abductive style captures two important aspects of the Organization Bank data: the orientation to the concrete encouraged by the bank's uncertainty-amplification practices and the supra-individual nature of cognitive processes in which the person's resources are supplemented with situational resources.

In both identity-induced and direct involvement, as we have described them, self-interpretations influence cognition, emotion, and motivation. The influence does not go only one way, however. Either type of involvement includes a system of processes that are reciprocally related. Identity-induced involvement orients the person toward abstractions and individual resources and favors a deductive style. The person starts with his or her own concepts and molds the situation accordingly. This means that the person consistently uses his or her own ideas, which reinforces a dualistic self-interpretation as being an entity that is separate from surrounding context. Because psychological processes are consequently directed inward, toward the person's ideas and goals, they function as the intramental faculties of a person and serve the person's interests. Direct involvement orients the person toward concrete, social resources and favors an abductive style. The person starts with concrete, social resources that exist outside of the individual and behaves as if knowledge is the property of a system, even when the individual is working alone. Because psychological processes are consequently directed outward, toward the concrete aspects of specific situations, they function in more relational ways, serving the interests of the system that includes but is not limited to the person.

The two different types of involvement create a different relation between psychological and social resources. The psychological processes of both Individual and Organization Bankers connected in different ways with social resources, and this constrained how social resources could contribute to solving problems. In identity-induced involvement, bankers used objects, such as pitch books, to transmit their own expert knowledge to another person. In meetings, Individual Bankers often went through a book page by page. The clients typically asked clarification questions and then left the meeting to make their decision about whether to retain the bank. In this arrangement, people were the main decision makers and they acted relatively independently. One person, such as the banker, merely gave input into the thought processes of another person, the client. The book was a passive container that represented the banker's thoughts. In direct involvement, on the other hand, social resources played a more active role in cognitive processes. Organization Bankers sometimes came to meetings with only a spreadsheet, which became the focus of a joint problem-solving discussion between banker and client. The spreadsheet participated in the cognitive accomplishments, making essential contributions that would not have been possible without such a tool. The evolving structure of the spreadsheet, as the banker entered new assumptions that emerged in the discussion, provided new perspectives on the situation and prompted next steps, interacting seamlessly with the participants' psychological resources.

Our concept of involvement captures the interrelations among self, psychological processes, and social resources. Our descriptions of two distinct types of involvement show that cognition can operate differently depending on how organizations such as investment banks orient psychological processes. When a person's psychological processes orient toward abstractions, as at Individual Bank, social and psychological processes enact the assumptions and principles of traditional cognitive theory –the person is seen as the primary actor and the context as a relatively independent set of inputs and outputs. When a person's psychological processes orient toward the concrete, as at Organization Bank, social and psychological processes enact the assumptions and principles of sociocultural theory – knowledge is a property of a social system that includes but is not limited to the individual.

CENTRAL INSIGHTS

We are arguing, then, that human cognitive processes are relatively plastic. Basic psychological processes can function differently when people engage in differently organized activities, and even similar organizations located in the same society and the same industry culture can sometimes push people toward distinct modes of psychological functioning. Organizations such as investment banks are important settings for studying psychological processes because people spend much of their time at work and because these settings can be organized in very different ways. Such organizations are also interesting because they are under competitive pressures to change their work practices more quickly than are many other collectives. As they institutionalize new ways of organizing psychological processes, organizations sometimes create new modes of psychological functioning. The Organization Bank data show how a new way of working catalyzed a distinct psychological form.

Our account of Individual Bank and Organization Bank has implications for both practitioners and scholars. The rest of this chapter explains four of our investigation's central ideas – uncertainty amplification, persistent uncertainty, clearing away the self, and theories as practices – and articulates their often counterintuitive practical and theoretical implications. We first discuss how uncertainty amplification challenges deeply engrained notions about decision making and offers an effective alternative. We also describe the limitations of such an approach. The second subsection shows how the persistent uncertainty caused by uncertainty amplification differed from the more transient uncertainty described in both academic and commonsense accounts of uncertainty. Prior work has assumed that transient uncertainty is necessary for learning to occur. We argue that persistent uncertainty can also catalyze beneficial learning in which people do not *accumulate* general concepts, as existing work assumes, but *suspend* the automatic activation of such general concepts.

Persistent uncertainty catalyzed a novel type of psychological transformation among Organization Bankers – what we call "clearing away the self" – and the third subsection explores this in more detail. Existing theories conceptualize learning as what Packer (2001) calls the "social production of persons," a process through which newcomers acquire subject positions, skills, dispositions, and concepts that make them socially recognizable people. Our description of clearing away the self shows how organizations can also "unproduce" persons, making them less likely to behave in socially recognizable ways. We discuss the dynamics of this process, reasons why it was uncomfortable for the participants, and ways that it could be made less painful.

Our accounts of Individual Bank and Organization Bank allow us to reframe the debate between the predominant theories of cognition – traditional cognitive theory and sociocultural theory. The last section of this chapter describes how we treat these theories as practices. The two theories live in the world as both explicit and tacit beliefs about how people function. We argue that each theory has limited scope – accurately describing one organizational context but not the other – and we explore how the theories do work for the organizations that enact them. We suggest that the theories should be evaluated using a less common criterion: not just for their scientific accuracy but also for their practical and moral consequences, including the transformative potential they offer the people who adopt them.

Uncertainty is one of the fundamental problems that organizations and their top managers face (Thompson, 1967). It is also of critical concern to other collectives, including the military (Wong, 2004), schools (Wortham, 1994), and a broad set of other socializing institutions (Levy, 2001). In the twenty-first century, uncertainty has reached an extreme level (Whetten and Cameron, 2005). These extreme conditions are likely to make uncertainty management an even higher priority for practitioners and a topic of increased interest to scholars. Our research presents an alternative to existing models of uncertainty reduction, and we offer managers a broader range of choices as they prepare their organizations and their employees for uncertainty. Our work also contributes to psychological and organizational research, which traditionally has focused on uncertainty reduction and not considered uncertainty amplification.

We challenge the assumption that organizations can manage uncertainty only by reducing it. This untested assumption is deeply embedded in both practical and academic work on organizational and psychological processes, including both cognitive and sociocutural approaches, as well as commonsense assumptions about how good decision making works. Our account of uncertainty amplification suggests several counterintuitive conclusions. We argue that the uncertainty-reduction practices commonly used to enhance decision making can in fact impede employees' thinking. Despite both academic and everyday assumptions that would lead one to see uncertainty amplification as a route to impaired individual decision making, we have shown that Organization Bank's uncertainty amplification in fact helped bankers think. In a professional service firm, which supposedly sells the expertise of its individuals, it can be better for a person not to know something than to know something too well.

When one hears about chaos in organizations, one might imagine a breakdown of the fundamental elements of the organization. One envisions task-related communications disrupted, employees distracted and trying to make sense of what they do not understand, and factions mired in conflict trying to shape ambiguous situations to their own advantage. Communication and coordination, one could argue, only proceed in a productive way when they are designed purposefully and executed according to plan. In contrast, the chaos at Organization Bank both strengthened communication and helped coordinate problem solving. Precisely because there was a dearth of formal plans – few strategies, role expectations, and purposeful training, and no matching of experts to tasks – bankers did not have the tools to do their jobs and were forced to collaborate with one another.

Similarly, when one observes organizational "strategies," one cannot necessarily conclude that they result from purposeful planning by top management. At Organization Bank, strategies happened when lower-level bankers coped with chaos. Strategy in this context, such as the bank's healthcare industry focus, often emerged when cognitively uncertain bankers consulted peers and compared lower-level information (e.g., "my healthcare client complained that I know too little about his industry") and discovered commonalities ("my healthcare client said the same thing"). As bankers noticed and seized such opportunity clusters, patterns became visible retrospectively – not prospectively, as is the case with traditional strategies.

Professional service organizations initially emerged to deal with situations that were too complex for traditional mechanistic organizations to handle. One cannot produce investment banking or legal advice with the same invariant procedures that one uses to produce a car. Professional service client situations have unique elements that seem to require the judgment of an individual expert. Our account draws attention to a paradox, however. The more of an expert one becomes, the less likely one is to notice the uniqueness of situations. Individual experts are prone to acting just as mechanistically as are traditional organizations, relying on relatively invariant scripts and procedures. The Organization Bank data show that uncertain environments require more reliance on organizations. Organizations have the resources and internal complexity to match and manage environmental complexity, even when this complexity overwhelms the resources of an individual mind. The type of organization that is required is, however, not a traditional mechanistic one. Organization Bank coped efficiently with external complexity not through planned procedures, nor by using the judgment of individual experts, but instead through the ad-hoc coordination of individuals each of whom lacked relevant expertise.

Organization Bank is still relatively unique. But a wide variety of other organizations have also begun to use uncertainty amplification. The question remains: can other types of collectives use uncertainty amplification with the same kinds of positive effects that Organization Bank achieved? A diverse set of organizations have in fact successfully implemented processes comparable to Organization Bank's, and many of these have also created a similar kind of adaptability in their participants.

Sutton and Hargadon (1996) describe how the innovative product design firm IDEO amplified the uncertainty of its designers – who were already struggling with the complexity of their work – by asking them to design products with which they did not have prior experience. Like Organization Bank, IDEO used this staffing process so that designers would look at a product from a fresh perspective, draw on colleagues, and design unexpected solutions. Similarly, Wong (2004) documents how the U.S. military tried in vain to create adaptive officers by teaching the deductive application of plans – a typical uncertainty reduction approach. In Iraq, however, situations "outpaced army doctrine" (Wong, 2004: 15) and, like the Organization Bankers, officers experienced persistent uncertainty as they were forced to fill diverse and unfamiliar roles. When the military saw that this yielded more adaptable officers, it changed its combat training intentionally to amplify soldiers' cognitive uncertainty and cultivate an inductive "situational awareness on the move" (Wong, 2004: 1) that resembled the Organization Bankers' abductive cognitive style. Schools are typically designed to reduce uncertainty by asking teachers to teach what they know and students to learn what they need to pass the test. A few contemporary approaches to schooling, however, have begun to practice uncertainty amplification. Haroutunian-Gordon (1991, in press) and Wortham (1994, 2006), for example, describe classroom conversations in which the teacher does not offer definite answers and in which students explore "essentially contestable questions" that continue to have more than one plausible answer. By maintaining both teachers' and students' uncertainty, such conversations can enrich students' understanding of subject matter and lead them to explore new ideas.

Together, these studies suggest that uncertainty amplification might be a viable strategy for other organizations. It should be noted, however, that most of these organizations are all-consuming. Like the investment bankers, the IDEO designers and the military officers worked unusually long hours, and this limited the counterbalancing influence of nonwork practices. Similar isolating practices are adopted by "total organizations" (Etzioni, 1975), "total institutions" (Goffman, 1961), and "greedy organizations" (Coser, 1967) and are known to render members unusually susceptible to organizational influence. Other types of organizations consequently need to be studied to establish the boundaries of the principles developed here.

Practitioners who are interested in adopting uncertainty amplification probably will not succeed if they simply emulate one specific practice – for example, fungible staffing or limited training. Uncertainty reduction and uncertainty amplification involve systems of interdependent practices. One thus cannot follow the standard approach of adopting discrete "best practices." Even practices that might seem universally valid can have unintended negative consequences when used within a contradictory approach. For example, organizations with a superstar culture such as that of Individual Bank would be ill advised to implement the more ad hoc conversations characteristic of Organization Bank, despite what management gurus have claimed (e.g., Waterman, 1990; Mandel, 2005). By seamlessly interacting with others on an ad hoc basis, Organization Bankers implicitly enact a more contextualized identity. If bankers at a place like Individual Bank adopted this practice, they might stop thinking of themselves as experts and expecting to have all the answers. As a result, they might be less motivated to invest the effort required to be a superstar and they probably would fail to meet the expectations of clients who were expecting to be serviced by a superstar. Facilitating such ad hoc conversations can also be expensive because it requires bankers' time. Organization Bank could afford this because it could recoup the cost in other ways – by, for example, staffing more junior, less expensive bankers on deals, an option that a superstar-dominated bank does not have.

We have observed that firms sometimes aspire to Organization Bank's collaborative approach while their employees remain hampered by work practices that resemble Individual Bank's – for example, well-defined managerial territories that incite political infighting and "not-invented-here" mindsets. As one McKinsey consultant observed: "Professionals are still managed as if they were in factories, in organizations designed to keep everybody siloed" (Mandel, 2005: 62). Davenport, as cited in Mandel (2005: 62) summarizes the predicament: "We've added a new set of [collaborative] standards without fully dropping the old [individual-centered ones]." In order to be successful, each approach relies on a set of mutually reinforcing practices. It requires attention to how the entire organization is structured, not the adoption of one or two discrete practices.

Similarly, not all types of chaos qualify as the artful uncertainty amplification we observed at Organization Bank. In many organizations, such as start-up companies, participants experience persistent uncertainty because the organization is resource-constrained and they do not know where to turn for answers. This is fundamentally different from the situation at Organization Bank, which had an extensive set of resources that newcomers could draw on. Because of the many complex deals it had done, the bank had deep collective knowledge in the form of bankers' knowledge, connections to players in the market, and deal templates. It may well be that Organization Bank's approach could only work in such a resource-rich setting.

PERSISTENT UNCERTAINTY: AN ALTERNATIVE DEVELOPMENTAL TRAJECTORY

Most existing research, as well as common sense, considers persistent uncertainty to be bad for individuals and organizations. According to the organizational socialization literature, uncertainty implies that an individual has not learned the content that the organization wants him or her to learn and that the goals of socialization have not been accomplished (e.g., Chao et al., 1994). The cognitive developmental literature assumes that people learn and develop to the extent that uncertainty is resolved so that they can apply new concepts and skills to similar situations in the future (e.g., Acredolo and O'Connor, 1991; Piaget, 1985). Our research questions these assumptions. We believe that researchers currently hold these views because persistent uncertainty has not been studied empirically. As a result, scholars misunderstand what persistent uncertainty is and how it works. We contribute to a more complete understanding by distinguishing persistent uncertainty from the more familiar notion of transient uncertainty. This allows us to recognize the positive influence that persistent uncertainty can have on human development.

Despite uncertainty's important influence on human development, work across various traditions has "very little knowledge of [cognitive uncertainty's] true prevalence [and] duration" (Acredolo and O'Connor, 1991: 208). Instead, researchers simply assume that people experience uncertainty only as transient. For example, the literature on legitimate peripheral participation assumes that, as newcomers' status changes from peripheral to central, newcomers become more certain of their knowledge (Lave and Wenger, 1991). This assumption did not hold at Organization Bank, where even senior bankers experienced uncertainty. As one Organization Bank director said, "You learn from experience that even things that you take for granted can change dramatically so, if anything, you constantly become more unsure of what you know and watch more parameters with suspicion."

The common though untested assumption that uncertainty is always transient also fails to address the many descriptions in the popular business press of employees who claim to experience persistent uncertainty. Recent commentaries suggest that persistent uncertainty has attained the status of a new *Zeitgeist* (Walker, 2003) – heralded, for example, by such advertising slogans as Apple Computer's "uncertainty is the new certainty." Persistent uncertainty has also been documented, though not well conceptualized, in other ethnographic work. For example, "'If one thing is constant, it is change' is an often heard and apparently respected cliché," writes Kunda (1992: 30), quoting his informants, who also describe the high-tech company they work for as "vague, decentralized, chaotic, ambiguous, a controlled anarchy."

Such reports do not contradict academic accounts of uncertainty once we distinguish between transient and persistent uncertainty. Uncertainty has different durations depending on the social setting. Transient uncertainty occurs often, and it is often followed by productive, stable conceptualizations and patterns of behavior. In such circumstances, extending the uncertainty would be counterproductive because that would block the useful resolution of uncertainty and the subsequent development of stable concepts and strategies. But more persistent uncertainty also occurs, and the Organization Bank case shows how it, too, can be productive. We argue that persistent uncertainty is not just an extended version of transient uncertainty. It has different antecedents in the form of the distinct social practices that we described at Organization Bank. It also has a different object and results in novel types of learning. Our account shows how human development can take different forms in different organizational contexts, with transient uncertainty sometimes giving way to stable concepts – in contexts such as Individual Bank – and with persistent uncertainty sometimes fostering a completely different approach to cognition, one that does not apply stable concepts to a class of situations but instead opens the person to the specifics of a situation.

Accounts of transient uncertainty typically focus on a specific concept or skill, describing, for example, how people experience uncertainty when they encounter new or contradictory information. Persistent uncertainty, however, does not focus on specific concepts or contradictions. It involves a more fundamental attitude toward individuals' limitations and their inability to predict the environment. This more general attitude comes from being consistently in situations, such as those deliberately fostered at Organization Bank, in which one's existing concepts and skills are insufficient. People experiencing these two different types of uncertainty act in contrasting ways and learn distinct kinds of things. When people experience transient uncertainty about a particular concept or domain, they work to learn a more suitable concept that can henceforward be applied to similar situations. Existing work in cognitive and organizational psychology takes this scenario as a universal prototype of all uncertatinty, however, and assumes that becoming an expert involves *acquiring and storing* more or better information (e.g., Ericsson and Lehman, 1996; Simon, 1991).

But when people experience uncertainty as a more general, persistent inability to understand the environment, it does not make sense to learn different concepts for future application. To the contrary, Organization Bankers came to distrust both existing concepts and the resources of an individual mind. They learned, instead, to *suspend* their existing concepts and draw on a diverse set of resources tailored to particular situations, including but not limited to their own concepts. Our examination thus validates the assumption, made in almost all cognitive and organizational research, that persistent uncertainty can disrupt the accumulation of concepts. But we argue that such disruption does not necessarily imply a failure to develop. Instead, persistent uncertainty in a setting such as Organization Bank can catalyze a previously unknown developmental trajectory, one that moves people toward a sociocentric way of thinking, feeling, and acting in concert with others and the affordances of particular situations.

The value of this alternative trajectory was recognized in the market-place. Organization Bankers were highly marketable, in part because other firms valued their propensity for teamwork and their alertness – which resulted from an absence of automatically activated, preconceived con-cepts. When Organization Bankers left the bank they found employment in a wide range of occupations, not only in finance but also in government and more traditional organizations, as well as such unrelated fields as owning a store or forming a rock band. The Individual Bankers, in con-trast, tended to remain in finance positions, partly because they were not as broadly marketable and partly because they had little interest in venturing outside the familiar. As the economy moves toward knowledge work and as other organizations start to prioritize alertness over the accumulation of expertise, the experience of persistent uncertainty might make people increasingly more marketable, although research on a broader variety of occupations is needed.

CLEARING AWAY THE SELF

Persistent uncertainty thus can lead to a new developmental trajectory that we conceptualize as clearing away the self. Organization Bank designed clearing away the self as an alternative approach to learning that counteracts cognitive rigidity in bankers. This form of learning does not involve the accumulation of concepts, as most cognitive accounts of learning assume. Nor does it involve becoming a socially recognizable person, as many sociocultural perspectives assume. Clearing away the self is a third alternative, one that describes how learners can act with respect to concrete situations, not based on preconceived abstractions – whether those abstractions are intramental or collective.

To understand how clearing away the self reduces cognitive rigidity, one first has to understand how and why stable, abstract identities foster cognitive rigidity. Cognitive accounts of knowledge accessibility, which use a connectionist approach, help explain this (e.g., Smith, 1995). Connectionism conceptualizes learning as the strengthening of connections within a network (Boden, 1990). Similarly, cognitive research on knowledge representation conceptualizes knowledge as residing in the interconnection between concepts stored in memory. Some of this work suggests that identities have special cognitive properties because concepts strongly connected to the category "I" are used more frequently than other concepts and have stronger interconnections (Andersen et al., 1997). People use the self-concept more often than other concepts because they believe that the self is the most important object they have to monitor and regulate in order to survive (Higgins, 1996). The more frequently a concept is used, the more likely that it will become salient, either without the person's awareness of it or without the person's ability to control it. Because concepts about one's own identity are jointly stored in memory and frequently called up together, they become interrelated through a conditioning-like process. When one aspect is activated in memory – for example, when a banker interprets a client's challenging question as being about his or her expertise – this activation spreads with special efficiency to other elements typically activated by stimuli relevant to the self (Andersen et al., 1997; Baldwin, 1992).

The cognitive literature on knowledge accessibility has focused largely on the interrelations among concepts. Our work on identity-induced involvement also explores how identity concepts are linked to a set of typical emotion, motivation, and action patterns that are associated with a given self-concept. What comes to mind when Individual Bankers confront situations that may be relevant to their senses of themselves are not merely such thoughts as "I am an expert," but a holistic way of (mis-) perceiving and acting on a situation. When the identity construct is activated, the person supplies an integrated cognitive, emotional, motivational, and behavioral pattern, filling in information without being aware of doing so. As a result of this patterned transfer of concepts and reactions, "people see things that are not there" (Higgins, 1989: 79). This sort of wholesale transfer of concepts and reactions first was described by Freud (1958) as "transference," and subsequently has been demonstrated in experimental work (Andersen and Berk, 1998; Andersen and Cole; 1990; Andersen et al., 1995).

Clearing away the self is an ongoing social process designed to reverse these special cognitive properties of identities and to avoid the resulting cognitive rigidity. It has two components. First, it withdraws people's attention from an abstract identity. People usually monitor situations for aspects that may be relevant to their identity – looking for things that they know or believe could characterize the situation, looking for ways in which others' actions might have implications for their own standing, and so forth – because they believe that the self is the most important cause of action. Such constant monitoring helps a person manage the self and use existing concepts to ensure successful action. Organization Bank's practices reversed this pattern of attention. They made it unmistakably clear that the self is not a privileged cause of action and that it therefore does not require constant attention. The bank also made self-concepts less relevant because it prevented bankers from forming an identity that described who they were in this new context. Because bankers then used a trait-based identity less frequently to explain successes and failures, the chronic accessibility of self-relevant concepts and the resulting cognitive rigidity were reduced, and their grip over emotions, motivations, and behaviors was loosened. As a result, Organization Bankers were less likely to supply a predetermined psychological pattern to a situation. Their thoughts, feelings, and actions depended relatively less on their identities and relatively more on the unique aspects of different situations.

As the second component of clearing away the self, Organization Bank substituted a new explanation for the results of bankers' actions, namely the whole organizational resource system. As bankers realized that the larger organization was responsible for their successes, they shifted their attention even further away from self and toward the social situation. For the Organization Bankers this shift also helped to undo the centrality of their self-constructs, reversed the rigidity-inducing properties of this construct, and opened the bankers to the idea of using organizational resources more often.

As we described in Chapter 6, this second aspect of clearing away the self developed in a somewhat paradoxical way. During the first six months, new Organization Bankers strenuously resisted the bank's sociocentric culture. Before their trait-based identities became less important to them, these identities became more important. The new Organization Bankers wanted desperately to prove themselves, and they worked extraordinarily hard to show how smart and competent they were. In other words, before these new bankers changed qualitatively and learned to clear away the self, they first focused even more intensely on their self-concepts. This developmental pathway differs completely from the developmental processes described in both cognitive and sociocultural literatures, which describe no such vigorous resistance. In these literatures, participants are assumed to be eager to learn the new ways of being that will make them successful at their jobs and become more central participants in new settings (e.g., Ashford and Black, 1996; Lave and Wenger, 1991). While researchers acknowledge that individuals can resist an organization's culture, the effects of such resistance have not been studied systematically. It is simply assumed that a person who resists the culture will not adopt it.

But when one studies resistance over a period of time in a setting such as Organization Bank, a surprising dynamic can emerge that contradicts this commonsense assumption. Because new Organization Bankers initially resisted the culture so vigorously, they eventually adopted it wholeheartedly. The more the new Organization Bankers wanted to do the impossible by themselves – acting against the bank's sociocentric culture – the more errors they made and the more stress they experienced. The trait-based identity found in identity-induced involvement entails a sense that the self is an agent who can bring about desired outcomes. This notion was challenged when new Organization Bankers' escalating failures and mounting weakness forced them to draw on other resources. Because these social resources became more critical for accomplishing tasks than the personal resources that the bankers previously focused on, the bankers began to attend more to these social resources and less to their identity traits, thereby eroding the power of the self-concept.

The Organization Bankers' experiences of failure represented an important step on the way toward clearing away the self. In contrast to the Organization Bankers we studied, who were hired as new associates, in more senior or "lateral" hires the clearing away process never took place. These senior transfers never adopted Organization Bank's culture, partly because they were not forced to confront their own failures. Because of their prior work experience they had enough knowledge to complete assignments relatively independently. Even though they often produced suboptimal solutions, they rarely had the spectacular failures and breakdowns of the junior bankers and, if they did, they blamed it on others.

They thus continued to maintain a notion of themselves as experts and as the primary agents for bringing about valued outcomes. These bankers often defended their independent decision making and actions with such comments as "that's why they pay me the big bucks," "that's why they hired me and not Joe-Schmo-MBA," and "if you just want someone who does what everyone is telling them to do you should give this job to my secretary." Because the individual person thought his or her own attributes were the primary explanation for success and failure, lateral hires at Organization Bank continued to focus on the self-as-object, thus reinforcing its influence on thought, feeling, and action. They considered social resources to be less important and attended much less to them.

Organization Bank's practices of amplifying uncertainty and clearing away the self are not the same as "tolerating employee mistakes" to facilitate learning, a practice adopted by many organizations including Google. Organization Bank did not tolerate mistakes, but rather intentionally set new bankers up to make them. The bank's primary goal was not to let employees learn a different way of doing an activity – for example, how to do a cash-flow analysis right the next time around – but instead to make them deeply insecure about their own knowledge and abilities and therefore more likely to attend closely to and mindfully choose appropriate resources in the future. This strategy is only possible in an organization-centered system where others can compensate for the errors of particular individuals.

As Organization Bankers cleared away the self, they traveled a relatively uncommon developmental pathway, and they also were subject to social influence. Our account describes not only what people learn in such an organizational setting – which is the primary focus of cognitive developmental research – but also how organizations compel people to learn. The practices at Organization Bank differ in important ways from other social influence processes. Clearing away the self did not depend on semantic transmission or more explicit statements about appropriate action, which have been emphasized by previous work on organizational socialization (e.g., Chao et al., 1994). New Organization Bankers looked in vain for helpful directives and narratives during their first six months. It also differed from the three types of influence processes described by the traditional cognitive literature: compliance, which is motivated by rewards and goes away when rewards and supervision go away; identification, which is motivated by attraction to a set of values or beliefs; and internalization, which is motivated by the need to be right (e.g., Kelman, 1958; Aronson, 1992). Organization Bankers did not comply. They drew on resources beyond the self because the task forced them to do so. When people comply, they experience reactance and sometimes change their behavior in ways opposite to those demanded by authority (e.g., Worchel and Brehm, 1971), even exhibiting behaviors that the individual, under other circumstances, would not endorse (e.g., Karpf, 1978). Because the Organization Bankers did not experience the bank's tacit demands as imposed by another person, they did not develop the resistance or unhappiness that sometimes accompany compliance. Because the bank's sociocentric culture was explicitly articulated only in a very rudimentary way – through such concepts as task-orientation – the newcomers did not have access to conscious beliefs and values that they could embrace intellectually, as is the case with identification and internalization.

These more typical cultural change processes – semantic transmission, compliance, identification, and internalization – differ from Organization Bank's in two ways. Organization Bank's practices did not give the bankers a choice but forced bankers to act differently through high demands and limitations on time and energy. And these practices continued to constrain bankers' behavior even when they already were enculturated. In compliance, in which a person exhibits culturally desirable behaviors but does not necessarily accept them, the person makes the decision to exhibit a behavior because the rewards outweigh the costs. In all other typical forms of enculturation (semantic transmission, identification, and internalization), the organization does not need to constrain behaviors because the person has adopted underlying values and principles. Organization Bank's ongoing behavioral constraints were necessary because "people forget to ask others, we become complacent and satisfied with what we think we know," as one Organization Bank director said. The bankers believed that such undesirable self-reliance is a deep part of the typical banker's psychology and that people are prone to lapse back into it, even though it was maladaptive in the Organization Bank context. Clearing away the self was thus an ongoing accomplishment, not an outcome that can be achieved once and for all.

One important benefit of clearing away the self is the cognitive flexibility it affords because people do not automatically supply preconceived notions in new situations. Can this benefit be achieved only through the relatively painful process of clearing away personally meaningful cognitive structures? Prior work suggests less painful alternatives that involve working with the self rather than against it. According to one perspective, organizations can encourage people to internalize a more flexible self-concept. They can encourage participants to identify with being adaptable, as in the notion of a "chameleon self" (Ibarra, 2000) or a "protean" self (Lifton, 1993). We predict that this strategy would not work. When people develop a chameleon or protean self – or any other type of stable, abstract self-concept – they are likely to become preoccupied with living up to this image and distracted from the concrete cues in a given situation. Not all contexts call for a chameleon. Organization Bankers did not think of themselves as flexible. They did not think of themselves as an abstract type of self at all.

Clearing away the self also sounds somewhat like patterns described by cross-cultural psychologists. Some have opposed a Western individualistic self to an Eastern collective self (e.g., Triandis, 1995). This collective self does not insist on being the same person in different settings, but flexibly adjusts to different expectations in distinct settings. This research, however, shows that people with a collective self are more flexible across – but not within – settings (Chen et al., 2006). That is, a person may have one way of being at home and another way of being at work. But the behaviors at home are relatively stable in one way and the behaviors at work are stable in another way, reflecting the different role expectations in these settings. This differs from clearing away the self, which allowed Organization Bankers to be more flexible even within a given setting and did not establish clear role expectations at all. Supplying individuals with diverse sets of role expectations and allowing them to shift among them does not accomplish clearing away the self. Organization Bankers did not build up sets of role expectations, however diverse and heterogeneous these might be, but instead cleared away the influence of such expectations on perception and behavior.

This process of clearing away the self was painful for Organization Bankers. It was more painful than other social influence processes because it involved a more profound type of change. New Individual Bankers began with an implicit sense that being a self means being a type of entity that has attributes, such as "I am smart." The bank simply required that bankers elaborate and add to their existing attributes. New Individual Bankers learned what counted as "smart" at the bank and they learned other concepts to help them act effectively in their new environment. But their underlying notions about what it means to be a person remained unchanged. In contrast, clearing away the self required a qualitative shift in Organization Bankers' existential stance. They had to learn a different way of being and knowing that contradicted habitual practices in the larger society, habitual practices that they had followed their entire lives. They no longer could define themselves in terms of the stable attributes that previously had given meaning to their lives and helped them pursue goals. They had to give up the sense that life was largely predictable and that they could make sense of and master experience by developing expertise. Moreover, unlike other processes that destroy parts of a person's existing worldview, such as "identity divestiture" (Van Maanen, 1976), clearing away the self did not offer a replacement view that new bankers could adopt instead.

Such a profound change in a person's most fundamental attitudes toward self and experience probably cannot be achieved without some pain. It might be possible to ameliorate this pain somewhat by taking more time to accomplish the shift. The Organization Bankers progressed more quickly toward giving up their trait-based selves when they experienced more traumatic crises. In one case an associate who had been with the bank for three months tried to complete work on a high-profile transaction independently. When it was time for the first internal meeting, the associate had slept in the office for almost a month on a vice president's couch, rarely sleeping for more than two or three hours per night. He had missed his child's birthday, his wife had threatened to leave him, and he experienced worrisome chest pains. Despite all this effort and sacrifice, he had fallen behind schedule and had made major mistakes in his uncompleted work. Looking back on this situation, he said:

> I had known all the way along that there was another way to work even though I did not really know what it was because I had not bothered to look. I wanted to wow people with how I was doing things. But clearly the associates ahead of me didn't kill themselves and that night I vowed that I will stop doing things my way and be open to that other way, whatever it might be.

For many other associates this type of insight came a few months further into their time at Organization Bank, and it was induced by less severe crises. This suggests that organizations could intervene in severe crisis situations, slowing down the developmental process but ameliorating some of the worst stress. It is also possible that more explicit intellectual understandings about clearing away the self would have helped the bankers cope. But offering the requisite narratives could also risk orienting bankers toward a set of abstractions that could be used for intellectualizing the experience and avoiding any meaningful change in behaviors.

As they cleared away the self Organization Bankers were able to adopt a distinctive stance toward their work, a stance that we have called direct involvement. Direct involvement involves a more genuinely social relation between mind and world than the one typically described by sociocultural theories of cognition. Sociocultural research provides a more social account of identities than cognitive psychologists, who focus on inter-mental contents, and sociocultural researchers have begun to describe interconnections between the self and social situations. But existing socio-cultural research shares one fundamental assumption with traditional cognitive research. Both types of research conceptualize identities in terms of abstractions, such as subject positions or narratives that are relatively stable within a particular context (Lave and Wenger, 1991; Shotter and Gergen, 1989; Wortham, 2001). The more fully contextualized self-enacted in direct involvement represents a more social account of identities. The Organization Bank data show how people can identify themselves by how they use resources in situation-specific ways through what Dreyfus (1999) calls "conspicuous action." Conceptualizing identities in terms of concrete resources and situations helps avoid artificial abstractions and helps describe how people can become different kinds of persons as they engage in different situations. A banker is a different kind of banker when equip-ped with a relatively open-ended spreadsheet than with a presentation book. A spreadsheet is a less open-ended kind of object when merely used as input into a presentation book and more open-ended when used to facilitate joint problem solving with the client. The systems within which self and cognition take shape can be more fluid and less sedimented than existing sociocultural accounts would lead us to believe.

Our account does allow for the power of abstractions and relative independence from particular situations. We describe such processes in our account of Individual Bank's practices, for example. We explain the Individual Bankers' abstract identities by delineating the bankers' preferred situation-independent resources. Our approach captures more of the variance in how people enact identities than existing accounts, however. Identities take the form of abstract traits, roles, and expectations – both intramental and social ones – but *only under certain social conditions*. Identities do not always take the form of a contextualized self, nor do they always take the form of an abstract subject. We argue, then, that research-ers must attend not only to the dimension that considers individual as opposed to social aspects of identities, but also to the dimension that considers accumulating abstractions as opposed to clearing away the self.

The typical account of how social concepts and intramental concepts relate involves some form of internalization. Psychological processes have been conceptualized as "social" when individuals internalize or replicate social concepts or processes. Notions such as internalization (Bourdieu, 1984/2000; Davydov, 1999; Schafer, 1968), social identification (Moretti and Higgins, 1999; Tajfel, 1981), role taking (Cooley, 1902/1964; Mead, 1934; Vygotsky, 1962), and incorporation and introjection (Schafer, 1968) all involve social resources – such as concepts, patterns, or cues – that become part of a person's inner realm. These notions do help link the individual to society. But the concept of internalization also directs attention away from investigating how resources operate differently inside and outside the person. Davydov (1999: 44) argues that we must investigate such differences:

> Numerous versions of activity theory admit the existence of an internalization process, that is, of the process of formation of individual activity on the basis of collective activity. While doing this, they notice that the structures of these two forms of activity are to a certain degree similar. But they pay very little attention to their difference. However, it is exactly the characteristics of this very difference that pose a particular problem for activity theory.

Our research speaks to this difference, showing how internalization sometimes can distract an individual from the social – not connect the person to it.

Our description of Individual Bank shows that social concepts can be integrated into a person's set of identity concepts, where they become infused with personal meaning that diverts the person's attention away from the social world. Against the typical account, which describes individuals as becoming "socialized" into a common group and linked by virtue of internalizing collective concepts, we argue that the internalization of concepts can distract individuals from attending to others and thus distance them from social situations – even though everyone else in the setting may have internalized similar concepts. When Individual Bankers activated abstract identity concepts, they did not attend closely to what others were saying and doing. Their self-concepts operated at a precognitive level that the bankers were not aware of and could not control. Different bankers may have articulated similar visions of who they were and what they valued, but their behaviors, especially under stress, isolated them from others and focused them on their own selves. Organizations might try to overcome this antisocial focus by trying to add more social concepts to the bankers' existing store. Our findings show that such efforts often have the opposite effect from what is intended, contributing to trait-based senses of self that separate the person further from the concrete social reality within which he or she needs to make decisions.

Social concepts that are integrated into a person's mental realm, then, are likely to be social only in the narrow sense that they originated in a social space. Internalization and other forms of psychological integration achieve only an incomplete alignment between the individual and the social. The notion of direct involvement points to another path, one in which an individual's cognitive structures – whether they are originally individual or social – are cleared away. In direct involvement, the person's mental contents become less personally meaningful. As a result psychological resources orient outward, toward concrete situations, and operate fungibly with other types of social resources. Then the person can attend more deeply to other people and external situations and can align internal psychological processes more seamlessly with social ones. This represents a different way in which the personal and the social can be linked. It does not bring the social world inside a person's mind, but instead makes the mind part of the social world.

THEORIES IN THE WILD

Our descriptions of Individual Bank and Organization Bank have allowed us to articulate a new way in which organizations and individuals can function. We have summarized this by describing the organizational practice of uncertainty amplification, the experience of persistent uncertainty, and the developmental process of clearing away the self. While describing these uncommon but promising forms of organizational practice and individual functioning, we have both drawn on and moved beyond existing cognitive, organizational, and sociocultural accounts of cognition, identity, and development. We hope that our account can contribute to academic discussions of these processes, but we do not intend in this book to adopt one existing theoretical perspective or another. Instead, we are interested in reframing these theories as things in the world.

Many distinguish between theoretical and practical knowledge. Dewey (1916) distinguishes between everyday, practical "knowing-how" and theoretical "knowing-why." Heidegger (1962) and Dreyfus (1999) argue that we are socialized into a background understanding of the world that we use in practical actions but might not understand intellectually. Building on Heidegger, Bourdieu (1977) formulates a theory of practice that centers on the notion of *habitus*, or embodied understandings. Polanyi (1962) elaborates a notion of "tacit knowing." Lave and others (Chaiklin and Lave, 1993; Lave, 1988) show how individuals' practical understandings inform their actions, even when they do not have relevant theoretical understandings. All of this work argues that theoretical knowledge and practical knowledge develop along different trajectories. People know things in practice that they do not know in theory. People walk without mentally representing the biological processes that make this possible, for example, and they can open doors without knowing why turning the doorknob causes the door to open.

Despite the differences between practical and theoretical understandings, however, they can have similar contents. We have argued that Individual Bankers enacted something resembling traditional cognitive theory in their practices and that Organization Bankers enacted something resembling sociocultural theory in theirs. We claim that practitioners sometimes use the same principles and assumptions as do scholars. This can happen because managers learn academic theories in school, or from consultants, and then implement them. This may explain why Individual Bank adopted cognitive theory, which underlies much of the subject matter in MBA programs and also is used by consultants that the bank hired. But it cannot explain why Organization Bank adopted a sociocultural approach, which was unfamiliar to most bankers and not commonly taught in business schools.

Both academics and others have to formulate an explicit or implicit understanding about the causes of action in everyday life. We argue that practitioners enact theories that resemble academic ones partly because both scientists and practitioners develop accounts of the causes of action, albeit through different routes. Practitioners do not need to represent these theories or accounts mentally, but can instead enact them as tacit guides for action. Whether explicitly or tacitly, scientists and practitioners develop theories that focus on a unit of analysis. Social scientists choose a unit of analysis that comprises processes and mechanisms that vary at the same time for the same reason in relation to the outcome variable of interest (Freeman, 1978). Underlying many of the differences between cognitive and sociocultural theories, for instance, is a disagreement about whether the appropriate unit of analysis is the individual, as cognitive psychologists argue, or whether it is a hybrid that includes the individual and aspects of the social situation, as sociocultural theories argue. Many important differences between the theories follow from these different units of analysis.

We suggest that Individual Bankers and Organization Bankers enact traditional cognitive theory or sociocultural theory, respectively, because they first arrived at distinct accounts of action that presupposed one or another of these units of analysis. Individual Bankers and Organization Bankers' divergent self-interpretations reflected distinct views of what causes action. Consistent with the assumptions of cognitive theory, the

Individual Bankers enacted an individual-centered type of self in which the person was seen as the primary cause of action. They saw social resources as playing a secondary role. Consistent with the assumptions of socio-cultural theory, the Organization Bankers enacted a sociocentric kind of self in which the social system, including but not limited to the person, was the primary cause of action. Many other important differences between the two patterns of involvement followed from these different units of analysis. As we have described in Chapters 5 and 6, the choice of more individual or more social explanations for action then worked together with diver-gent patterns of cognition, emotion, and motivation in systems that were mutually reinforcing.

Our account of Organization Bank describes how self-interpretations had to change before bankers began to think, feel, and act as sociocultural accounts predict they would. During their first six months, Organization Bankers exhibited identity-induced involvement. They construed the self as an abstract identity, a property of the individual separate from the world. Like cognitive theorists, they believed that the most important resources for action were a person's mental resources, and they overrelied on these while using organizational resources reluctantly and ineffectively. The bankers' behavior changed when they noticed that they could solve problems despite their own limited knowledge. They then became less preoccupied with their abstract identities, and they started to notice more opportunities for engaging organizational resources.

From this developmental point onward, the Organization Bankers enacted sociocultural theory. They acted as if they were trying to make sociocultural theory's claims about distributed cognition come true, although they were not familiar with the academic theory. They acted this way because they more fully recognized the potential contributions of social resources and they saw the use of heterogeneous resources as the best way to solve client problems. Sociocultural theories often construe all cognition as "situated," as woven into systems of resources that include other people and objects that extend beyond the individual. We argue that the potential contributions of social resources can be more or less realized in action, depending on the extent to which people notice situational affordances. Cognition at Organization Bank was relatively more situated once the Organization Bankers became aware of and exploited the cogni-tive contributions of social resources.

At Individual Bank cognition was less situated because the bankers often ignored the potential contributions of social resources. The Individual Bankers did of course rely on some social resources, including other people and the bank's reputation and procedures. Unlike Organization Bankers, however, Individual Bankers never were forced to confront how helpless they were without social resources. They never recognized the fundamental interdependence between personal and social resources, and they kept attributing cognitive accomplishments to their own skill and effort. Because the Individual Bankers' kept interpreting the self as the primary resource for action, they continued to pay close attention to this self. Their preoccupation with their identities distracted them from engaging with the situation and blunted the potential contributions of many social resources. As a result, the cognitive systems at Individual Bank were truncated and mostly limited to the resources of the individual. Thus, the bankers enacted the individual-centered principles of traditional cognitive theory.

We are suggesting that practitioners and scientists solve the same epistemological and ontological problems, but via different routes. While scientists use abstract reflection to develop an appropriate unit of analysis, practitioners develop their intuitions through a cycle of acting and reflecting. This means that practitioners have the upper hand in formulating a useful account because the means at their disposal are richer. We believe that scholars should pay attention to the conceptual advances made by practitioners, both explicit and tacit, to articulate our accounts of psychological functioning. Practitioners at Organization Bank developed an intuition about what it means to be a contextualized self – the kind of situated unit of analysis that sociocultural theory talks about – by drawing on richer input than theorists have available and by refining their intuition through direct experience. Through this process, the Organization Bankers discovered and implemented a type of situated, contextualized self and an approach to cognition that have not been captured fully by scientists' abstract reflection.

The fact that Individual Bankers act like naïve cognitive theorists does not mean that all cognitive scholars enact identity-induced involvement, nor do we mean to imply that all sociocultural scholars enact direct involvement. In fact, because uncertainty reduction is the norm in our society, it is likely that academic settings, including those peopled by sociocultural researchers, encourage identity-induced involvement. Sociocultural scholars have recognized the interdependence between the person and the social situation and should know better than to attribute successes to their own resources alone. But scholars' insights are based on abstract reflection and relatively impoverished data. Mere intellectual insight into the interdependence between personal and social resources generally does not suffice to catalyze direct involvement. Self-interpretations have to change too. This requires the painful experience of clearing away the self.

Much sociocultural theory has been generated by researchers who identify as socioculturalists, a group normally conceived in opposition to the abstract identity of cognitive researchers (Lave, 2003). These groups are defined by people's attachments to a set of abstract principles that come to define the researcher. The principles are not normally tested and are not subject to revision. We would describe this as an instance of identity-induced involvement in which sociocultural researchers work to advance their theories and overthrow cognitive theory. This is different from noticing opportunities to build sociocultural theory by observing concrete empirical phenomena, which Lave (2003) recommends as a more fruitful path. We are not arguing that any reference to a theoretical tradition is a problem, however. Researchers always have to use resources, such as theoretical frames, for understanding phenomena. From the perspective of Organization Bankers, the problem occurs when sociocultural researchers identify with and become attached to an abstract set of assumptions instead of focusing on the affordances of concrete situations.

Theories are things in the world as well as descriptions of the world, and those of us who work with theories are also engaged in practices. One can evaluate theories by how well they describe the world, and such evaluation is often useful. It is also useful to adopt pragmatic and moral criteria for evaluating theories. Tacit and explicit psychological theories influence how people and communities function, and they have ethical implications. We propose that these theories should be evaluated with respect to the ways of life that they both facilitate and justify. In this we follow others who have asserted that our theories of the world should be evaluated based on their moral consequences (e.g., Danziger, 1997; Gergen, 2001a,b; Gergen and Kaye, 1992). Exploring cognitive and sociocultural theories from this perspective opens a different type of debate between them. The two theories are normally construed as competing explanations. Even though a productive dialogue between the two theories has been sought (Anderson et al., 1996, 1997, 2000; Greeno, 1997), an integrated perspective has not been achieved. We take an alternative angle on the debate, treating the theories not as mutually exclusive competitors but as things that live side-by-side in the world. Instead of taking sides, we wish to examine the theories' practical and moral consequences. From this perspective, our account of Organization Bank presents a new world for us to evaluate and possibly learn from.

Our descriptions of Individual Bank and Organization Bank sketch the kinds of social conditions that gave rise to more cognitive and more sociocultural ways understanding the self and its social context. These different theories arose in different organizations because of mundane, practical choices that the organizations made. The divergence between individual-centered and contextualized selves does not reflect some major cultural difference, or some transformation in contemporary society – as implied by such phrases as "the turn to postmodernity." The contextualized self that the Organization Bankers developed does not reflect some epochal shift. It emerged from a pragmatic insight: abstract identities are not helpful if one wants to get certain kinds of work done. Having had this insight, Organization Bankers developed everyday practices that counteracted the cognitive rigidities of individual-centered work processes. Our account of Organization Bank thus explores some empirical conditions under which a sociocultural approach can become the tacit or explicit organizing principle for action. Such work can help us understand theories in the wild, and it can provide resources for evaluating and perhaps changing them.

There are many different practical and ethical dimensions according to which we could evaluate the alternative way of life found at Organization Bank, as well as the more familiar practices found at Individual Bank. Here, we employ two criteria that were important to our informants: adaptability and developmental freedom. Bankers at both banks were interested in the banks' differential ability to adapt to a changing environment. Our analysis has shown the Organization Bankers to be more adaptive. When Individual Bankers relied on abstractions, which was most of the time, they paid less attention to concrete situations and failed to notice opportunities for innovation. As a result, minor problems sometimes expanded into crises and forced top management to intervene. Because top management was removed from everyday practice, its typical response was to change leadership and organizational structures. These changes left the root problems unaddressed, such that performance deteriorated and eventually demanded another cycle of reorganization. During the two years of our study, Individual Bank underwent fifteen changes in leadership and organizational structure, while task processes remained unchanged. In contrast, Organization Bank prevented its bankers from using their abstract knowledge by putting them in unfamiliar situations. They consequently attended more to details of particular situations and they were more likely to recognize opportunities for innovation. Organizational change thus occurred more continuously at Organization Bank. During the two years of our study, there was no change in leadership or structure at Organization Bank. Yet there were many successful innovations in how Organization Bankers completed tasks, all initiated by bankers who were alert to opportunities that arose in particular situations. Organization Bank, then, was more adaptive than Individual Bank.

A second criterion that mattered to our informants was developmental freedom. This sort of freedom is described in some constructionist approaches that favor conditions under which people have the greatest possible freedom for transformation (Gergen, 2001a,b). Our informants at the two banks differed in their conceptions of developmental freedom, reflecting the different opportunities that their bank opened up for them. Individual Bankers often criticized Organization Bank because its processes robbed bankers of their individuality, transforming them into "people without personality" or "clones." One Individual Bank associate said: "That is an important criterion for me. That a place gives you the freedom to be the kind of person that you are." The Individual Bankers agreed that Individual Bank was such a place. They also sometimes mentioned trade-offs: "Any kind of freedom comes at a price. In our case, it comes with the extremely high stress of maintaining the reputation that you are creating." The Individual Bankers agreed that this was a price worth paying.

Organization Bankers, on the other hand, felt that Individual Bank limited a person's freedom precisely because of its "personality cult." Organization Bankers sometimes referred to the industry's superstars as "caricatures of themselves," by which they meant that superstars enacted their public personae with such effort that they appeared artificial and contrived. As one Organization Bank director remarked, in reference to Individual Bank, "I don't equate personality with freedom. People with big personalities actually do *not* have a lot of freedom to behave in a way that differs from this personality. So I think that settings that encourage people to indulge in that kind of complacency are the ones that limit people." An associate said: "For me freedom has more to do with what you can actually do [than with who you are]. The greatest feeling of freedom for me was to discover the kinds of things that you can do here because no one really cares about who you are. We don't limit people because they are too young or because they haven't had a certain set of experiences or education or because you don't have the right personality." The Organization Bankers also valued the freedom they achieved from the powerful and typically negative emotions that overcame bankers when they felt that their abstract, trait-based selves were at stake. One Organization Banker explained his relatively lower stress level after six months:

> I still have plenty of stress because I have to work insane hours, I don't
> see my family, unexpected events come up, I eat shitty food and too

much of it. But it is a little bit like becoming a parent. Somehow being sucked into such a frantic whirl of activity also feels good because you stop worrying. You are into doing mode, just tackling whatever comes up. You are not constantly thinking about how someone is judging you or what someone's expectations are and that you are not good enough or that you are not as good as you want to be or not as good as someone else. You just don't have the luxury to do that.

The Individual Bankers' freedom was *freedom for the self*: they were free to pursue the goals that they identified with, the abstract goals and traits that they had articulated or internalized. The Organization Bankers' freedom was a *freedom from the self*: they were free from the compulsions that accompany a high-priority identity that requires one to act on its behalf. Neither of these approaches to freedom is inherently better than the other. But our data raise questions about whether Individual Bankers did achieve the freedom for the self that they desired. Our data also reveal contradictions and constraints in the Organization Bankers' freedom from the self.

Freedom for the self is freedom to be a particular kind of person, to behave in line with the personality attributes that one has chosen. Our data indicate that this freedom is a mirage. As we have described in our account of identity-induced involvement, abstract identities work through a conditioning-like process in which the activation of an identity concept habitually calls up a predetermined pattern of emotions, motivations, and behaviors (Bargh; 1982, 1984, 1989, 1996). What feels like a personal choice is in significant part a mechanistic process. We do not mean to make a philosophical argument about whether free will is possible. We merely point out that, when an abstract identity concept is activated, people most often do not freely choose their behaviors.

Moreover, abstract identities themselves are often not freely chosen. Identities are often socially constructed in ways that do not always allow for choice (cf., Gergen and Kaye, 1992). For example, one Individual Bank associate said:

> During the first few days in training I think I said things that others saw as aggressive, but you know that isn't really me. I was just nervous and maybe even a bit intimidated. . . . But then I noticed how people started to treat me like I was some kind of jerk, making faces or rolling their eyes when I said something and that then *did* start to piss me off and I felt that I had to be forceful just to defend myself. . . . And now I feel that I am locked into being this kind of person and into acting in a way that I actually do not want for myself.

This quotation illustrates the self-fulfilling nature of an abstract identity. When a banker repeatedly behaved in a particular way, others created social situations that brought this pattern out in the focal banker. This process then limited the associate's freedom because it compelled him to keep displaying the same kinds of behavioral responses despite his desire to break out of this cycle.

Individual Bankers themselves often cherished their abstract identities, feeling that such an identity made the banker unique and constituted his or her essence. Even when an identity led to maladaptive behaviors, Individual Bankers expressed no desire to change. For example, one Individual Banker explained his aggressive treatment of a client with reference to his personality: "I don't like it when people dick me around. That's who I am and that's how I am going to respond, whether you like it or not." Other Individual Bankers did not appreciate such responses in their colleagues. The senior bankers who helped us code transcripts of client meetings argued that such an aggressive response is not only inappropriate but also "a sign of weakness. You cannot just act on any whim you have. You need to be able to control yourself." But they acknowledged that impulsive actions were relatively frequent at Individual Bank, were linked to the bank's superstar orientation, and were tacitly accepted. "There is a lot of this going on and we tolerate that stuff as part and parcel of the whole superstar mentality. When your whole business is about building up big egos you have to accept what comes with the territory." The bankers who displayed these behaviors gladly accepted the costs, such as client dissatisfaction and their colleagues' mild disapproval, in order to be "authentic," "true to who I am," and "able to live with myself."

This last set of quotations shows that the Individual Bankers' viewed their demeanor as a personal choice, claiming that they were free to be the kind of people they wanted to be. Our account of identity-induced involvement would suggest, however, that they were not as free as they thought. Freedom for the self fails against its own standards. People are not free to choose their identities. Once they identify with a set of traits, norms, and narratives, these generally become mental concepts that compel the person to enact them automatically, without noticing this compulsion and without being able to stop, even when these behaviors and narratives are not appropriate. Such abstract identities trap people in a repetitive and increasingly confining reality. Individual Bankers who were aggressive, for example, were more likely to be staffed with "tough" clients who would not be alienated by the banker. These bankers therefore had many opportunities to establish further their aggressive way of being and fewer opportunities to notice and cultivate more cooperative alternatives. Having a "personality," then, is not a way to be unique, but could instead be construed as a handicap that blocks alternative ways of being.

The freedom that Organization Bank made possible was a *freedom from* such identity-induced compulsions. When identities are cleared away, the person is freed from the influence of abstract identities. He or she is less likely to experience situations as predictable and less likely to employ monolithic cognitive, emotional, motivational, and behavioral responses. In direct involvement, people notice more decision making cues and thus break situations down into more and smaller decision making moments. An analyst writing a memo recognizes that writing a particular introduction constrains what can be presented in the main body. A poet notices how writing one word constrains the choice of the next word. And a scientist recognizes how the result of one experiment calls for a specific type of follow-up experiment. Each cue that a person notices provides an opportunity to direct the situation in a new way. A person using the deductive style of identity-induced involvement would not notice as many of these cues because he or she would attend to a few initial cues and then apply a relevant schema to the situation that would foreclose alternatives.

When the person in direct involvement notices and responds to situational demands, he or she distributes decision making responsibility across a diverse set of psychological and social resources. Situations unfold in relatively unique ways partly because of the diversity of the resources contained in them. These resources also interact with one another. In identity-induced involvement, the person uses resources in a way that silences their contributions and imposes an abstract vision brought from outside the situation. A pitch book, for example, merely manifests what already exists in the banker's mind. Because of how the banker uses it, it cannot contribute new ideas or prompt new courses of action. Even though a given pitch book might be a great creative accomplishment, one can hear the banker's distinct voice through it. A person in direct involvement can produce creative work that is not as limited by the position and preconceptions of its creator. The bankers uses resources in a way that brings forth their *voices* and lets situations play out as a *conversation* between the voices of other people, objects, and task constraints. This conversation can yield unexpected, emergent possibilities that cannot be anticipated by any one person's expectations.

Because the Organization Bankers were free from the compulsion to project a relatively stable psychological template onto situations, they *experienced* more situational diversity. Their responses then were called forth by these specific, diverse situations, and so Organization Bankers' responses were themselves more diverse. These diverse responses, in turn, allowed the bankers opportunities to notice their own freedom from – their flexibility to exhibit different ways of acting and being. As one associate said, "Here they throw you into different situations that you would never freely choose and you are forced to act the part. . . . But that's how you learn about what is possible for you." When the associates saw that they could handle each of these different situations, regardless of their own attributes, they were also freed from the fear of failing:

> I mean when you think about it, this job is incredibly daunting; it's actually terrifying. We are advising the top organizations worldwide and you constantly have to deal with senior managers who are a lot older than you are and they rely on you to handle things that really matter and that could influence the lives of many people. . . . You learn to trust the system. You realize that there is no hole deep enough that you cannot be dug out from.

Freedom from the self also has paradoxical elements. It is a "freedom to be dominated by the object" (Bruner, 1962). Direct involvement is about being free from one's preconceived notions, from fear for one's own self, so that one can notice and submit to the affordances of situations. Instead of being able to dominate the situation and impose one's preferred way of behaving, one is dominated by that situation. One notices how a situational cue demands a particular type of response within a given cultural frame, and one is more responsive to this demand. Such situational constraint on the person, however, is an artifact of a particular way of thinking that is characteristic of an individualistic psychology. In direct involvement, the person is part of the situation. Through his or her input, the person contributes toward shaping the situation. The person is a participant who acts in a situation, but not an agent who designs the outcome. In identity-induced involvement, the objective of freedom is to bring about a desirable outcome. In direct involvement, outcomes are not under the individual's control but are instead in the hands of a more competent system.

The Organization Bankers' freedom was the freedom to recognize constraint and use it constructively. This framing removes part of the stigma that "constraint" carries in a more individualistic framework, where it is seen as an impediment to the person's agency. Even though the Organization Bankers eventually relished freedom from the self, they did not initially choose this type of transformation. As described in Chapters 4 and 6, the Organization Bankers entered seeking freedom for the self. They wanted to become a certain type of socially recognizable person – the accomplished and competent Wall Street expert. To become this kind of person, they were willing to pay high costs in terms of their health and family relations. Unbeknownst to the bankers, this was precisely the type of transformation that Organization Bank undermined – while letting the bankers work hard and separating them from their families anyway. Still, the bankers might have been forced into the only freedom possible.

REFERENCES

Abbott, A. 1988. *The system of professions*. Chicago IL: The University of Chicago Press.

Acredolo, C. and J. O'Connor. 1991. On the difficulty of detecting cognitive uncertainty. *Human Development* 34: 204–223.

Adler, P.S. and S. Kwon. 2006. The evolving organization of professional work. Working paper, University of Southern California.

Andersen, S.M. and S.W. Cole. 1990. "Do I know you?": The role of significant others in general social perception. *Journal of Personality and Social Psychology* 59: 384–399.

Andersen, S.M., N.S. Glassman, S. Chen, and S.W. Cole. 1995. Transference in social perception: The role of chronic accessibility in significant-other representations. *Journal of Personality and Social Psychology* 69: 41–57.

Andersen, S.M., I. Reznik, and S. Chen. 1997. The self and others: Cognitive and motivational underpinnings. In *The self across psychology: Self-recognition, self-awareness, and the self-concept*, edited by J.G. Snodgrass and R.L. Thompson, 233–275. New York: New York Academy of Science.

Andersen, S.M. and M.S. Berk. 1998. Transference in everyday experience: Implications of experimental research for relevant clinical phenomena. *Review of General Psychology* 2(1): 81–120.

Anderson, J.R., L.M. Reder, and H.A. Simon. 1996. Situated learning and education. *Educational Researcher* 25(4): 5–11.

Anderson, J.R., L.M. Reder, and H.A. Simon. 1997. Situative versus cognitive perspectives: Form versus substance. *Educational Researcher* 26(1): 18–21.

Anderson, J.R., J.G. Greeno, L.M. Reder, and H.A. Simon. 2000. Perspectives on learning, thinking, and activity. *Educational Researcher* 29(4): 11–13.

Aronson, E. 1992. *The social animal*. 6th ed. New York: W.H. Freeman.

Asch, S.E. 1952. *Social psychology*. Englewood Cliffs, NJ: Prentice-Hall.

Ashford, S.J. and J.S. Black. 1996. Proactivity during organizational entry: The role of desire for control. *Journal of Applied Psychology* 81(2): 199–214.

Baldwin, M.W. 1992. Relational schemas and the processing of information. *Psychological Bulletin* 112: 461–484.

Barab, S.A. and J.A. Plucker. 2002. Smart people or smart contexts? Cognition, ability, and talent development in an age of situated approaches to knowing and learning. *Educational Psychologist* 37(3): 165–182.

Bargh, J.A. 1982. Attention and automaticity in the processing of self-relevant information. *Journal of Personality and Social Psychology* 43: 425–436.

Bargh, J.A. 1984. Automatic and cognitive processing of social information. In *Handbook of social cognition*, vol. 3, edited by R.S. Wyer Jr. and T.K. Srull, 1–43. Hillsdale, NJ: Erlbaum.

Bargh, J.A. 1989. Conditional automaticity: Varieties of automatic influence in social perception and cognition. In *Unintended thought*, edited by J.S. Uleman and J.A. Bargh, 3–51. New York: Guilford.

Bargh, J.A. 1996. Automaticity in social psychology. In *Social psychology: Handbook of basic principles*, edited by E.T. Higgins and A.W. Kruglanski, 169–183. New York: The Guilford Press.

Bartunek, J.M., J.R. Gordon, and R.P. Weathersby. 1983. Developing "complicated" understanding in administrators. *Academy of Management Review* 8: 273–284.

Bauer, T.N., E.W. Morrison, and R.R. Callister. 1998. Organizational socialization: A review and directions for future research. *Research in Personnel and Human Resources Management* 16: 149–214.

Baumeister, R. and M.R. Leary. 1995. The need to belong: Desire for interpersonal attachments as a fundamental human motivation. *Psychological Bulletin* 117: 497–529.

Beck, A.T. 1976. *Cognitive therapy and emotional disorders.* New York: International Universities Press.

Bem, D.J. 1967. Self-Perception: The dependent variable of human performance. *Organizational Behavior and Human Performance* 2: 105–121.

Berger, P., B. Berger, and H. Kellner. 1974. *The homeless mind: Modernization and consciousness.* New York: Vintage Books.

Berlyne, D.E. 1970. Children's reasoning and thinking. In *Carmichael's manual of child psychology*, 3rd ed., edited by P.H. Mussen, vol. 1, 939–981. New York: Wiley.

Boden, M.A. 1990. *The creative mind: Myths and mechanisms.* London: Weidenfeld & Nicholson.

Bourdieu, P. 1977. *The logic of practice.* Stanford CA: Stanford University Press.

Bourdieu, P. 1984/2000. *Distinction: A social critique of the judgment of taste.* Cambridge, MA: Harvard University Press.

Brewer, M. and W. Gardner. 1996. Who is this "we"? Levels of collective identity and self representations. *Journal of Personality and Social Psychology* 71(1): 83–93.

Brewer, M. and A.S. Harasty Feinstein. 1999. Dual processes in the cognitive representation of persons and social categories. In *Dual process theories in social psychology*, edited by S. Chaiken and Y. Trope, 255–271. New York: Guilford Press.

Brown, J.S., A. Collins, and P. Duguid. 1989. Situated cognition and the culture of learning. *Educational Researcher* 18(1): 32–42.

Bruner, J.S. 1957. Going beyond the information given. In *Contemporary approaches to cognition*, edited by J.S. Bruner, E. Brunswik, L. Festinger, F. Heider, K.F. Muenzinger, C.E. Osgood, and D. Rapaport, 41–69. Cambridge, MA: Harvard University Press.

Bruner, J.S. 1962. *On knowing: Essays for the left hand.* Cambridge, MA: Belknap Press of Harvard University Press.

Budner, S. 1962. Intolerance of ambiguity as a personality variable. *Journal of Personality* 30: 29–50.

Burton, D.M. 1998. *The firmwide 360° performance evaluation process at Morgan Stanley.* Cambridge, MA: Harvard Business School Press.

Campbell, R.L. and M.H. Bickhard. 1986. *Contributions to human development, vol. 16: Knowing levels and developmental stages.* Basel: Karger.

Carver, C.S. and M.F. Scheier. 1981. *Attention and self-regulation: A control-theory approach to human behavior.* New York: Springer Verlag.

Carver, C.S. and M.F. Scheier. 1990. Principles of self-regulation: Action and emotion. In *Handbook of motivation and cognition: Foundations of social behavior,* edited by E.T. Higgins and R.M. Sorrentino, vol. 2, 3–52. New York: Guilford.

Chaiklin, S. 1993. Understanding the social scientific practice of understanding practice. In *Understanding practice: Perspectives on activity and context,* edited by S. Chaiklin and J. Lave, 377–402. Cambridge: Cambridge University Press.

Chaiklin, S. and J. Lave (eds.). 1993. *Understanding practice: Perspectives on activity and context.* Cambridge: Cambridge University Press.

Chao, G.T., A.M. O'Leary-Kelly, S. Wolf, H.J. Klein, and P.D. Gardner. 1994. Organizational socialization: Its content and consequences. *Journal of Applied Psychology* 79(5): 730–743.

Char, R. 1995. *Oeuvres complètes.* Rev. ed. Paris: Gallimard (Plèiade).

Char, R. 1996. *Dans l'atelier du poète.* Edited by Marie-Claude Char. Paris: Gallimard.

Chase, W.G. and H.A. Simon. 1973. Perception in chess. *Cognitive Psychology* 4: 55–81.

Chen, S., H.C. Boucher, and M.P. Tapias. 2006. The relational self revealed: Integrative conceptualization and implications for interpersonal life. *Psychological Bulletin* 132(2): 151–179.

Chiu, C., Y. Hong, and C.S. Dweck. 1997. Lay dispositionism and implicit theories of personalities. *Journal of Personality and Social Psychology* 73(1): 19–30.

Cole, M. 1996. *Cultural psychology: A once and future discipline.* Cambridge, MA: Harvard University Press.

Colvin, G. 2006. Managing chaos. *Fortune* 154(7): 76–82.

Cooley, C.H. 1902/1964. *Human nature and the social order.* New York: Schocken Books.

Coser, L. 1967. Greedy organizations. *European Journal of Sociology* 8: 196–215.

Covaleski, M.A., M.W. Dirsmith, J.B. Heian, and S. Samuel. 1998. The calculated and the avowed: Techniques of discipline and struggles over identity in big six public accounting firms. *Administrative Science Quarterly* 49: 293–327.

Daft, R.L. and N.B. Macintosh. 1981. A tentative exploration into the amount and equivocality of information processing in organizational work units. *Administrative Science Quarterly* 26: 207–225.

Damon, W. 1984. Peer education: The untapped potential. *Journal of Applied Behavioral Psychology* 5: 331–343.

Danziger, K. 1997. The varieties of social construction. *Theory and Psychology* 7(3): 399–416.

Davydov, V. 1999. The content and unsolved problems of activity theory. In *Perspectives on activity theory*, edited by Y. Engeström, R. Miettinen, and R. Punamäki, 39–2. Cambridge: Cambridge University Press.

Dennett, D.C. 1991. *Consciousness explained.* Boston MA: Little, Brown, and Company.

Deutsch, M. and H. Gerard. 1955. A study of normative and informational social influence upon individual judgment. *Journal of Abnormal and Social Psychology* 51: 629–636.

Dewey, J. 1916. *Democracy and education.* New York: Free Press.

Dreyfus, H.L. 1999. *Being-in-the-world.* Cambridge, MA: The MIT Press.

Drucker, P.F. 1993. *Post-capitalist society.* New York: HarperCollins.

Dweck, C.S. 1986. Motivational processes affecting learning. *American Psychologist* 41: 1040–1048.

Dweck, C.S. 1999. *Self-Theories: Their role in motivation, personality, and development.* Philadelphia PA: Psychology Press.

Dweck, C.S. and E.L. Leggett. 1988. A social-cognitive approach to motivation and personality. *Psychological Review* 95(2): 256–273.

Eccles, R. and D.B. Crane. 1988. *Doing deals: Investment banks at work.* Boston MA: Harvard Business School Press.

Engestrom, Y. 2003. Activity theory and individual and social transformation. In *Perspectives on activity theory*, edited by Y. Engestrom, R. Miettinen, and R.L. Punamaki. Cambridge: Cambridge University Press.

Ericsson, K.A. and A.C. Lehman. 1996. Expert and exceptional performance: Evidence of maximal adaptation to task constraints. *Annual Review of Psychology* 47(1): 273–305.

Etzioni, A. 1975. *A comparative analysis of complex organizations: On power, involvement, and their correlates.* New York: Free Press.

Festinger, L. 1954. A theory of social comparison processes. *Human Relations* 7: 114–140.

Fiske, S.T. and S.E. Taylor. 1991. *Social cognition.* 2nd ed. New York: McGraw-Hill.

Fransman, M. 1994. The IBM paradox. *Industrial and Corporate Change* 3: 713–758.

Freeman, J.H. 1978. The unit of analysis in organizational research. In *Environments and organizations*, edited by M.W. Meyer, 335–351. San Francisco CA: Jossey-Bass.

Freud, S. 1958. *The dynamics of transference.* Standard ed., vol. 12. London: Hogarth.

Gergen, K.J. 2001a. Construction in contention: Towards consequential resolutions. *Theory and Psychology* 11(3): 419–432.

Gergen, K.J. 2001b. Psychological science in a postmodern context. *American Psychologist* 56(10): 803–813.

Gergen, K.J. and J. Kaye. 1992. Beyond narrative in the negotiation of therapeutic meaning. In *Therapy as social construction*, edited by S. McNamee and K. Gergen, 166–185. London: Sage.

Gibson, J.J. 1977. The theory of affordances. In *Perceiving, acting, and knowing: Toward an ecological psychology*, edited by R.E. Shaw and J. Bransford, 67–82. Hillsdale NJ: Lawrence Erlbaum.

Gibson, J.J. 1986. *The ecological approach to visual perception*. Hillsdale NJ: Lawrence Erlbaum.

Gioia, D.A. 1992. Pinto fires and personal ethics: A script analysis of missed opportunities. *Journal of Business Ethics* 11: 379–389.

Goffman, E. 1961. *Asylums: Essays on the social situation of mental patients and other inmates*. Garden City: Doubleday.

Greeno, J.G. 1997. On claims that answer the wrong questions. *Educational Researcher* 26(1): 5–17.

Greeno, J.G. and The Middle-School Mathematics Through Applications Project Group. 1998. The situativity of knowing, learning, and research. *American Psychologist* 53(1): 5–26.

Hardin, C.D. and E.T. Higgins. 1996. Shared reality: How social verification makes the subjective objective. In *Handbook of motivation and cognition*, vol. 3, edited by R.M. Sorrentino and E.T. Higgins, 28–84. New York: Guilford Press.

Haroutunian-Gordon, Sophie. 1991. *Turning the soul: Teaching through conversation in the high school*. Chicago IL: The University of Chicago Press.

Haroutunian-Gordon, Sophie. (in press). *Cultivating questions: A focus for schooling in the twenty-first century*. New Haven, CT: Yale University Press.

Harrison, J.R. and G. Carroll. 1991. Keeping the faith: A model of cultural transmission in formal organization. *Administrative Science Quarterly* 36: 552–582.

Haslam, A. 2004. *Psychology in organizations: The social identity approach*. 2nd ed. Thousand Oaks, CA: Sage.

Heidegger, M. 1962. *Being and time*. New York: Harper and Row

Heise, D.R. 1979. *Understanding events: Affect and the construction of social action*. New York: Cambridge University Press.

Heise, D.R. 1989. Effects of emotion displays on social identification. *Social Psychology Quarterly* 53: 10–21.

Higgins, E.T. 1989. Knowledge accessibility and activation: Subjectivity and suffering from unconscious sources. In *Unintended thought*, edited by J.S. Uleman and J.A. Bargh, 75–123. New York: Guilford.

Higgins, E.T. 1996. The 'self digest:' Self-knowledge serving self-regulatory functions. *Journal of Personality and Social Psychology* 71(6): 1062–1083.

Higgins, E.T. and J.A. Bargh. 1987. Social cognition and social perception. *Annual Review of Psychology* 38: 369–425.

Higgins, E.T. and A.W. Kruglanski (eds.). 1996. *Social psychology: Handbook of basic principles*. New York: Guilford Press.

Higgins, E.T., I. Loeb, and D.N. Ruble. 1995. The four A's of life transition effects: Attention, accessibility, adaptation, and adjustment. *Social Cognition* 13(3): 215–242.

Hogg, M.A. and B.A. Mullin. 1999. Joining groups to reduce uncertainty: Subjective uncertainty reduction and group identification. In *Social identity and social contagion*, edited by D. Abrams and M.A. Hogg, 249–279. Malden: Blackwell.

Hogg, M.A. and D.J. Terry. 2000. Social identity and self-categorization processes in organizational contexts. *Academy of Management Review* 25(1): 121–141.

Hogg, M.A. and J.C. Turner. 1985. Interpersonal attraction, social identification and psychological group formation. *European Journal of Social Psychology* 15: 51–66.

Hutchins, E. 1991. The social organization of distributed cognition. In *Perspectives on socially shared cognition*, edited by L.B. Resnick, J.M. Levine, and S.D. Teasley, 283–307. Washington, DC: American Psychological Association.

Hutchins, E. 1995. *Cognition in the wild*. Cambridge, MA: The MIT Press.

Ibarra, H. 1999. Provisional selves: Experimenting with image and identity in professional adaptation. *Administrative Science Quarterly* 44: 764–791.

Ibarra, H. 2000. *Making partner*. Cambridge, MA: Harvard Business School Press.

John-Steiner, V. and H. Mahn. 1996. Sociocultural approaches to learning and development. *Educational Psychology* 31: 191–206.

Karpf, R.J. 1978. Altering values via psychological reactance and reversal effects. *Journal of Social Psychology* 106: 131–134.

Katz, R. 1985. Organizational stress and early socialization experiences. In *Human stress and cognition in organization*, edited by T.A. Beehr and R.S. Bhagat, 117–139. New York: Wiley.

Kelly, G.A. 1955. *The psychology of personal constructs*. New York: Norton.

Kelman, H.C. 1958. Compliance, identification, and internalization: Three processes of attitude change. *Journal of Conflict Resolution* 2, 51–60.

Kitayama, S. and H.R. Markus. 1994. The cultural construction of self and emotion: Implications for social behavior. In *Emotion and culture*, edited by S. Kitayama and H. Marcus, 89–130. Washington, DC: American Psychological Association.

Kitayama, S., H.R. Markus, and H. Matsomoto. 1995. Culture, self, and emotion: A cultural perspective on "self-conscious" emotions. In *Self-conscious emotions: The psychology of shame, guilt, embarrassment, and pride*, edited by J.P. Tangney and K.W. Fisher, 439–464. New York: Guilford Press.

Knee, J. 2006. *The accidental investment banker*. New York: Oxford University Press.

Kunda, G. 1992. *Engineering culture: Control and commitment in a high-tech corporation*. Philadelphia PA: Temple University Press.

Lashinsky, A. 2006. Chaos by design. *Fortune* 154(7): 86–98.

Latour, B. and S. Woolgar. 1979. *Laboratory life: The social construction of scientific facts*. Beverly Hills, CA: Sage.

Lave, J. 1988. *Cognition in practice: Mind, mathematics and culture in everyday life*. Cambridge: Cambridge University Press.

Lave, J. 1991. Situating learning in communities of practice. In *Perspectives on socially shared cognition*, edited by L.B. Resnick, J.M. Levine, and S.D. Teasley, 63–84. Washington, DC: American Psychological Association.

Lave, J. 2003. The practice of learning. In *Understanding practice: Perspectives on activity and context*, edited by S. Chaiklin and J. Lave, 3–34. New York: Cambridge University Press.

Lave, J. and E. Wenger. 1991. *Situated learning: Legitimate peripheral participation*. Cambridge: Cambridge University Press.

Lawrence, P.R. and J.W. Lorsch. 1967. *Organization and environment: Managing differentiation and integration*. Cambridge, MA: Graduate School of Business Administration, Harvard Business School.

Le Bon, G. 1911. *Psychologie der Massen*. Stuttgart: Kroener.

Leonard-Barton, D. 1992. Core capabilities and core rigidities: A paradox in managing new product development. *Strategic Management Journal* 13: 111–125.

Levine, J.M., L.B. Resnick, and E.T. Higgins. 1993. Social foundations of cognition. *Annual Review of Psychology* 44: 585–612.

Levy, R.I. 2001. Bateson and Academia: Reflections on the fit of different kinds of visions with the business of departments of anthropology. Paper presented at 7th Biennial Meeting of the Society for Psychological Anthropology, Decatur, Georgia.

Lifton, R.J. 1993. *The protean self: Human resilience in an age of fragmentation.* Chicago IL: The University of Chicago Press.

Linton, R.J. 1936. *The study of man.* New York: Appleton-Century Co.

Lyotard, J.F. 1984. *The postmodern condition.* Manchester: Manchester University Press.

Mael, F. and B.E. Ashforth. 1995. Loyal from day one: Biodata, organizational identification, and turnover among newcomers. *Personnel Psychology* 48: 309–333.

Mandel, M. 2005. The real reasons you're working so hard . . . and what you can do about it. *Business Week*, October 3, 60–67.

Mandel, M. 2006. Mr. Risk goes to Washington. *Business Week*, June 12, 46.

March, J.G. and H.A. Simon. 1958. *Organizations.* New York: Wiley.

Markus, H. 1980. The self in thought and memory. In *The self in social psychology*, edited by D.M. Wegner and R.R. Wallacher, 102–130. New York: Oxford University Press.

Markus, H. and S. Kitayama. 1991. Culture and the self: Implications for cognition, emotion, and motivation. *Psychological Review* 98: 224–253.

Markus, H. and R.B. Zajonc. 1985. The cognitive perspective in social psychology. In *The handbook of social psychology*. 3rd ed., edited by G. Lindzey and E. Aronson, vol. 1, 137–230. New York: Random House.

Mead, G.H. 1934. *Mind, self, and society.* Chicago IL: The University of Chicago Press.

Molden, D.C. and C.S. Dweck. 2006. Finding "meaning" in psychology: A lay theories approach to self-regulation, social perception, and social development. *American Psychologist* 61(3): 192–203.

Moreno, J.L. 1953. *Who shall survive?: Foundations of sociometry, group psychotherapy, and sociodrama.* Beacon, NY: Beacon House Publishers.

Moretti, M.M. and E.T. Higgins. 1999. Own versus other standpoints in self-regulation: Developmental antecedents and functional consequences. *Review of General Psychology* 3(3): 188–223.

Nanda, A. 2005. *Who is a professional?* Cambridge, MA: Harvard Business School Press.

O'Reilly, C.A. and J.A Chatman. 1996. Culture as social control: Corporations, cults, and commitment. In *Research in Organizational Behavior*, edited by B.M. Staw, 18: 157–200. Greenwich, CT: JAI Press.

Packer, M.J. 2001. *Changing classes: School reform and the new economy.* New York: Cambridge University Press.

Packer, M.J. and J. Goicoechea. 2000. Sociocultural and constructivist theories of learning: Ontology, not just epistemology. *Educational Psychologist* 35(4): 227–241.

Palincsar, A.S. 1998. Social constructivist perspectives on teaching and learning. *Annual Review of Psychology* 49: 345–375.

Park, R. 1955. *Societies*. Glencoe, IL: The Free Press

Peirce, C.S. 1934. Pragmatism and abduction. In *Collected papers of Charles Sanders Peirce, vol. 5: Pragmatism and Pragmaticism*, edited by C. Hartshorne and P. Weiss, 112–131. Cambridge, MA: Harvard University Press.

Piaget, J. 1967. *Six psychological studies*. New York: Vintage.

Piaget, J. 1980. *Experiments in Contradiction*. Chicago IL: The University of Chicago Press.

Piaget, J. 1985. *The equilibration of cognitive structures: The central problem of intellectual development*. Chicago IL: The University of Chicago Press.

Polanyi, M. 1962. The republic of science: Its political and economic theory. *Minerva* 1: 54–74.

Pratt, M.G. 1998. To be or not to be: Central questions in organizational identification. In *Identity in organizations: Building theory through conversations*, edited by D.A. Whetten and P.C. Godfrey. Thousand Oaks, CA: Sage Publications.

Prawat, R.S. 1996. Constructivisms, modern and postmodern. *Educational Psychologist* 31(3/4): 215–225.

Prawat, R.S. 1996. Ideas and their objects: A reply to Garrison. *Educational Researcher* 25(6): 23–34.

Rogoff, B. and J. Lave (eds.) 1999. *Everyday cognition: Development in social context*. Cambridge, MA: Harvard University Press.

Rose, N. 1999. *Governing the soul*. 2nd ed. New York: Cambridge University Press.

Rubin, R. 2003. *In an uncertain world: Tough choices from Wall Street to Washington*. New York: Random House.

Ruble, D.N. 1994. A phase model of transitions: Cognitive and motivational consequences. *Advances in Experimental Social Psychology* 26: 163–214.

Salancik, G.R. and J. Pfeffer. 1978. A social information processing approach to job attitudes and task design. *Administrative Science Quarterly* 23: 224–253.

Schafer, R. 1968. *Aspects of internalization*. New York: International University Press.

Schatzki, T.R., K. Knorr Cetina, and E. von Savigny. 2001. *The practice turn in contemporary theory*. New York: Routledge.

Schein, E.H. 1978. *Career dynamics: Matching individual and organizational needs*. Reading, MA: Addison-Wesley.

Scribner, S. 1999. Studying working intelligence. In *Everyday cognition: Development in social context*, edited by B. Rogoff and J. Lave, 9–40. Cambridge, MA: Harvard University Press.

Scribner, S. and M. Cole. 1981. *The psychology of literacy*. Cambridge, MA: Harvard University Press.

Scott, W.R. 1992. *Organizations: Rational, natural, and open systems*. 3rd ed. Englewood Cliffs, NJ: Prentice Hall.

Sender, H. and K. Kelly. 2007. Blind to trend, Quant funds pay heavy price; computer models failed to see increasing global alpha of 16%. *Wall Street Journal (Eastern Edition)*, August 9, C1.

Sfard, A. 1998. On two metaphors of learning and the dangers of choosing just one. *Educational Researcher* 27(2): 4–13.

Shotter, J, and K. Gergen (eds.) 1989. *Texts of identity*. London: Sage

Shweder, R. 1991. *Thinking through cultures*. Cambridge, MA: Harvard University Press.

Silver-Greenberg, J. 2008. More muscle for risk manager. *Business Week*, February 25, 62.

Simon, H.A. 1976 *Administrative behavior*. 3rd ed. New York: MacMillan.

Simon, H.A. 1991. Bounded rationality and organizational learning. *Management Science* 20(1): 125–137.

Smith, E.R. 1995. What do connectionism and social psychology offer each other? *Journal of Personality and Social Psychology* 70: 893–912.

Strange, S. 1994. *States and markets*. London: Pinter.

Suchman, L.A. 1987. Plans and situated actions. *The problem of human machine communication*. Cambridge: Cambridge University Press.

Sutton, R.I. and A. Hargadon. 1996. Brainstorming groups in context: Effectiveness in a product design firm. *Administrative Science Quarterly* 41(4): 685–718.

Tajfel, H. 1981. Human groups and social categories: Studies in social psychology. Cambridge: Cambridge University Press.

Tajfel, H. and J.C. Turner. 1979. An integrative theory of intergroup conflict. In *The social psychology of intergroup relations*, edited by S. Worchel & W.G. Austin, 33–47. Monterey: Brooks–Cole.

Thoits, P.A. 1991. Merging identity theory and stress research. *Social Psychology Quarterly*, 54: 101–112.

Thompson, J.D. 1967. *Organizations in action*. New York: McGraw-Hill.

Triandis, H.C. 1995. *Individualism and collectivism*. Boulder, CO: Westview Press.

Trope, Y. and A. Liberman. 1996. Social hypothesis testing: Cognitive and motivational mechanisms. In *Social psychology: Handbook of basic principles*, edited by A.W. Kruglanski and E.T. Higgins, 239–270. New York: Guilford Press.

Turner, J.C. 1975. Social comparison and social identity: Some prospects for intergroup behavior. *European Journal of Social Psychology* 5: 5–34.

Turner, S. 1994. *The social theory of practices: Tradition, tacit knowledge, and presupposition*. Chicago IL: The University of Chicago Press.

Turner, J.C., M.A. Hogg, P.J. Oakes, S.D. Reicher, and M.S. Wetherell. 1987. *Rediscovering the social group: A self-categorization theory*. Oxford: Basil Blackwell.

Tushman, M., and L. Rosenkopf. 1992. On the organizational determinants of technological change: Towards a sociology of technological evolution. In *Research in organizational behavior*, edited by B. Staw and L. Cummings, 311–347. Greenwich NJ: JAI Press.

Van Knippenberg, D. and N. Ellemers. 2003. Social identity and group performance: Identification as the key to group-oriented effort. In *Social identity at work: Developing theory for organizational practice*, edited by S.A. Haslam, D. van Knippenberg, M.J. Platow, and N. Ellemers, 29–42. New York: Psychology Press.

Van Maanen, J. 1976. Breaking-in: Socialization to work. In *Handbook of work, organization, and society*, edited by R. Dubin, 67–130. Chicago IL: Rand McNally.

Van Maanen, J. and E.H. Schein. 1979. Towards a theory of organizational socialization. In *Research in Organizational Behavior*, edited by B.M. Staw, vol. 1, 209–264. Greenwich, NJ: JAI Press.

Voss, J.F., J. Wiley, and M. Carretero. 1995. *Acquiring intellectual skills*. 46–81.

Vygotsky, L.S. 1962. *Thought and language*. Trans. by E. Hnafmann and G. Vakar. Cambridge, MA: The MIT Press.

Vygotsky, L.S. 1978. *Mind in society: The development of higher psychological processes*. Edited by M. Cole, V. John-Steiner, S. Scribner, and E. Souberman. Cambridge, MA: Harvard University Press.

Walker, R. 2003. The guts of a new machine. *New York Times Magazine*, November 30, 78–84.

Walsh, J.P. 1995. Managerial and organizational cognition: Notes from a trip down memory lane. *Organization Science* 6(3): 280–321.

Waterman, R.H. Jr. 1990. *Adhocracy*. New York: W.W. Norton & Company.

Weick, K.E. 1979. *The social psychology of organizing*. 2nd ed. New York: McGraw-Hill.

Weick, K.E. and R.E. Quinn. 1999. Organizational change and development. *Annual Review of Psychology*, 50: 361–386.

Weick, K.E. and K.H. Roberts. 1993. Collective mind in organizations: Heedful interrelating on flight decks. *Administrative Science Quarterly* 38: 357–381.

Wertsch, J.V. 1991. A sociocultural approach to socially shared cognition. In *Perspectives on socially shared cognition*, edited by L.B. Resnick, J.M. Levine, and S.D. Teasley, 85–100. Washington, DC: American Psychological Association.

Wertsch, J.V. and A. Stone. 1985. The concept of internalization in Vygotsky's account of the genesis of higher mental functioning. In *Culture, communication, and cognition: Vygotskian perspectives*, edited by J.V. Wertsch, 162–179. New York: Cambridge University Press.

Whetten, D.A. and K.S. Cameron. 2005. *Developing management skills*. 6th ed. Upper Saddle River, NJ: Pearson, Prentice Hall.

White, M. and D. Epston. 1990. *Narrative means to therapeutic ends*. New York: Norton.

Whitehead, A.N. 1938. *Modes of thought*. New York: Free Press.

Whitehouse, K. 2007. The buzz: One quant fund sees shakeout for the ages – "10,000 years." *Wall Street Journal (Eastern Edition)*, August 11, B3.

Wicklund, R.A. 1986. Orientation to the environment versus preoccupation with human potential. In *Handbook of motivation and cognition: Foundations of social behavior*, edited by R.M. Sorrentino and E.T. Higgins, 64–95. New York: Guilford Press.

Williamson, O.E. 1981. The economics of organization: the transaction cost approach. *American Journal of Sociology* 87: 548–577.

Wong, L. 2004. *Developing adaptive leaders: The crucible experience of Operation Iraqi Freedom*. Carlisle, PA: Strategic Studies Institute, United States Army War College. http://www.strategicstudiesinstitute.army.mil/pubs/display.cfm?pubID =411 (accessed 12 June 2008).

Worchel, S. and J.W. Brehm. 1971. Direct and implied social restoration of freedom. *Journal of Personality and Social Psychology*, 18: 294–304.

Wortham, S.E.F. 1994. *Acting out participant examples in the classroom*. Amsterdam: John Benjamins.

Wortham, S.E.F. 2001. *Narratives in action: A strategy for research and analysis*. New York: Teachers College Press.

Wortham, S.E.F. 2006. *Learning identity*. New York: Cambridge University Press.

INDEX